Unconscious Intelligence in Cybernetic Psychology

This important book examines how the growing field of cybernetic psychology – the study of the creative complexity of the mind – can be applied to a range of different realms, tapping into the unconscious potential within us all.

Cybernetic psychology integrates theories from various schools of thought, bringing them together in one unified theory. First developed and described by Danish author and psychotherapist Ole Vedfelt, it can be used in therapeutic practice, in relation to learning and pedagogics, and as a tool for better leadership. The 15 chapters within this volume apply the theory to these as well as other areas, including ecology, creativity, mindfulness and scientific enquiry itself.

Insightful and wide-ranging, the book will appeal to psychotherapists and those working within mental health, as well as students and researchers across education, psychology and beyond.

Torben Hansen is Head of Education at the Vedfelt Institute, Copenhagen. He is a psychotherapist MPF and supervisor. He is editor of and contributor to *Potentials of the Unconscious – Cybernetic Psychology in Practice* and, furthermore, co-author with Henrik Hass of *Cybernetic Psychology – Unconscious Intelligence in Psychotherapy and Everyday Life*.

Henrik Hass is a psychotherapist and supervisor at the Vedfelt Institute, Copenhagen. He is the author of *Numen* and co-author with Torben Hansen of *Cybernetic Psychology – Unconscious Intelligence in Psychotherapy and Everyday Life* and has contributed an article in "Potentials of the Unconscious".

Unconscious Intelligence in Cybernetic Psychology

Edited by
Torben Hansen and Henrik Hass

Routledge
Taylor & Francis Group

LONDON AND NEW YORK

Designed cover image: Altedart as rendered the owner of the
images on Getty Images.

First published 2024
by Routledge
4 Park Square, Milton Park, Abingdon, Oxon OX14 4RN

and by Routledge
605 Third Avenue, New York, NY 10158

Routledge is an imprint of the Taylor & Francis Group, an informa business

© 2024 selection and editorial matter, Torben Hansen and Henrik
Hass; individual chapters, the contributors

British Library Cataloguing-in-Publication Data
A catalogue record for this book is available from the British Library

Library of Congress Cataloging-in-Publication Data
Names: Hansen, Torben (Psychotherapist), editor. | Hass, Henrik, editor.
Title: Unconscious intelligence in cybernetic psychology / edited by
Torben Hansen, Henrik Hass.
Description: Abingdon, Oxon; New York, NY: Routledge, 2024. |
Includes bibliographical references and index. |
Identifiers: LCCN 2023011051 (print) | LCCN 2023011052 (ebook) |
ISBN 9781032418926 (hardback) | ISBN 9781032418919 (paperback) |
ISBN 9781003360247 (ebook)
Subjects: LCSH: Subconsciousness. | Cybernetics. | Cognition. |
Human information processing. | Cognitive science.
Classification: LCC BF311 .U63 2023 (print) | LCC BF311 (ebook) |
DDC 153—dc23/eng/20230321
LC record available at https://lccn.loc.gov/2023011051
LC ebook record available at https://lccn.loc.gov/2023011052

ISBN: 978-1-032-41892-6 (hbk)
ISBN: 978-1-032-41891-9 (pbk)
ISBN: 978-1-003-36024-7 (ebk)

DOI: 10.4324/9781003360247

Typeset in Times New Roman
by codeMantra

Thanks to Henriette Løvdal, Janus Mortensen and Pernille Bjerrum for their constructive feedback in the creation of this book and, last but not least, heartfelt thanks to all the contributors and clients for sharing their life stories.

Contents

Contributors

Mikkel Anthonisen is a medical doctor specialising in general medicine and neurology, a psychotherapist MPF, founder of the non-profit sailing organisation Oceans of Hope (www.oceansofhope.org), Denmark, and author of *Oceans of Hope, Around the World – Back to Life* (2016).

Lisa Carew Dahlager has MA and PhD degrees and is a psychotherapist MPF and a supervisor at the Vedfelt Institute, Copenhagen.

Torben Hansen, Head of Education at the Vedfelt Institute, Copenhagen is a psychotherapist MPF and supervisor. He is co-author with Henrik Hass of the book *Cybernetic Psychology – Unconscious Intelligence in Psychotherapy and Everyday Life* (2022, Frydenlund).

Henrik Hass has a BA degree and is a psychotherapist, MPF, and a supervisor at the Vedfelt Institute, Copenhagen. He is co-author with Torben Hansen of *Cybernetic Psychology – Unconscious Intelligence in Psychotherapy and Everyday Life* (2022, Frydenlund).

Anne Hjort has a PhD degree in media and literature and is a documentary film director and psychotherapist, MPF.

Britta Karlshøj has an MA degree in educational psychology and is a psychotherapist MPF from the Vedfelt Institute, Copenhagen.

Charlotte Lindvang has a PhD degree; she is a music therapist and an associate professor at Aalborg University, a GIM therapist (EAMI), a psychotherapist, MPF, and author of *Resonant Learning in Music Therapy. A Training Model to Tune the Therapist* (Pedersen, Lindvang & Beck, 2022, Jessica Kingsley).

Henriette Løvdal has an MA in literature and is a psychotherapist MPF and supervisor at the Vedfelt Institute, Copenhagen.

Dorte Mikuta is a psychotherapist educated at the Vedfelt Institute and is a parish priest and priest of diaconia in the Danish National Church, Copenhagen.

Anne Maj Nielsen has a PhD degree and is an associate professor in educational psychology at the Danish School of Education, Aarhus University. She is a psychotherapist MPF and a supervisor at the Vedfelt Institute, Copenhagen. She is the author of several articles.

Lone Nissen has a BA degree and is a psychotherapist, MPF, from the Vedfelt Institute, Copenhagen.

Maria F. Sejersen is a nurse and psychotherapist MPF from the Vedfelt Institute, Copenhagen.

Solveig Thorborg has an MA in sociology and is a psychotherapist MPF and external examiner at the Vedfelt Institute, Copenhagen.

Christian Uhrskov has an MA from the Danish Music Conservatory and is a psychotherapist, MPF, from the Vedfelt Institute, Copenhagen.

Anders Vogt has an MA degree and is a psychotherapist MPF and supervisor at the Vedfelt Institute, Copenhagen.

Introduction

Cybernetic psychotherapy is empathetic and growth oriented with a consistent method of combining cognitive, existential, psychodynamic, art and body-oriented psychotherapies and mindfulness. Cybernetics being a science of nature as well as a science of information allows for a unifying theory for the psychologies with a new overall perspective to psychotherapy. A main interest is uncovering the unconscious intelligence, designing our dreams, structuring our daily life and playing a defining role in the dimensions of psychotherapy. True to the values of the therapies of the 20th century, cybernetic psychology is compatible with the age of information.

The Orchard of Psychotherapy

This book is primarily about nature, about the cybernetics of human nature. Cybernetics is a theory of communication, a theory that gives us a science of the delicate complexity of the many layers in the communication of the living. Over the now 30 years that have seen the development of cybernetic psychology at the Copenhagen-based Vedfelt Institute, American forest ecologist Suzanne Simard conducted a series of experiments uncovering the communication paths connecting trees and plants on the forest floor. Strikingly similar results were found in the two seemingly very different fields of nature – the forest and the human. Simard found that the forest thrives optimally with a variety of trees in a community with the rich biology that belongs to the forest, and that the trees are connected in highly intricate, complex communication networks. The Vedfelts, psychotherapist Lene and author-psychotherapist Ole, likewise insisted that in the orchard of the psychotherapies we need all the valuable research programmes to understand the human and to best tend the growth of the client. And, like in Simard's forest where non-trees – fungi – were found to play a fundamental role in integrating the trees, in the Vedfelts' psychology the integrating mediator was a non-psychology – namely, cybernetics – a science suited to describing the delicate dimensions of our presence in psychotherapy and everyday life.

The mosaic formed by the 15 chapters of this book presents the main theories and methods of cybernetic psychology. In the course of reading it, the fascinating

DOI: 10.4324/9781003360247-1

phenomenon emerges that our existence is built on an intelligence far exceeding our everyday rational mind. An intelligence we unconsciously rely on from moment to moment, day and night. The science around the unconscious intelligence peaking around the millennium is of decisive and refreshing significance. This applies to therapeutic treatment, bodily health, pedagogy, science, arts, and creative processes, in communication and in everyday wisdom.

Cybernetics is a theory of information processes in complex systems such as flocks of birds, pine forests, vast ecosystems, and the human in its environment. For most of us, we unknowingly speak and think cybernetically when we use everyday terms such as feedback and self-reference.

It is a theory that allows us to understand the beauty and depths of conversation flowing in multiple layers of images, feelings, bodily gestures, movements, facial expressions, the rational, the wisdom of the irrational, and the importance of the faint perceptions of moods on the brink of our awareness. Cybernetic psychology and psychotherapy have been developed to match and resonate with the simple and yet immensely complex reality of human interactions in our everyday life and especially the relations and communications that unfold in the psychotherapeutic relationship.

Cybernetics was the answer to the search for a theory that would serve as a platform for the integrative project merging the cognitive, the existential humanistic, the psychodynamic, the Eastern contemplative traditions, art therapies and body-oriented psychotherapies. Systems theory and cybernetics would in this process be both an overarching scientific paradigm and a critical analysis tool for the various psychologies, merging them into a new person model built around the science of unconscious intelligence. On top of that, the integrative project would provide a safe passage for the psychologies of the 20th century into our age of cybernetics and information theory.

The achievements in artificial intelligence (AI) during the 1990s kept mirroring the human mind in more and more complex ways, which seemed to insist that, if we humans were to be considered an information system, it would be of extreme proportions and there would have to be some kind of system intelligence regulating it at levels that went far beyond the everyday mind – a kind of unconscious intelligence. And, if the human should be considered a true living information system, it would be self-optimizing, meaning self-healing. These fundamental elements would have far-reaching consequences for psychotherapy since, if the system is self-optimizing, we would be better looking for impulses to self-sustainability and personal development than for what is wrong. And, if unconscious intelligence was the general master of self-optimization, getting closer to the language of the unconscious would be a first priority.

The unconscious intelligence obviously had an extreme capacity for organizing information, expressing this in a variety of forms, from the rational to the poetic abstract. The reason for these variations is that the rational only expresses a very low rate of information, whereas the poetic and body language have a far higher information capacity. This comes out in our everyday life in the use of metaphors, whenever we are in need of words and, likewise, regarding the seemingly irrational poetic imagery of dreams that yet appear to reveal deep meaning beyond the rational. So, observing the language and conversation style of the client gives an indication of the relationship between the unconscious intelligence and the I-centred everyday consciousness. But this is where things get more interesting – for what actually is communication? There are pauses in speaking, posture, gestures, mimicking, bodily warmth, face colour changes, glances. And then there are words with images and choice of style and nuances of meaning and, not least, how all these and maybe many more flow and change together in the aim of expressing the complexity of life situations. Cybernetic psychotherapy is about our ability to navigate the depths of conversation, making way for the natural self-unfolding of personality. These themes are summoned in the Vedfelts' 1996 *Consciousness* and 2000 *Unconscious Intelligence.*

We have considered the repetition in descriptions of the key concepts of cybernetic psychology in the different chapters a learning tool, giving the reader, to whom the concepts may be new, a better chance to become familiar with the theories. By coming across the same concepts, in different contexts and in different interpretations, it is our hope that a familiarity with cybernetic psychology can gradually be created.

As a final remark, Suzanne Simard gathers her research around a single concept – complexity, the rich interwoven communication network below ground defining the health of the forest. She strongly advocates including complexity science in the study of the living. The necessary complexity is precisely the key concept the reader will meet over and over again. The defining idea in the orchard of psychotherapies.

Selected Characteristics of Cybernetic Psychotherapy

- Personal growth and maturity are considered the aim of psychotherapy.
- The atmosphere of therapy is loving and warm. The relationship between therapist and client is considered to be a vital part of the process.
- The focus is on resources and growth potentials rather than on finding faults and shortcomings. This is called salutogenesis and is basic to personal growth.
- The therapist sets the framework, but the real authority lies with the client's conscious and unconscious self-expression and self-assessment.
- Meeting people in their distinctiveness is a prerequisite for the process and the therapist's noblest task.
- So-called resistance on the part of the client is considered an intelligent natural constraint or self-protection.
- The therapist's foremost task is to sense the communication that constantly flows from the client's unconscious intelligence.
- The practical implementation of cybernetic psychotherapy is a creative fusion of scientifically approved therapies – cognitive, psychodynamic, existential-humanistic, art therapies and mindfulness.

- Dreams, feelings, body sensations, gestures and inner images are considered as worthy and important as rational thinking.
- The basic attitude of cybernetic psychotherapy is that there is always a network of causes for a client's symptoms and problems.
- There are therefore always several routes to the solution of a given problem. This is called equifinality and calls for creative, empathetic listening to the client.

Henrik Hass and Torben Hansen, December 2022

1

The Necessary Complexity

Key Elements of Cybernetic Psychology

Henrik Hass

Adventuring into the age of cybernetics and information theory an inconvenient question arises around the foundations of psychotherapy. An overall cybernetic premise is that a more complex system can control and facilitate a less complex system – not the other way round. The central premise of cybernetic psychology turns out to be that the everyday conscious mind is a subsystem of lower complexity, meaning less information capacity, than the entire conscious-unconscious person-system. The central premise of cybernetic psycho*therapy* thus becomes that, unless the more complex, higher-order unconscious levels of the client's person-system are engaged, the therapeutic process will yield no real psychotherapeutic gain – that is, no reorganising of the conscious mind. The problem is obviously that these premises seen together seem to leave the promising new idea of cybernetic psychology with an inconvenient problem: According to the laws of cybernetics stated above, it seems impossible for the therapist's less complex rational everyday conscious mind to influence the far more complex intelligent unconscious levels of the client's person-system – necessary for a therapeutic process. More worryingly, it would seem that this problem applies to psychotherapy in general. Analysing the therapeutic setting with the tools of systems theory and cybernetics, this chapter portrays psychotherapy as a highly complex 'system of systems' with the needed explanatory power to solve the inconvenient problem.

From Reductionism to Laws of Complexity

A Few Key Concepts

Complexity

The concept of complexity has been with us for thousands of years. Roman emperor and philosopher Marcus Aurelius speaks in his *Meditations* of how the world is divinely *woven together* (*cum plectere*; Aurelius 1996, Book 7), and American forest ecologist Suzanna Simard, in her *Finding the Mother Tree*, talks about the *intricacy* and *complexity* of the communication networks between the trees in the forest (Simard 2021, p. 4). In this chapter, the concept of complexity is likewise

DOI: 10.4324/9781003360247-2

about information processing capacity. High complexity is the positive state of an open mind that will enable smooth handling of complex matters, whereas a lack of complexity is when things get complicated. In this light, psychotherapy becomes a work of establishing a communication network of high complexity between the everyday person and the unconscious intelligence, in order to restore the connection to the resources of the unconscious. Hence the quest for *the necessary complexity*.

Constraints and Freedom

Contrary to what we might think, control and constraints are the basis of freedom and creativity. Imagine any ordinary conversation. Such is only possible because the unconscious intelligence gives you a sense of what is relevant in the face of the time at your disposal. If you have time to engage in a conversation around matters dear to you with a wise friend, you might widen the landscape of the topics, but only so that new perspectives resonate with the theme you investigate. The newly opened perspectives will be sensed as relevant guided by subtle feelings that serve as enabling constraints and controlling facilitators for the focus and creativity of the conversation. In the cybernetic sense, psychotherapy is, in this way, a process towards mind states of higher complexity and personal freedom, working with the often too tight constraints in the relationship between the everyday consciousness and the unconscious intelligence.

Purpose and Direction

Contemplating the conversation again: On the way to the meeting, there is the very practical goal of getting there on time. The purpose or aim of the meeting is the hope of achieving the tranquil inspirational excitement experienced in previous talks and the more specific goals of getting a little wiser about specific stuff. Deep into contemplating complex matters with your friend, the guiding goal orientation is abiding in the subtle, nonverbal variations of sentiments of meaningful connections. Cybernetic psychology insists that we are permanently purposeful and goal oriented, but purpose varies from practical matters to the far more complex here and now conversation and long-sighted growth of personal development.

An Overview

In the search for a solution to the initially stated problem, the chapter sweeps briefly through the history of the science of reductionism and complexity leading up to the present-day biology of homeostasis, artificial intelligence, and the concept of unconscious intelligence. This points to a scientific basis for understanding psychotherapy as processes in a self-optimising cybernetic information system.

From here on, the chapter shows how the core ideas of cybernetic psychology arose out of an attempt to establish an integrative theory for the main schools of psychology. Viewing the human as basically a communication phenomenon, the different schools of psychology could be seen as descriptions of various modes of communication, thus integrating everyday language and the rational and poetical, images and metaphors, emotions, core body sensations and the wide range of postures, mimicking and gestures, with a special regard to the language of dreams. Cybernetics being a theory of communication fitted the need for an integrative theory and could, on top of that, be a meta-theory that would be free of the scientific barriers that separated the main schools. The cybernetic view of personality as a self-optimising system would further yield new interpretations of classical themes such as resistance being intelligent systems constraints and conscious–unconscious being a matter of information bandwidth, and the gains of mindfulness would be a matter of accessing higher system processes. It is pointed out that the concept of complexity is a question concerning information processing capacity. High complexity is the positive state of an open mind that will enable smooth handling of complex matters, whereas a lack of complexity is when things get complicated. Hence the quest for *the necessary complexity*.

From theoretical landscapes, the chapter zooms in on the therapeutic setting. As a comment on the initial problem, surprisingly, it turns out that the higher unconscious levels of the client's person-system are actively seeking contact with the therapist, even, in various ways, bypassing the client's conscious mind. In this way, psychotherapy turns out to be a system of communication patterns between the different levels of two highly complex communication systems – even, often, outside the conscious minds of both therapist and client. The key to understanding this lies in the biological concept of homeostasis turning into the psychological concept of *unconscious intelligence*.

This leads to therapeutic methods of opening the conscious mind to the influence of the problem-solving creative unconscious – this very capacity of human homeostasis and self-optimisation that, throughout this anthology, is referred to as *unconscious intelligence*. The chapter sums up this prospect, showing how the therapist can train and unfold the ability to observe and engage in these unconscious processes of higher order through which the therapy unfolds. Counterintuitively maybe – and most likely thought-provoking – this leads to showing how aspects of be it Jungian deep psychology, cognitive therapy or body-oriented therapy will work in fine-tuned concert, enhancing the bandwidth and complexity of the everyday mind and enabling its opening to the unconscious intelligence. All together, this finally drives the key message that psychotherapy is not about fixing faults but about tending the natural growth of the person's self-actualisation and self-expression in the social network. And this is the underlying premise that carries all the chapters of this anthology.

So, what at first glance might have looked like a game-over argument against a cybernetic psychology, on its own premises, slowly loses its grip when we see the client–therapist relationship as an integrated self-optimising system of a yet higher order than the two separate person-systems. As an unexpected gift, this furthermore renders scientific support to the age-old humanistic psychology claim – it is the relationship that heals.

A Brief History of Complexity and Reductionism

When Italian mathematician Galileo Galilei (1564–1642) described the accelera-
tion of falling bodies as independent of their weight, it was a landmark event. Not
so much because it was a mathematical description of nature – examples of that
were known from ancient Pythagoreans and Babylonians. What was new was that
Galileo, from an experiment, had demonstrated a law in nature that broke with a
nearly 2,000-year-old, widely accepted belief of the Greek philosopher Aristotle
(384–322 bc). Galileo was aware of the scientific parameters of the experiment,
such as discussion of sources of uncertainty and requirements for it to be repeat-
able. The scientific revolution that Galileo became an exponent of consisted of
a description of nature that would totally rule out the contemporary reference to
inherent properties or moving forces in things. According to Galileo, nature could
and should be understood and described entirely using pure mathematics based on
elementary observations (Knudsen 2006, p. 743).

Of the inherent qualities of matter Galileo sought to rule out, the *cause of intent*
must be emphasised. In Latin, this cause of movement was called *causa finalis*,
meaning goal orientation. The theme of the *causa finalis* is known as *teleology*
after the Greek *telos*, for goal. Aristotle famously described the teleological cause
of motion, the cause of purpose or intention. What motivated, directed and caused
the movement was the goal. The movement of an acorn towards the realisation of
an oak tree was caused by this cause of intention. It was the intention of the acorn to
realise the tree; it was a purposeful movement that worked from the determination
or nature of the acorn. Galileo and many of his contemporaries admired Aristotle,
but the contemporary use of Aristotle's causes and natural properties as inherent
in things led to a speculative philosophy of nature. For Galileo, the experiment
of direct observation and mathematical description became the method of natural
philosophy. His method led to a number of epoch-making observations and was to
become the design of science as we know it today. Most crucial was his discovery
of Jupiter's moons, which became the main argument in the controversy over the
heliocentric world-view (Jones 1970, p. 224).

The French mathematician René Descartes (1596–1650) went a bit further along
this path, expelling absolutely the inner forces of nature and introducing the idea
of *mecanicism* that would rule Western natural science to the present day. For
Descartes, all movement in matter was the expression of mechanical pushes or
pulls between the parts of matter. The world was like a clock, one big ingenious
mechanical device. According to Descartes, the task of the natural scientist was to
demonstrate the mechanics of things. The mechanical conception of nature became
such a strong theory that even a giant such as the British mathematician Sir Isaac
Newton (1642–1726) almost apologised when he introduced the law of gravity
in his description of the planets' orbits, because gravity, no matter how well it
could explain the motion of celestial bodies, could not be seen as pull or shock –
and, hence, was a very suspicious entity (Knudsen 2006, p. 752). With Descartes's
mechanicism and Galileo's descriptive method, methodical reductionism –

meaning modern science – was born. The scientist's task was to break nature down to its smallest parts in order to understand how it works – like clockwork. A small slice of the world's mechanics would not be affected by the larger mechanism or the whole it was functioning as a part of. In the movement, the mechanics of the individual parts do not vary as a function of the rest of the movement. Another important thing was that, as with the clockwork model, the mechanics of nature are locked in like fine gears. This movement does not have options.

Complexity Intrudes

Fast forward to the 1930s when Austrian biologist Ludwig von Bertalanffy (1901–1972) was engaged in the struggle between mechanicists and vitalists. As mentioned, the mechanicists believed that in the end everything could be broken down into mechanics. Vitalists believed that in biology, in addition to mechanics, there was a vitalising life force. Bertalanffy chose a position that broke with both positions. He believed that a living organism should be considered as an *organised whole*. It was no longer central what the single biological element might be. The central effort was about describing the organisation of the biological phenomenon. The position was further developed to apply not only to individual organisms, but to organised systems in general, such as the ant hill or the ecological niche. Bertalanffy called the theory the *general systems theory* (GST; hereafter just systems theory) and presented it for the first time in 1937. It was an emerging paradigm contrasting with mechanicism when systems theory claimed that the function of the individual part was affected by the whole system. Thus, one could not exhaustively describe an anthill based on the material parts of the individual ant. The ant as an organism was defined by the organisation of the whole ant community. Bertalanffy called it the problem of *organised complexity* (Bertalanffy 1973) The popular wording has become that "the whole is more than the sum of the individual parts" – in other words, a contradiction of the basic idea of mechanicism, which claims that we can understand the whole thing when we understand the mechanics of the individual parts.

Systems theory was a new science with a new subject field and a new terminology. The complex system itself became the scientific object. The features of the system that now came into focus were themes such as identity in change, self-organising and self-optimising, control and adaptation, as well as purposeful or teleological behaviour, elements that largely describe what is called homeostasis – the inner dynamic balancing towards an optimal state of the system in communication with its environment (Ølgaard 2004, p. 52). It is notable that the teleological or purposeful motives in nature, which Galileo and Descartes had excluded from natural science, are back again with systems theory and cybernetics as concepts necessary to explain the properties of systems. Even more, the key parole of systems theory being that the system is more than the sum of its parts was in a head-on collision with the central paradigm of the natural science method, namely reductionism. According to systems theory, the system as the scientific object should be studied as a whole as a structure of purposeful motion. By reducing the system to its elements, you would in fact lose what you were trying to observe. After encountering quite some headwind in its early days, systems theory proved a strong paradigm and, as of today, is indispensable in climatology, biology and the social sciences (Ølgaard 2004, s. 52).

Cybernetics, Feedback and Self-reference

While Bertalanffy was struggling to introduce systems theory in Europe, American mathematician Norbert Wiener (1894–1964), working with communication in electrical networks – the very early states of computer-aided mechanics – stumbled upon the concept of *feedback*, which would become the defining concept of cybernetics and prove a core element in systems theory. Feedback refers to a system of events around the discovery that the systemic entity constantly has to tell itself where it is in relation to its goal in order to know what to do, to move in the direction of its goal. An example that inspired Wiener was the hand that reaches out to get hold of a thing – a pencil dropped on the floor. The movement of the hand must be constantly regulated according to the knowledge of where the hand is in relation to the target. This means that there must be a circling flow of information in the system for it to work. An observation unit sends information feedback to the assessment control unit, which then sends information feed-forward to the action unit, which creates a new situation, which is then observed, and then new information is given back, all related to the goal (Wiener 1948, s. 7). This flow of goal-oriented assessment and adjustments would later become central to the works of American psychologist Daniel Stern (Stern 2004, s. 75) and, in the form of homeostasis, would define the later works of Portuguese biologist Antonio Damasio (Damasio 2012). With Mexican physician Arturo Rosenblueth and American computer engineer Julian Bigelow, Wiener wrote the short groundbreaking paper "Behavior, Purpose and Teleology" (1943), and here we are again looking at the concept of teleology in cutting-edge science of nature.

The concept of feedback, so common today, was revolutionary when it was launched in the 1940s. Systems refer to themselves in order to correct themselves in their directed purpose and in order to maintain the optimal balanced state in relation to themselves. Wiener's book *Cybernetics* (Wiener 1948) was to become one of the most influential books of the 20th century. Wiener gave this new science the name cybernetics after the Greek *kybernetes* for helmsman – a helmsman symbolising the controlling capacity of a system in its environment. Cybernetics is the science of controlling information in complex communication systems, whatever they may be – computer networks, pine forests or humans in their milieu.

Today, the word cybernetics most likely calls to mind the increasingly all-encompassing world of information technology, the elements of which we refer to as cyber-this or cyber-that, such as the internet, nicknamed cyberspace, or the computer-enhanced human being, a cyborg. But cybernetics, like systems theory, was originally thought of as an interdisciplinary meta-theory (Wiener 1948, p. 159), and, for the English philosopher-anthropologist Gregory Bateson

(1904–1980), cybernetics provided a possibility to describe the biosphere as basically communication structures. A pine forest, according to Bateson, has a mental structure because it has communication. Where a mechanistic biology would see the forest primarily as chemical mechanical processes, Bateson saw the forest as a system of mutual information exchanges in different reference structures which he called *mind*, a structure of consciousness, a work that has now been confirmed and widely extended by forest ecologist Suzanne Simard (Bateson 1980, p. 101, Simard 2021). The new insight was that, in living systems, there are no linear causal chains, as there are in mechanical aggregates. Living systems are seen as self-referential; they are circularly causal – as we saw with the hand reaching out, the assessment–adjusting process is a circular process. An interesting aspect of this is the *equifinality*, meaning there are many ways to the goal; the hand on the way to the pencil can be disturbed in many ways, but the control unit will readjust (Hass & Hansen 2022, p. 23). Bateson would later use cybernetics for analysing language structures behind mental illness (Bateson 1973, p. 167) and, late in life, seek a new language for the holy based on cybernetics (Bateson & Bateson 1987). At the Macy Conferences on Cybernetics (1946–1954), alongside Bateson and Wiener would sit American neurophysiologist Warren McCulloch, famous for the first mathematical design of neural networks, and next to computer pioneer John von Neuman, in the company of the highly influential anthropologist Margaret Mead and researchers from scientific fields ranging from physics to education (Heims 1991, s. 16). The Macy Conferences would summon scientists from various sciences because the new paradigm of communication was an analytical tool that would apply to a wide array of sciences (Hass & Hansen, s. 42). Systems theory and cybernetics were new sciences because they did not deal with the classical material aspects – mass, power and electricity – but with information necessary for communication in and between the subsystems of systems, be they machines or living organisms. This was coined in Wiener's famous dictum that cybernetics is a new science because "information is information, not matter or energy". Cybernetics was, from its founding days, a field that was seen to be able to cross-pollinate technology, nature and the humanities (Wiener 1948, p. 18).

Laws of Complexity

In his *An Introduction to Cybernetics* (1957), the English cybernetic psychiatrist William Ross Ashby (1903–1972) derived, from game theory, the basic cybernetic rule that a more complex system can regulate or control a less complex system – *not* the other way around. This basic rule is known as the *Law of Requisite Variety*, often shortened to *the necessary complexity*. That is, in complex systems with layers of system complexity, there is a kind of hierarchy of control systems that determines which system can regulate which (Vedfelt 1996, p. 114). But, in contrast to the classic concept of hierarchies where control becomes narrower towards the top, the regulatory capacity of systems depends on the level of complexity or *bandwidth* of the system, as given with the Ross Ashby rule. This means that one should not understand the helmsman metaphor as in the traditional corporate management hierarchy, but rather in the sense that, in order to function as a unit, larger systems have levels of regulation that are superior to the smaller individual subsystems, and yet the subsystems are a part of the control system. Such systems are also called holarchical systems (Koestler 1967).

As an everyday example of system levels, cybernetics and holarchical systems, we could choose the overall structure of a family going on a holiday trip. Picturing the family as a system and the family members as subsystems, a whole lot of intents and communication are circling round and have to play together for the thing to work. The whole mega-complex of a holiday trip is governed by creative meta-structures in the family system that accommodate and optimise the wishes, obligations and possibilities for the various persons as subsystems. Although a child with a stomach ache or an empty gas tank can have a major impact on the trip, these subsystems (car-in-traffic-system, child-needing-care-system) are unable to actually regulate the trip. The controlling system of a family of combined minds and coordinated sub-goals finds out something (assessment and adjustments) and reorganises (equifinality – many ways to the same goal) based on the overall optimisation of the totality of the subsystems under the goal orientation of the entire family system's holiday. Cybernetically, we say that the individual subsystems have lower complexity than the overall system, which, with its higher complexity, can regulate the lower ones – bring them into harmony with the overall goal realisation. In our example, we can say that the individual person-systems are regulated and optimised within the constraints and possibilities of the total family holiday system homeostasis.

A Cybernetic Psychology: The Intelligence of the Unconscious

The Integrative Project

Cybernetic psychology was developed at the Copenhagen-based Vedfelt Institute in the 1990s and was originally a research programme into a paradigm suitable for integration of the main schools of psychology. The leading idea was that the main schools all have important views on the human to offer. And, while it seemed that the different schools would define themselves in contrast to each other, practitioners would very often be multi-methodic in therapy. Based on systems theory and cybernetics, Vedfelt argued that the spectrum of psychological schools – be they psychodynamic, body-psychological, cognitive, human existential or neurologically based, each with highly skilled special competences – still only addressed constricted domains of personality. If seen together, these would produce a more diverse image of the human, far better fitting the rich complexity of the total human body–mind–language–social being that we experience as ourselves and our fellow beings. In this view, all the relevant major schools of psychology make important contributions to the image of the human, but we seem to miss a scientific mutual ground on which to assemble the values and methods of the separate schools. The breakthrough came in considering the human as primarily a communication phenomenon where, until now, the different schools had concentrated around a certain aspect of the complex of interwoven layers of communication inside the human and in the social web. Looking at the communication phenomenon as a cybernetic system, the different schools could be considered representatives of different *information processing channels*. Largely speaking, Freud and Beck would be about rational conversation, Jung would be into imagery, Perls would focus on emotions, the Reich–Lowen–Levine path would focus on the muscular body, Boadella would be more into the organ system, cognitive therapy and cognitive science, and the neurologists would look at patterns of connections between these information channels. Central to all this was the acknowledgement of a formidable creativity of balancing the process channels to resonate with the situation. To give voice to the creativity of the person-system, art therapy around writing, music-playing and drawing and painting was integrated. The different schools and lines of research, despite their proclaimed different systems, would all be seen as doing therapy inside the unified web of information channels, only mainly focused on their own perspective – meaning reduced complexity. In picturing the person-system as an information-system, these layers of information channels would dovetail beautifully, and the neutral cybernetics paradigm would supply the much-needed scientific mutual ground for integrating the psychologies. The person-system would further include preprogrammed structures in the line of Jungian archetypes, Piaget–Beck schemata, Vedfelt adult schemata and Chomsky–Fodor modules. On top of this, skills of creating subpersonalities as personified communication interfaces – that is, schemata as distinct modes of interaction – developed to balance and optimise adaptation to the ecological niche of, for example, childhood or workspace (Vedfelt 2000, p. 223, Hass & Hansen 2022, p. 73).

This seemingly well-functioning idea would, however, raise a far-reaching question, namely *how* this highly creative, complex communicating unity of process channels and sub-persons was regulated. The hypothesis of the unconscious intelligence as an overall controlling entity of the person-system, as stated by Vedfelt around the year 2000 (Vedfelt 2000), would become the central claim of cybernetic psychology and psychotherapy. The research into unconscious intelligence would later be the theme of New York-based journalist Malcolm Gladwell's influential book *Blink* (Gladwell 2005) and would become central to the works of highly influential psychologists Gerd Gigerenzer (Gigerenzer 2007) and Daniel Kahneman (Kahneman 2011). In cybernetic psychology, the unconscious intelligence is considered a mutual ground for psychodynamic and cognitive psychology.

Cybernetic psychology is thus an attempt to formulate a groundwork for an integrative interpretation and convergence of classical and current Western- and Eastern-inspired psychologies under an information theoretical meta-theory, a theory that could forge a passage for the psychologies of the 20th century into the age of AI and information theory (Hass & Hansen 2022, p. 75).

A Science of Communication

A central systems theory claim in cybernetic psychology is the perception of personality as a self-regulating, self-optimising and intelligent problem-solving information system. The systems theory perspective is the aforementioned homeostasis, which denotes the system's ability to regulate itself in order to obtain the optimal internal balance in relation to the stress and development opportunities in the surrounding environment. Transferred to cybernetic psychology, this means that the entire conscious–unconscious person-system in its social web is a hyper-complex, multilevelled, self-optimising, problem-solving entity, meaning that psychotherapy is a function to facilitate the client's innate highly skilled problem-solving capacities. The system-optimising entity necessary for the function of the cybernetic self is labelled, as mentioned, the *unconscious intelligence*. The central claim of cybernetic psychotherapy is that the art of therapy is a facilitation of the communication between the unconscious intelligence and the everyday mind of the client, since the problem-solving capacities lie mainly in the unconscious intelligence guiding the entire system, the greatest part by far of which is unconscious. The state of conscious versus unconscious is thus a matter of information processing compatibility, where the whole system capacity far exceeds the conscious mind and therefore remains unconscious, just as what you see on the computer screen is immensely less complex than the systems running the apps. Cybernetics is a science of communication, and cybernetic psychology is a theory of communication viewing the human as primarily a hyper-complex communication phenomenon, meaning again that the problems or crises in a person's life are primarily problems concerning styles of communication – in short, the bandwidth for communication between the everyday mind and the unconscious intelligence is too narrow. And further, this is owing to a lack of complexity in the personal environment – or, cybernetically speaking, a lack of complexity in the personal *ecological niche*. So, a person seeking psychotherapy is a person seeking an environment supporting the necessary complexity for personal growth.

Patterns of Communication

The cybernetic psychotherapist will thus regard the client's problems or symptoms as intelligent communication from higher-order information processes. And, although it can be difficult to find the special key to grasping the intelligence of the 'rhetoric' of the client's sufferings, dreams or bodily states, this is exactly the main aim of the cybernetic approach – seeing the complex network of verbal language, body language, dream images, feelings, social situation and so on as a unity of expressions of the unconscious intelligence (Vedfelt 2017). The client view of cybernetic psychotherapy is thus far from the classical apparatus-error model; rather, it is a picturing of the therapeutic process as an unfolding of complex communication structures, continuously unfolding personality at various levels of consciousness. This means that a symptom such as anxiety or a feeling of alienation, shame or guilt must be seen as an intelligent expression of a developmental process directed at problem-solving. The symptom is a flag drawing attention to the zone of personal development, asking for help to manage the unfolding of personality.

So, this is where we meet our initial problem: From the perspective of our well-trained yet still relatively low-complexity rational psychotherapist mind, how do we meet and engage with the unconscious intelligence of the client? The following will point to various therapeutic ways of conscious communication with the unconscious intelligence. Psychotherapists will most likely recognise their work owing to both the integrative nature of cybernetic psychology and the idea that what we do as therapists comprises variations on the unfolding of natural healing communication, be it psychodynamic or cognitive (Stern 2004, p. 97).

In the following, the argument from cybernetic psychology vis-à-vis the Ross Ashby theorem of necessary complexity will be that the client's higher system levels will seek contact and willingly engage in connecting with the therapist. This may be recognised as transference but being conscious about it in the present moment it becomes communication. This process will broaden the client's mind, lessening the mental constraints and yielding more inner freedom and personal growth. It is important to also recognise that the concept of complexity throughout signifies the highly interwoven, smooth collaboration of layers of information processes. Where we, in everyday life, experience matters to be complicated is actually where there is a lack of complexity – a lack of capacity to contain conflicting opposites as a meaningful dynamic. In the following chapters, the keywords *enhanced bandwidth* will signify the process in therapy whereby the everyday mind opens up to the influence of the higher system levels – that is, the unconscious intelligence.

Second Part: Solving the Dilemma – Cybernetic Psychotherapy

Working with the Unconscious Intelligence

According to cybernetic psychology, a human being is endowed by nature with a lifelong ability to unfold a still broader embracing of life's controversies in step with age and personal development. The mark of this higher-complexity open-mindedness is the ability to embrace opposites and develop creative syntheses. Still, the simple, natural, goal-oriented development of maturity will often create difficulties for the person in the close environment that is experienced as a crisis and can take many different forms at the symptom level.

A main reason for a lack of openness of personality is that the person-system has skills to tune its filtering of the outside world in such a way that the person-system is spared harm – an ability to fluently reduce the information pressure from the surrounding environment so that it matches the bandwidth of the person's information processing capacity. In this way, a balance – or homeostasis between the individual and the outside world – can be created that prevents overloading of the system. We know this from everyday life: When complexity becomes too deep in one area of the surrounding environment, other information intakes are shut down. When we unexpectedly dive into an important conversation, we need to turn off the music or the television set in the next room. In more serious contexts, it is seen that, when the mother and father undergo a marital crisis, the child will often be so preoccupied with finding an inner and outer balance in relation to that that there is not sufficient information capacity left to concentrate in school.

If the child, at an early age, has thus to ongoingly narrow the bandwidth in the face of a lasting adverse influence in the environment, the reduced bandwidth may become permanent in life (Vedfelt 1996, p. 115). Thus, there will be a tendency for the system's setting in adulthood to continue to match the childhood environment. The constraints of the homeostasis and self-reference determined by the protective lower bandwidth the child needed will remain as a default background mode in adulthood. What was once a necessary and optimal regulation will often, later in life, be limiting and disruptive to the person when the reduced processing capacity does not match the complexity required in adult life. So, why do the settings not just change to match the new environment? In cybernetic therapy, we would tend to think that what appears to be the client's reason for enquiry is the aftermath of a strategy that was once the best possible problem-solving method, a solution that may have been crucial to the person's psychological survival. The thing is that this self-protecting coding of constraints on the person-system has had such a high security level that it needs a matching environment to unlock it, and that might eventually be the therapeutic setting. The case is that the unconscious intelligence that once set up the constraints still has the passwords to the coding and so needs to be engaged to unlock the childhood constraints. The focus on the meaningful aspect of what is a burden to the client is thus not just an expression of encouraging recognition but primarily a way to open the field of communication with the unconscious intelligence that was the engineer behind the childhood rescue system settings. Recalibrating the settings of the person-system requires collaboration with the client's unconscious intelligence, starting with listening to signals from the inner silent child-sub-person who has never had a voice and, by listening in a warm and welcoming way, creating an increasing bandwidth for the therapeutic relationship to engage the unconscious (Vedfelt 2000, p. 57).

Cybernetic psychology often refers to the therapeutic space as an ecological niche; in the introduction, we used the images of forest and orchard as poetic models for the therapy's ability to create an environment enabling the growth of the self-optimisation processes of the client's higher-order systems by first recognising the work of the unconscious intelligence in the problems the client is facing. Any therapeutic results are achieved owing to this process, since it is not possible to fix the highly complex person-system – it is only possible to facilitate self-optimisation. A warm, welcoming attitude is the first step in the direction of establishing a collaboration with the client's unconscious intelligence, overcoming the Ross Ashby dilemma of psychotherapy. As put by Vedfelt,

Entering the therapeutic process somehow beneath the surface, one constantly senses something else in the client's personality, which, as it were, tries to break through, express itself and start a dialogue with the client's ego or the therapist. This "other", which manifests itself in dreams, body language, and imaginative material and transference processes, is not treated as malfunctions in the psychophysical apparatus, but as signals from superior, integrative levels, and their attempts at self-regulation and homeostasis.

(Vedfelt 1996, p. 112)

Process Channels and Bandwidth

As we saw, systems theory arose from the assumption that individual parts of systems could not be studied without reference to the whole system. Similarly, one can, with reference to systems theory, say that the different communication channels – verbal, facial, bodily and so on – cannot be understood otherwise than as aspects of a highly complex, organised communicational *intent*, with an overall control system translating this intent from the status of information processes into the mind–body–social world. This relationship is expressed in the above quote about the multiple communication pathways in the therapeutic relationship. This exemplifies the dilemma of the relationship between the communication capacity of the overall system and the reduced bandwidth of the client's rational communication pathways. In the quote, the client's higher communication bandwidth is awoken in the therapeutic setting, but the client ego or everyday conscious mind is too narrow a passage, and therefore the communication is conducted in ways that are beyond the control of the personal self. So, the central point of the quote is that what might be experienced as awkward or disruptive in the session is by no means considered so but rather is welcomed as communication, indeed as creative utterances from the unconscious intelligence. In this way, the therapist can increase the client's communication bandwidth by being aware of and responding to the expressions of unconscious communication that the client is showing. Regarding the initial problem of this chapter, the important aspect is *from* – that is, the communication comes from the client's higher level of complexity. The therapist's being there effects an activation of the client's higher processing levels solely by being available to the client's unconscious intelligence and by the therapist being aware of the communication that comes from there. Systemically speaking, the therapeutic setting thus constituting a favourable ecological niche allows the client's higher control system to communicate with the aware therapist's conscious level. This means that, in therapy, the client's higher processing level will contact the therapist, bypassing the client's conscious self, and the therapist can then lead this communication back to the client's conscious self, step by step.

It is thus important to emphasise that the different process channels – the rational, poetical, visual, bodily and so on – are not to be understood as being like separate tubes that are communicated through, but are rather to be understood as an interwoven yet distinct unity of multiple languages – verbal–visual–bodily – unfolding the intended highly complex information laid out in the field of communication. Speech communicates the meaning of words, while the vibrations of the voice move the body, while the sound of the voice expresses emotions, while the client's gestures, facial expressions and so on together convey a unity of complex meaning. It is Vedfelt's point that our awareness is usually focused on one channel at a time – and preferably the rational verbal channel (Vedfelt 2000, p. 58). But the cybernetic therapeutic perspective here is the attempt to consciously engage communication on several process channels simultaneously and hereby expand the bandwidth in the client's consciousness. This can be done by simply asking, for example, how the dream image feels? And how is this feeling experienced in the body? This is perhaps recognised as elements from cognitive therapy, but the cybernetic practitioner will go further by, for example, asking the colour and shape of the feeling and will often invite the client to move to the floor and draw the feeling, thereby engaging creativity and the body in motion. By attention thus being maintained on several processing channels simultaneously, the client's higher level of consciousness is answered and invited in, because the higher level of complexity that is now opened allows a higher system level to express itself. What the unconscious intelligence of the higher system level has been constantly trying to say can now be better expressed because the client has an open mind – that is, a mind open to intent that would otherwise not be processed in the narrow mindset. Along with the drawing, the client might suddenly sense new images or memories, reach a new vision of the problem, finding simple, comforting words covering the pain felt just by leaving it to the unconscious while drawing. And bear in mind that drawing the colour alone can be a highly information-dense process that allows unconscious processes to reorganise the personal self beyond the rational mind. The argument here regarding necessary complexity is that, even by methodically engaging the process channels with low complexity, the therapist can, from the conscious perspective, establish an opening for the work of the client's higher-complexity organising system levels.

Channel Switching, Mental Leaps and Holes in Consciousness

The therapeutic relationship is thus considered a web of communication networks where one can engage the various processing channels in ways that transcend everyday possibilities. The client has the opportunity to express intricate emotions that the everyday environment might not allow. This alone – an extension of the emotion processing channel – is an extension of the communication bandwidth – that is, higher complexity. During the therapeutic session, breaks or gaps in continuity will occur. These can be a pause in the conversation, a sudden hand movement, the gaze becoming distant or more alert, or the position of the whole body changing. The therapist sees that there has been an issue that has not been able to pass from the client's unconscious to present awareness owing to the limited channel capacity of the conscious self-reference. The higher information control has released an amount of information that the personal self is not able to contain and thus refuses to communicate. The information therefore moves to another channel to get through (Vedfelt 1996, p. 131). What happens in these leaps is that the overall control, which cannot be blocked by the limitations or constraints of the personal self, moves the information to another channel and thereby bypasses the limited bandwidth in order to reach the therapist. Mostly, the client is unconscious of this communication pattern but can become conscious of it through the mirroring by the awake therapist. The general pattern is that the overall operating system will move the communication to a channel where the conscious I of the client does not notice it, and therefore the information gets through to the therapist, be it through body expressions, odd metaphors, 'random' whims, transmissions or dreams that bypass conscious control. These leaps in the conversation designs by the client's overall control system will be able to give the therapist access to essential material. This then gives the client the opportunity, together with the therapist, to gain awareness of the content that could otherwise not be communicated. By thus following and responding to the expression that the client's higher operating system offers, the therapist will be precisely influencing or enabling the work of the client's unconscious intelligence. So, again regarding the Ross Ashby problem, simply by establishing an open listening and welcoming environment and awareness of the communication patterns of the client's unconscious intelligence, the therapist is able to facilitate engagement between the client's higher-order information levels and everyday self-awareness. In this process, we begin to see that what the therapist does is not so much change the higher levels of the client's unconscious intelligence but rather establish a kind of – very roughly put – triangular communication cycle between the client's unconscious intelligence, the therapist's conscious awareness and the client's conscious self, which opens the client's everyday mind to the unconscious intelligence. This is the basis of cybernetic psychotherapy, engaging all processing channels in the integrative process of the communication patterns, and this is why the integrative project is so central. So, what we see is a higher-order system of communication patterns emerging as the relationship deepens. This is cybernetic psychology's version of the idea of the talking cure and existential psychology's idea that it is the relationship that heals. This is, furthermore, a really broad view of the occasional 'Freudian slip', seeing instead how the intelligent, creative unconscious is highly skilled in continuously slipping around the client's conscious constraints. Importantly, this pattern is expanded only when the therapist engages, viewing it as an intelligent step towards a self-optimisation in the client's personal ability to embrace the seemingly unembraceable. It is very important also to understand the delicacy of this situation since it is only if the therapist engages with an unconditional growth-minded embracing of the client's expressions that the process will open. It takes quite some bravery on the part of the client to accept this level of being observed, not to feel exposed but to feel cared for. This is why we emphasise the importance of a warm, welcoming atmosphere in the setting.

Second-Order Cybernetics

When we consider personality as a cybernetic information system, two people communicating will create a second-order cybernetic system – two communication systems in communication (Vedfelt 2000, p. 94). If we thus consider the therapeutic relationship as a second-order systemic entity, then, when the client's higher system level bypasses the client's conscious subsystem, this can be seen as an expression of the second-order homeostasis of the client–therapist system. As mentioned, homeostasis is a term for the system striving to maintain an optimal internal balance under the influence of its milieu. In the therapeutic relationship as a system, the imbalance manifests itself in the fact that the client's need for communication is greater than the client's normal consciousness channel capacity allows, meaning the client-system is carrying a concealed communicational imbalance. The client's communication thus becomes an imbalance matter for the entire therapeutic second-order cybernetic system, and the regulation of this matter spreads throughout the whole therapist–client system. Significant in this context is that the second-order cybernetic system is of a greater complexity than the systems of the two persons separately. Again turning to the law of necessary complexity, this means that a higher-bandwidth control system emerges between the two, which in itself has a regulating and problem-solving effect on both subsystems. In this way, the therapeutic relationship itself activates and regulates the client's overall levels of control.

According to systems theory, the second-order cybernetics of the therapeutic relationship must in itself be considered an emerging unified field. The law of necessary complexity states that the control in the therapeutic setting is of a higher complexity than the two individual ones, and it must follow that the deepening of the therapeutic relationship in general is an emergence towards greater bandwidth in the relationship control system and, as such, engages the client's unconscious intelligence. Here, we come close to a solution to the initial problem. The second-order unified information system of a higher order engages the client's higher self-organising levels, which were exactly what seemed to be missing. The problem seems to originate from a mechanistic thinking considering therapist and client as separate entities. Here, again, we see how the second-order homeostasis can be considered the facilitating of the self-actualising processes of psychotherapy central to Carl Rogers (1957), Karen Horney (1991, p. 15) and I.D. Yalom (2003, p. 35). Cybernetic psychology would likewise here identify the push behind and organisation of the Jungian concept of individuation (von Franz 1991, p. 161, Jung 1989, p. 86).

Introspection and Supramodal Space

As mentioned earlier, the person-system communicates in its ecological niche in different communication languages – poetic and rational, body, facial, and so on. I have argued that a communication modality – what has been called a processing channel – does not stand alone but is to be seen as an element in a complex, but that the everyday consciousness is mostly aware of one of the processing channels – rational thinking. We have seen how the overall control can simultaneously

communicate through a channel other than the conscious one, and how holes or la-
cunae in the communication stream on a channel can point to images or memories
that seem awkward to the client in the situation but may turn out to be a guide or
Ariadne thread into the communication. In understanding the second-order cybernetic system, the therapist may be aware of this communication across multiple
channels. But being aware of communication on several channels simultaneously
is not only for the trained therapist. It is – as mentioned – an ability that we all
have, and it is part of the therapeutic process to develop this in the client. This
is important for therapy because it expands the bandwidth of the client self. The
higher bandwidth will consequently be able to accommodate and communicate the
issues raised in the second-order cybernetic homeostasis of the session. Being consciously aware of several communication channels – for example, being aware of
body sensations at the same time as reflections and inner images in a conversation –
recalls Vedfelt's supramodal awareness. It is *supra*modal because we somehow, as
in mindfulness practice, have a mindful overview of the interplay between the processing channels or modes of experience. When the therapist asks the client to repeat a sentence and hand movement and, while doing so, to carefully note feelings,
images, bodily sensations – for example, warm or cold feet – the client is invited to
access the supramodal viewpoint, enhancing the bandwidth, and, with the opened-
up complexity or layers of network, inner imagery might leap to a whole other situation or memory that has a special explanatory relevance. The supramodal point
is Vedfelt's term for the mental point of view from which we view the experience
modalities or processing channels and it is, furthermore, a mental space where we
have a special awareness of feeds from the unconscious intelligence, be it images,
memories or the connected emotions (Vedfelt 2000, pp. 84 and 90). It is important
to note that what we see here is a merger of cognitive therapy, mindfulness and the
psychodynamic notion of the unconscious (Arendt & Rosenberg 2012, p. 48). The
cognitive therapy linking feeling, body sensations, thoughts and imagery opens up
higher complexity in the supramodal space opening for the self-organising work of
the unconscious intelligence, in the auspicious milieu of the second-order homeostasis. This is, according to cybernetic psychology, the genius of cognitive therapy
and why mindfulness is an obvious tool in cognitive therapy.

Mindfulness practices help establish the supramodal viewpoint as a key element in
therapy. In a cybernetic psychotherapeutic process, there will thus often be direct am-
plification of unconscious processes. During supramodal sensory training, the therapist might point the client's awareness to a specific hand movement that accompanies
the client's speech and invite them to an investigation into what the hand movement
'means' or how the movement is connected to inner-body states. Or the therapist
might ask the client to go back in their account and notice what happens in the body
at a certain passage in the account. This is what is called guided introspection. This
process of opening the supramodal mind space is an extension of the bandwidth
of the client's conscious mind, consciously being aware of several communication
processing channels simultaneously. The point in connection to the initial problem
is that opening the supramodal space is an opening to processes of self-organisation.

Note that this is a central element in the answer to the initial question: The sufficient psychotherapeutic method will open the necessary complexity in the client's conscious mind, rendering possible the reorganising of cognitive schemata by the unconscious intelligence. These are highly intricate information coding processes, more like growth processes, that we as therapists work to facilitate.

Transference, Countertransference and Homeostasis

Systemically seen in the therapeutic relationship is one system, a second-order cybernetic system. There is an imbalance locally in the system, as the client system contains a conflict that cannot be communicated through the client's conscious self. Therefore, the overall operating system communicates around the client's conscious self. Part of this communication takes place in a transference process. By transference it is meant that the client transfers figures from their own inner gallery to the therapist – mother, father, teacher and so on. The therapist becomes a screen for projections of persons important to the client's personal history or projections of the client's positive development potentials. In this way, unconscious material emerges in the therapeutic relationship so that it can be examined. Owing to the second-order system, unconscious information in the form of emotions, mental images and body states can be transferred from the client to the therapist. Here, again, it is a matter of there being an issue in the client-system that cannot come into contact with the client's consciousness but still finds its way to the therapist. It can be a mental image but also a physical feeling, such as a tension in the shoulders, or a mindset of, for example, sadness or high spirits. If the therapist, through introspection skills, is aware of this transference and is able to process it back to the client, it is of very great value for the widening of the therapeutic space – that is, the complexity of the communication network. This is a cybernetic merger of classical transference theory and the Heinz Kohut theory of empathy (Vedfelt 2000, p. 104). In other words, the homeostasis of the second-order cybernetic system has brought, for example, bodily information that could not be manifested consciously in the client to conscious awareness of, for example, a bodily sensation in the therapist. The therapist will then be able, together with the client, to search back in the client's report and find out the content where the feeling originates. In the case of transfer, the client gets a chance to consciously integrate the complexity of the feeling and body states in the setting (Vedfelt 1996, p. 144). Returning here to the initial Ross Ashby question, it is noted that, simply by being aware of the transference, the therapist is in communication with the client's overall higher control system. Often it will be the case that the meeting with the therapist alone evokes higher levels of complexity in the client because the therapist will tend to represent a model for the higher level of personality in the client. The transference thus often takes the form of an idealisation of the therapist. It may reflect a fixation on a necessary stage of development in childhood, but it is also the image of the client's processes at higher levels, which may slowly realise itself as client identity (Vedfelt 1996, p. 145). So, again, the cybernetic hypothesis is that it is the homeostasis of the therapeutic setting that drives the transference. This salutogenesis of the relationship is further suggested by Stern to be a foundation of the human – meaning, in a sense, that we are designed for psychotherapy (Rogers 1957, Stern 2004, p. 97).

Sub-persons and Enhanced Complexity

In cybernetic therapy we recommend – as a theme throughout this chapter – considering *the other* behind the client's conscious self as an intelligent conversation partner trying to get through. This intelligence is unconscious to the client, but conscious to the therapist. One must regard it as a personality that unfolds as if behind the conscious self. As described earlier, cybernetic psychology sees this *other* as a subpersonality related to the niche of the therapeutic setting working towards optimising the balance and utilising the possibilities in the situation. In the history of psychotherapy, it has been observed and studied how the personality is a set of persons rather than one single person. Hypnotherapy has shown how 'inside' a person there could be other personalities and that these did not necessarily know each other. Systems of subpersonalities we know from, for instance, Freud's tripartite model of the psyche, with the *ego, super-ego* and *id*. Jung worked with a model of the psyche with dynamically related subpersonalities such as the shadow, anima–animus, the inner child, mother–father archetypes and so on (Jung 1991a, p. 158). Along these lines, cybernetic psychology sees the person-system as a multilayered, hyper-complex information system where the system intelligence creates subpersonalities as information structures enabling diverse communication in various ecological niches. This has an important implication in relation to the problem of necessary complexity, because the rational I-centred consciousness is also considered a sub-person regulated by a higher system intelligence – the unconscious intelligence (Vedfelt 2000, p. 232, Jung 1991b, p. 266).

In cybernetic psychology, this is related to the necessary reduction in capacity previously mentioned in the child, which could become permanent and cause problems later in life. Aspects of the personality are split off to avoid harm. In therapy, this subpersonality will possess information that is essential for the healing of the personality.

Vedfelt mentions a case of a woman who grew up with an alcoholic father. As a child, she used a coping strategy to regulate her personality and states of consciousness according to her father's condition. This built up two subpersonalities corresponding to the protection the child needed. She had to shut down part of the consciousness according to what the situation offered. This became a permanently automatised, unconscious structure lingering into her adult life, when the woman would encounter problems arising from this double structure in her conscious attitude (Vedfelt 2000, p. 237). As the woman went into therapy, the two subpersonalities came to be present for the therapist's consciousness. From there, it was possible for the woman to learn to see the two structures together.

The important thing for our dilemma here is that it requires greater bandwidth in the client's consciousness to see both subpersonalities together – to become aware of the two from a higher conscious perspective. The integration of the two subsystems takes place under observation from a supramodal position, which, as we saw earlier, has greater bandwidth than the systems of the individual subpersonalities. Based on the above, it can be described as the emerging supramodality of consciousness necessarily having higher bandwidth than the previous consciousness setting. In the same way as Vedfelt acknowledges the client's unconscious body language, narratives, channel changes and so on as an intelligent move from the other that lies behind, so also a client exposes different subpersonalities in therapy – that is, it can be seen as a way in which the client's overall system communicates information to the therapist.

We have seen how personality can regulate information flows in relation to the surrounding environment by reducing bandwidth. It has been pointed out how the executing and operational outward function of the ego has a limited bandwidth. Bateson speaks of the fact that consciousness is digitised as opposed to the analogue form of communication of the higher levels of organisation. It has been discussed how consciousness in everyday life mostly rests on the modality of one communication channel, but that the communication channels are woven into each other, that every human being possesses a supramodal ability to perceive several modalities of experience simultaneously. And I have mentioned that the simultaneous awareness of transference requires a kind of two-way attention or supramodal perception.

The Therapist's Self-examination

On the whole, it seems that the example from Vedfelt of observing *the other* presupposes a consciousness that can function in different directions at the same time. The therapist must be present in the conversation's reflections, but, at the same time, attention must be open to their own body sensations, and, at the same time, the therapist observes the client's body language and senses different moods that accompany the client's account. And, as can be seen from the foregoing, this therapist supramodality requires a significantly increased consciousness bandwidth. The mere fact that the therapeutic relationship is a second-order cybernetic system entails that the therapist affects the client systemically – meaning there is no way around it – and that this obliges the therapist to work with self-examination (Vedfelt 1996, p. 110, Yalom 2003, p. 73). According to Vedfelt, this generally requires that the therapist, in addition to therapeutic learning analysis, enters into a work of contemplation and meditation in order to practise an ability to observe the client as open-mindedly as possible in the therapeutic moment. That is, the therapist should have a meditation practice that allows for the separation of self-perception from perception of the client in the field of transmission – in the session. Furthermore, Vedfelt believes that self-observation, with the right guidance, will be able to create access to increasingly information-dense states of consciousness. Just as a person who is being educated in music can start by learning simple harmonisation and then learn to distinguish ever more and more complex harmonies, in the same way, the therapist can deepen the listening to the diverse *music* of the conversation while keeping attention on the supramodal space. This is great support for the therapeutic relationship, where quite small mood nuances can be the moments where it is possible to connect to deeper levels in the client's personality.

Summary

Initially, this chapter raised the inconvenient situation around laws of cybernetics that seemed to entail that the therapist could not regulate the higher levels of the client's person-system. This is a crucial issue in view of the fact that Vedfelt and the Ross Ashby theorem point to precisely this as decisive for the possibility and effectiveness of therapy. The problem was inevitable since the law of necessary complexity states that a less complex system cannot regulate a more complex one, and the therapist's normal consciousness has far lower complexity than the client's overall information system.

Based on cybernetics and systems theory, it has been argued how the therapist *in* the therapeutic relationship consciously can participate in communication at levels of higher complexity than that of normal consciousness and so actually engages the client's higher, unconscious levels in the therapeutic process.

First, this has been shown by pointing to how the client's higher unconscious levels try to get in contact with the therapist by bypassing the client's constrained consciousness. So, the surprisingly simple answer to our question is that, in therapy, there is always an open opportunity to be in conscious contact with the higher levels of complexity in the client's unconscious intelligence.

Second, it has been shown that the therapeutic setting can be tuned to higher complexity by engaging a broader range of processing channels, primarily by including the nonverbal, non-rational processes of dreams, body language, feelings, and art forms such as drawing and music playing. This opens the everyday mind to the problem-solving capacities of the self-optimising system.

Third, and fundamental to the two previous items, the setting is a second-order cybernetic system generating a higher-order homeostasis that influences the higher levels of consciousness of both client and therapist.

The main theories carrying these arguments are complexity theory, systems theory, the homeostasis of second-order cybernetics, the natural tendency towards higher complexity of mind lying underneath the growth perspective and, last but not least, the hypothesis around the concept of unconscious system intelligence.

All in all, this invites us to the view that the therapist is an observer-participant, a guide in conversations at information levels far transcending the normal consciousness – changing both client and therapist. The two people as information systems merge to form a single unified field of communication of a far higher complexity than the two persons separately. In this way, the therapist is not an entrepreneur making an intervention to fix the client, but rather a guide and helmsman along the way in an ocean of information, of which both are the creators.

References

Arendt, M. & Rosenberg, N.K. (2012) *Kognitiv terapi – Nyeste udvikling*. Hans Reitzels Forlag, Copenhagen.

Aurelius, Marcus (1996) *Meditationer*. Det Lille Forlag, Copenhagen.

Ashby, William Ross (1957) *An Introduction to Cybernetics*. Chapman & Hall, London.

Bateson, Gregory (1973) *Steps to an Ecology of Mind*. Paladin, St. Albans.

Bateson, Gregory & Bateson Mary C. (1987) *Hvor engle ej tør træde*, Rosinante, Copenhagen.

Bertalanffy, Ludwig von (1973) *General Systems Theory*. Penguin University Books.

Damasio, Antonio (2012) *Self Comes to Mind*. Vintage, London.

Gigerenzer, Gerd (2007) *Gut Feelings – The Intelligence of the Unconsciousness*. Allen Lane, London.

Gladwell, Malcolm (2005) *Blink: The Power of Thinking without Thinking*. Little, Brown, Boston.

Hass, Henrik & Hansen, Torben (2022) *Kybernetisk Psykologi – ubevidst intelligens i psykoterapi og hverdag*. Frydenlund, Copenhagen.

Heims, J. Steve (1991) *The Cybernetics Group*. MIT Press, New York.

Horney, Karen (1991) *Neurosis and Growth*. Norton, New York.

Jones, W.T. (1970) *A History of Western Philosophy*. Harcourt, Brace.

Jung, C.G. (1989) *Jeg'et og det ubevidste*. Gyldendal, Copenhagen

Jung, C.G. (1991a) *Mennesket og dets symboler*. Lindhardt & Ringhof, Copenhagen.

Jung, C.G. (1991b) *Erindringer, drømme, tanker*. Lindhardt & Ringhof, Copenhagen.

Kahneman, Daniel (2011) *Thinking. Fast and Slow*. Penguin Books, London.

Koestler, Arthur (1967) *The Ghost in the Machine*. Hutchinson, London.

Knudsen, Ole (2006) Den videnskabelige revolution. In Hans Siggaard Jensen, Ole Knudsen & Frederik Stjernfelt (Eds.), *Tankens Magt – Vestens Idéhistorie*. Lindhardt & Ringhof, Copenhagen.

Rogers, Carl (1957) The Necessary and Sufficient Conditions of Therapeutic Personality Change. *Journal of Consulting Psychology*, Vol. 21, pp. 95–103.

Rosenblueth, Arturo, Julian Bigelow & Norbert Wiener (1943) Behavior, Purpose and Teleology. *Philosophy of Science*, Vol. 10, no. 1, pp. 18–24.

Simard, Suzanne (2021) *Finding the Mother Tree*. Alfred A. Knopf, New York.

Stern, Daniel N. (2004) *The Present Moment – in Psychotherapy and Everyday Life*. W.W. Norton, London.

Vedfelt, Ole (1996) *Bevidsthed*. Gyldendal, Copenhagen.

Vedfelt, Ole (2000) *Ubevidst Intelligens – du ved mere end du tror*. Gyldendal, Copenhagen.

Vedfelt, Ole (2017) *A Guide to the World of Dreams*. London, Routledge.

von Franz, Marie L.(1991) Individuationsprocessen. In C.G. Jung, *Mennesket og dets symboler*. Lindhardt & Ringhof, Copenhagen.

Wiener, Norbert (1948) *Cybernetics: Or Control and Communication in the Animal and the Machine*. MIT Press, New York.

Yalom, Irwin D. (2003) *Terapiens Essens*. Hans Reitzel, Copenhagen.

Ølgaard, Bent (2004) *Kommunikation og Økomentale systemer*. Akademisk Forlag, Copenhagen.

2

Academia through the Lens of Cybernetic Psychology

Anne Maj Nielsen

In this chapter, I will examine my experiences of the potential of unconscious intelligence in academia through the lens of cybernetic psychology and illustrate this with examples from my experiences as a researcher and teacher at the Danish School of Education, Aarhus University. I will apply Ole Vedfelt's cybernetic psychology, as it provides a well-founded integrative framework of dynamic systems theory for conceptualising consciousness as a set of emerging processes of various levels of complexity, where the more complex levels can integrate what appears contradictory at less complex levels. In this framework, it is possible to study specific units and processes by applying the unit-specific or process-specific knowledge provided by a variety of studies and theories. In particular, I highlight Vedfelt's conceptualisation of consciousness, especially unconscious intelligence, as interconnected with persons' lived experience and present circumstances in their sociocultural ecological niches, including their material, practical and cultural resources and discourses. I focus particularly on his concepts of 'supramodal space' and 'processing channels'. The sociocultural concept of 'mediating means and tools' further helps to qualify my analysis and reflections on the potential of unconscious intelligence in academia.

A Line from Passion in Practice to Research and Theory

As a child, I loved to draw and paint on all kinds of surfaces – paper, canvas, cloth – and, as an adult, I love to work with graphic and painting technologies and experience art. I vividly remember my encounter with a green painting by Cézanne at the Musée du Jeu de Paume[1] a long time ago. It was as if the painting approached me, and, in the moment, there was just a vibrant experience of being with this green appearance in a deep sense of meaning, while everything else was distanced. The sense of meaning in visual art drew me into certain lines of thought and interests throughout my education as a psychologist After a couple of years doing innovative social work that fused art, cultural work, counselling and therapy for socio-economically vulnerable women, a post for a doctoral fellow to study children's drawings was announced by the Royal Danish School of Educational

DOI: 10.4324/9781003360247-3

Studies, and I felt it was for me. In autumn 1988, I returned to academia and university and immersed myself in a world of drawings and theories that focused on children's development, age, socialisation, learning and art education, and gender studies in women's art.

A Dreaming Researcher

One morning in 1989, I woke from a vivid dream. I flew like a rapid bird over a wide landscape of high mountains and blue sky. As I flew, I looked down on the Earth and slowly came closer, so that I could see huge plains and fields. Birds and animals lived in these places. I flew at a steady speed, not slowing as I approached the fields, and I saw girls and women wearing old-fashioned dresses and bonnets, some of them riding small wild mustangs. I flew close to the grass – it almost touched my face – passed a high cliff and approached the endless blue ocean to fly like a fishing bird, directly into the water, and here I was flying-swimming slower, with two large, slow sea turtles. One of them approached me, and we had very intense eye contact, into which everything around us was absorbed.

At the time of the above-mentioned dream, I was halfway through my three-year PhD programme, and, as I contemplated the dream, it suggested a new and theoretically diverse approach distinguishing between different foci and, accordingly, different theories and conceptualisations to my study: "What does gender look like in children's drawings, and how can we understand it?" I had gathered collections of children's drawings that covered the 1900–1980 period, and these made it possible to identify various qualities specific to young children's drawings compared with those of older children. The older the children became, the more gendered were their drawings, but there were also distinct variations in that. I had struggled to find and select a theoretical approach to embrace these variations from the very diverse approaches applied at that time. In my environment of educational research, there was a well-documented interest in semiotic approaches, which emphasised how children seemed to learn and acquire certain codes and cultural images, which, in turn, was observable in their drawings (Hansson, Nordström, Pedersen, & Stafseng, 1991). Psychological theories reflected the well-documented interest in how a child's personal and existential experiences might be expressed in their drawings, thus providing information about their emotional and mental conditions (Goodnow, 1978; Larsen, 1979, 1989; Miller, 1989; Mortensen, 1971). Gender was part of the study, and at that time gender studies were influenced by theories of sociocultural gender roles and how such prototypes were communicated in children's social lives (Ethelberg, 1985; Haavind, 1987).

My dream made it clear to me that each of the above-mentioned approaches was important in terms of offering different perspectives on the same phenomenon. Analysing a child's drawing could develop knowledge about gendered images in children's drawings as mediating means that contribute to their sociocultural participation as subjects who were becoming gendered, as persons with specific life courses and existential experiences of being and becoming subjects and 'genders' in specific social environments (their local lifeworld) and with shared cultural ideas, values and images. As I applied the methods and theories to thematise and analyse the drawings that formed the body of my material, these mediating means simultaneously reduced focus and suggested potential new knowledge. I based the analyses on a sociocultural ontology in which every individual becomes a person by participating in societal activities and acquiring mediating means and tools in their specific culture (Karpatschof, 1989). This approach suggested that, throughout history, sociocultural arrangements have been gendered in specific ways, and societal conditions have developed gendered values that are expressed in everyday practices. One aspect of such expressions was the appearance of gendered motifs in cultural products for children, and in children's play and art when they participated in sociocultural activities, of which drawing is one. The sociocultural activity theory (Leontjev, 1983; Vygotsky, 1978, 1987) provided a good understanding of children's possible motives for learning and developing gendered expression to participate in social life. However, this approach was not as helpful for understanding and explaining why children's drawings of what seemed personally important seemed to be rendered with fewer gendered schemata. Instead of being formed by controlled schemata, such drawings appeared to be formed by emotionally saturated movements, lines and organisation. Drawings of directly observed objects and persons also differed from gendered schemata and appeared more descriptive and influenced by children's perceptions.

Three Layers of Symbols

The result of my attempts to theorise about the foregoing phenomena was the conceptualisation of three layers of symbols in children's drawings, comprising a cultural, a local and a personal layer. The cultural symbol layer includes conventions in pictorial expressions, including gendered images, and this symbol layer offers children 'visual semiotics' to communicate experiences and ideas by gendered schemata and conventional motifs. The local symbol layer includes the signs and visual expressions that reference experiences in the child's everyday life, in a specific local community and ecological niche, with their family and friends. The personal symbol layer includes the sensory and symbolic expression of the child's existential experience. The gendered visual semiotics provide children with gendering mediating means for expressing and reflecting on their personal, existential experiences of being and becoming in their local lifeworld and intersubjective encounters with others. In young children's drawings, the cultural, gendered signs were less apparent than in drawings by older children, who had mastered the conventions of visual culture to a greater degree. In drawings of existential experiences, the personal 'sense of being' saturated the expression, and culturally gendered signs were less dominant (Nielsen, 1992, 1995, 2012a, 2012b).

My dream was a turning point in my doctoral studies. Throughout more than 25 years of working life at university, dreams have often given me important insights. Not only dreaming, but also contemplation, meditation, a relaxing walk and even intensive gardening have given rise to sudden inspirations and ideas. Such activities have become essential parts of my research and teaching work. Similar activities seem to support creative researchers, not that I claim to be one (Gregersen & Køppe, 1985; Keller, 1985; Sadler-Smith, 2015). Researchers describe relaxation, rest or occupation with something completely different from the focus of their study as supporting the development of new knowledge through meaningful, difficult and joyful processes (Sadler-Smith, 2015).

Unconscious Creative Processes in Research

A model developed by Graham Wallas, and often referred to by creativity researchers, comprises four stages of creativity in research: *Preparation, incubation, illumination*, and *verification* (Sadler-Smith, 2015). The modes of thought in the first and last stages are conscious and voluntary – studies of existing knowledge in theory and practice during preparation, and examining new ideas/knowledge through the domain's verification processes (Sadler-Smith, 2015, p. 9). In contrast to the conscious and voluntary modes of thought of preparation and verification, Wallas described incubation as involving unconscious or subconscious processes, nested in the knowledge acquired during preparation. Illumination is also unconscious – it is impossible to plan or choose to be illuminated, as it is an unexpected "final 'flash'" (Sadler-Smith, 2015, p. 11). Although most subsequent accounts of Wallas's theory seem to have incubation lead directly to illumination, Sadler-Smith emphasises a fifth stage, that of *intimation*. The intimation stage comprises and distinguishes between conscious and unconscious states and "also between 'focal ("full luminosity") consciousness' and 'fringe (periphery) consciousness'" (ibid.). Intimation manifests as vague sensations of something emerging, as more or less clear images, and is described as slowly ascending towards the threshold of consciousness.

Neuropsychological, cognitive and psychoanalytic theories are applied to theorise about the above stages in creativity (Sadler-Smith, 2015). However, these approaches are different perspectives that are not really integrated into a coherent theory of inter- and intra-acting processes. Vedfelt's cybernetic psychology (1996) offers a coherent integrative framework of dynamic systems theory for conceptualising how the processes of neuropsychology, cognitive, emotional, developmental, analytical and social psychology inter- and intra-act, and how we may learn about, and understand, the dynamics of these processes. Cybernetic psychology accounts for intimation and illumination, as well as dreaming, as meaningful dynamics in creativity.

Unconscious Intelligence

Vedfelt's theory builds on the psychoanalytic idea of unconscious dynamics (Freud), the breach with Freud's concept of the unconscious as chaotic (Jung), and Jung's theory of a creative, independent and active unconscious in individuals and culture, working through personal and collective layers (Vedfelt, 1996). Vedfelt criticised Jung's theory for lacking sufficient clarity considering the relationships between person and lifeworld, body and mind, and levels and states of consciousness (Vedfelt, 2001). Based on extensive experience and studies, Vedfelt theorised that consciousness "can function on various levels, in different states and modalities such as bodily and emotional, and through visual imagery and thinking modes of experience" (Vedfelt, 2017, p. 39). The human psyche is understood as

> a multi-layered, self-optimising, complex information system. It functions as a parallel-processing neural network where many subsystems are active, simultaneously accessing differing yet overlapping memory systems that learn through practice. The system is open but swings rhythmically between states more or less in contact with the outer world.
>
> (Vedfelt, 2020)

This information system develops through practice in processing various sorts of information that demand different kinds of processing and levels of complexity. Experiences such as bodily impulses, affects, emotions, associations and flows of ideas are conceptualised as various forms of information mediated via processing channels in the system of consciousness.

In cybernetic psychology theory, our everyday, goal-directed consciousness is relatively low in complexity compared with states with a less focused and more open awareness of sensory, affective, emotional, associative and symbolic experiences. Unfocused awareness of diverse processing channels opens gateways to the supramodal space of consciousness, where memories, fantasies, embodied knowledge, emotional and affective patterns and theoretical understanding can unite in self-regulating processes (such as calming oneself in stressful circumstances) and self-organising processes (such as a sudden, new understanding of oneself or of something, as in 'illumination'; Vedfelt, 2017). These unconscious processes include and combine information from various modes of being, experiences and levels of consciousness in unforeseeable and intelligent ways related to the present life situation of the person and are termed 'unconscious intelligence'.

Mediating Means in the Supramodal Space

Although the cybernetic psychology concept that everyday goal orientation is a state of consciousness that is less complex than unfocused or dreaming states, cultural-historical psychology emphasises the individual's cultivation and acquisition of mediating means as the basis of complex psychological development. The cultivation and acquisition include "the process of 'ingrowing' of the external means", where external means and signs involved in activity turn into internal signs, by which "instrumented, significative [human] behavior" develops (Leontjev, 1994 p. 306), and, in this way, the person, influenced by social and cultural experience, masters a number of ways of behaving, which transform psychological acts into new and more complex acts and structures (Leontjev, 1994).

The sociocultural psychologist Vygotsky used the term conscious awareness to denote "an act of consciousness whose object is the activity of consciousness itself" (Vygotsky, 1987, p. 190). His focus on the functional aspects of consciousness and emphasis on mediating means gave rise to new ways of understanding the interconnections between the material and the mental (Edwards, 2005). In this approach, conscious awareness involves mediating means, particularly language acquired through communication – termed 'external speech' – which, as it becomes 'inner speech', also changes mental processes and allows reconfigurations of internal psychological structures, which in turn are externalised as actions in the world (Edwards, 2005). Although language opens the gates to sharing experiences with others, 'inner speech' provides means for directing attention to the experience of mental processes and other psychological phenomena, and for reducing an orientation towards the environment and increasing focus, to deliberately contemplate specific phenomena and experiences (Hart, 2004).

This cultural-psychological line of thought permits us to consider sociocultural mediating means as contributing to self-regulation and self-organisation through diverse forms of information and processing channels, such as embodied knowledge about how to act with artefacts and tools, music, dance, theatre, rituals and everyday practices (Cassirer, 1999; Nielsen & Petersen, 2021). The body of knowledge behind the cultural-historical approach focuses on the development of subjects, subjectivities and life courses through participation in societal, historical and cultural activities, and how practices and mediating means support and constrain potential development (McDermott, 2001; Køster & Winther-Lindqvist, 2018; Leontjev, 1983). Through this lens, contemporary society's dismissal of states of consciousness such as dreaming, contemplation and other aspects of unconscious intelligence as 'irrational' has profound implications for human development and well-being in everyday life, care and education (Gitz-Johansen, 20016; Tart, 1975; Thielst, 1990; Vedfelt, 1996, 2002).

Next, I will integrate the terminology of mediating means into the cybernetic psychology approach, to describe how theory, symbols and language intersect with conscious and unconscious intelligence. Mediating means denote cultural-historical tools (including mental tools such as language, other symbolic systems and theories), artefacts and their practical use, and practices for dealing with matters in everyday life (including how to deal with emotions, relationships etc.; Fuchs, 2011, 2017; Køster & Winther-Lindqvist, 2018; Leontjev, 1983; Vygotsky, 1978, 1987).

A Dreaming Researcher Online to Unconscious Intelligence

The various theories about children's drawings as either semiotic products of children's acquisition of cultural signs and symbols or symbolic expression to be interpreted according to stages of psychological development functioned as mediating means for me, as a researcher. The theories and methods were means for analysing the project data according to the rules for knowledge development

(Gregersen & Køppe, 1985). However, I did not consider these mediating means to be 'right' – something was missing. They gave me no tools to express the meaning saturation I experienced in my encounter with the painting by Cézanne, with children's drawings, or when I was drawing or painting. According to the 'rules for knowledge' developed by 'logical argumentation', the semiotic approach and the gender theories were consistent in their sociocultural focus on 'socialisation', but this seemingly good, logical framework for analyses appeared superficial and unsatisfying. The preparation did not provide a satisfying understanding of the 'whole', and this problem was the focus of my consciousness until I had the dream.

This foregoing situation resembled descriptions of creative discoveries in research related to relaxed, unfocused or unconscious states of mind, a phenomenon explained by the researcher's deep personal involvement with the subject of the research and with existing knowledge about it (Gregersen & Køppe, 1985; Keller, 1985; Sadler-Smith, 2015). In the cybernetic psychology approach, fringe consciousness is a relaxed and unfocused state in which various processing channels are open to the supramodal space of consciousness. In this highly complex state, it is possible for multiple modes of information to combine, and for possible insights to manifest, because a complex state may integrate what appears contradictory at less complex levels. Early-morning creativity exemplifies how a fresh and unfocused consciousness with great complexity offers a supramodal space for new knowledge, insights and possible problem-solving (Vedfelt, 2020). Dreaming is also considered a highly complex state of consciousness, in which matters important to us are addressed in symbolic and often personalised modes, as 'trial runs' in a safe place, as we do not act out a dream in the real world. "In the dreaming state, consciousness is online to unconscious intelligence" (Vedfelt, 2017, p. 95). Dreaming therefore opens gates to recognise patterns and communicate on high levels of complexity through condensed information, and to present experiences of wholeness in symbols and psychological energy landscapes (Vedfelt, 2017).

In my dream, I was flying over a landscape with mountains, plains and ocean. These changed as I approached them and as my perspective changed – from looking at them from a great distance to approaching closely and relating to them and to diving deep into the ocean. The flying movement made perspective changes evident, including an understanding of perspective as just a potential approach – the perception of matter changed as the observing eye changed perspective, approach and/or theory. The flying speed was a sensory trial run (in the safe place of my bed), an embodied demonstration of various energies in different perspectives: Very high speed over the mountains, down closer to the plains, and steady speed over female figures in old-fashioned clothes and directly into the ocean, where my speed was reduced, and I was flying-swimming with large, slow sea turtles. During my slow movements while immersed in the ocean, an absorbing contact emerged – very intense eye contact with an old being, the wise sea turtle. Speed and intensity had personal meaning for me and in children's drawings, where these characteristics are observable in the sensory qualities of colour and lines of movement (this I therefore termed the 'personal symbol layer' to denote the personal sense of meaning).

An inner psychological landscape included huge, steady, immovable mountains (they may symbolise 'fundamental values', 'grand theories', 'authorities' – solid as bedrock and difficult, or very slow, to change – which I term the 'cultural symbol layer') and plains and cultivated fields with living figures resembling settlers and the 'strong' girl, Laura, shaped by the settler's life with her family, described in Laura Ingalls Wilder's novels, some of my favourite childhood literature (the plains and fields could symbolise fertile land, ready for cultivation and formation by 'family', which I term 'the local symbol layer').

Something that mattered to me personally and was part of the 'bedrock' of my experience, but that until then could not be integrated into the 'established theory landscape', was transformed into a whole, as the dream made it possible for me to observe the 'grand' theories as 'just' perspectives. The various perspectives and theories were 'just' specific approaches, not the entirety of 'true knowledge'. They were also just right, as they gave knowledge of specific and important processes that contributed to the expression through drawing. Through the lens of cybernetic psychology, my dream was 'online' with my unconscious intelligence, and, through various processing channels, 'my research subject' self-organised from the separate phenomena of 'children's drawings and gender', 'theories' and 'me, as researcher' into a unified whole that could be addressed, explored and understood by applying various perspectives and terminologies. At that time, I did not know how to conceptualise the dreaming experience in theory, and I focused consciously on my PhD project. During the process of verification, not only knowledge of theory but also 'time' was a limited resource, and I attempted to include my personal, multidimensional, intensely meaningful experiences in a consistent, cultural-historical approach, as I argued for a terminology that described various layers of symbolic meaning (Nielsen, 1992). Years later, I became acquainted with cybernetic psychology and experienced a sense of truth – this is just right. At that time, I was an associate professor at a university, and the lens of cybernetic psychology offered new perspectives on my experiences of work-related tasks and myself.

Cybernetic psychology is a well-documented theory describing unconscious processes and dynamics and is a mediating means for guiding our orientation and actions. As a mediating means, cybernetic psychology guides our intentionality and understanding towards the phenomenology of experience through an appreciative approach to accepting and learning how our experiences may be governed by lived experiences, how unconscious patterns of experience and action may hold us back from developing, and how we may become consciously aware of (some of) these dynamics, and open ascending lines of individuation, self-regulation and self-organisation. This theory provided mediating means for conceptualising how personal sensory experience is fundamental to individuation, learning, development and understanding and therefore should be included in education, at two levels. The first level is that of the subject or domain that comprises theories and methods, how to think and how to act in the domain. The second level comprises the contemplation and observation of states of consciousness, online to unconscious intelligence, as an element of the educational domain. The second level is rarely an explicit part of university education. In the next section, I describe an example of university education online to the unconscious intelligence.

Dreams, Meditation and Other States of Consciousness

I feel excited and thrilled as I walk across campus towards the functionalist red-brick building in which the experimental education laboratory is situated. It is 8.40 a.m., and only a few colleagues and students are visible on campus on this warm and sunny September morning in a suburb of Copenhagen, where DPU, the Danish School of Education, Aarhus University, is located. I pull a small suitcase heavy with books, its wheels bumping over the grey tiles. A cotton bag with a thick roll of drawing paper and my yoga mat bump against the suitcase as I walk. This does not feel elegant and easy, but rather clumsy, and I remind myself of the potential of sensory inspiration for opening the supramodal space of body and mind. Lived experience and theoretical mediating means guide my orientation as they did when I planned the course I am going to teach.

The course I was going to teach was a master's-level elective in the educational psychology programme at DPU. Electives are shorter courses (ten ECTS) offered in the final year of the master's programme, and students choose the elective they prefer from various subjects. Thirty-three students chose this new elective, based on its title, aims and content. The title was "Dreams, Meditation and Other States of Consciousness – and Their Implications in Pedagogy, Education and Leadership". Aims and content emphasised knowledge and understanding of various theories of consciousness, both theoretically traditional and as experienced through student participation in guided practices such as meditation, relaxation and guided imagery. The course comprised eight four-hour teaching sessions and a final 'mini-conference', where participants could present their ideas for exam projects and have supervision. Before the course began, I sent each participant an email about the practical arrangements in the 'experimental education laboratory', with moveable furniture for flexibility, and information about how we should place our yoga mats and follow COVID-19-related safety recommendations and rules. The email also specified how students were expected to participate and presented a set of ethical guidelines that included listening mindfully and respectfully to each other and keeping confidential any personal information shared in class.

The first lesson of the eight teaching sessions was practical and began with a standing exercise for mindful balancing; then, students lay or sat on their yoga mats on the floor to join a guided relaxation exercise. In the first two sessions, this was succeeded by mindful breathing, in the third session, by guided imagery to recall a recent dream, in the fourth session, by focused mindfulness and, in the fifth, sixth and seventh sessions, by guided imagery for the students to follow their own paths and explore their inner landscapes. After each exercise, students were given a few minutes and some paper so that they could draw or make notes on their experience during the exercise, which was followed by time in which to share experiences in small groups of two or three, before sharing with the entire class and relating their experiences to the topic of the day – for example, 'dreaming' or 'meditation'. In each session, the first, practical lesson was succeeded by three lessons focused on the specific theories and studies of the topic of the day and reflections relating to the practical experiences.

Teaching Online to Unconscious Intelligence

Many participants arrived several minutes before the class started, and, as I approached the classroom for the second four-hour session, I saw a pile of shoes outside the door. This is quite unusual at a university. In the first session, I suggested that they change from outdoor shoes to something clean when they entered the room, and now there was this unusual pile of shoes outside the door. When I entered the classroom, participants were busy moving chairs and creating space for the yoga mats. Cybernetic psychology guided my perception of the class-community as self-organising its space to begin a day of teaching and learning activities that were rather unusual in the ordinary practices of academia.

Participants in this course were asked to evaluate each four-lesson session. After the first session, many commented on their varied bodily postures during classes, including their use of yoga mats and the possibility of sitting on either chairs or their mats on the floor. They found it comforting to be able to change position, and one wrote, "I was a bit worried that it would be strange to lie down and sit on the floor, but I felt very safe there during the entire session". Approximately half of the participants preferred to sit on their mats during every class except the final 'conference event'. Many participants said it was difficult to 'remain mindful' during guided mindfulness exercises, although some participants were trained in meditation and found these activities relaxing and, during the sharing rounds, were already applying mediating means of theory to explain their experiences. Thus, participants applied elements of theory from the course as well as other sources of knowledge and contributed to a distributed body of knowledge in class.

The guided imagery of a 'wisdom walk' was prefaced by gentle standing movements with a mindful awareness of the feet succeeded by reclining relaxation. Then, participants were invited to imagine standing at the beginning of a path, to feel it under their feet, to perceive smells, temperature, sounds, the weather, the landscape and then mindfully begin to walk along their path and observe what appeared. After walking for a few minutes, they would see a comfortable place to sit. Again, they were guided to observe how it was to sit there and how the place was experienced through their senses. After a little while, they were guided to look at the yet unexplored continuation of the path, then back to the place they were, and then to rise to their feet and, with mindful awareness, return to their path, walking back to where they began. In the sharing round, many had immediately found themselves on a path, although some found it difficult. Those who perceived a path described various transformations, some during one imagery walk, others between the first, second and third sessions of imagery walks. An example of the first imagery walk describes transformations of the imagined path:

> When I began, my path was not so pleasant, but as I went on, and you told us to be kind and accept what appeared, my path became more and more pleasant to walk along. When I returned, it had become a pleasant path.
>
> Statement by course participant, 2020)

An example of changes between the first, second and third sessions of imagery walks describes transformations of the imagined path:

> This time, my path passed through a landscape of green meadows, and the weather was sunny and warm. It was very different from last time, back then I was on the strip down the middle of a huge dual carriageway, with cars driving fast in the lanes on either side. And then, when we relaxed, I was suddenly transported to the hill beside the carriageway, where I could look out over the landscape and see green fields.
>
> Statement by course participant, 2020)

During the third guided imagery session, this particular student was not able to find her path, and most participants described similar difficulties, which they ascribed to approaching deadlines for exam projects, as worries about exams constantly distracted them from 'their paths'. Through students describing experiences of 'my path', it was possible to address aspects of their current situation, of their experiences of 'being', expressed symbolically, and the potential for understanding through the mediating means of various theories from 'the subjective turn' in psychology. This changed the perspective from focusing on their personal abilities and worries, and the guided imagery turned out to be a mediating means for describing their experiences of their 'being-in-situation'. Through the lens of cybernetic psychology, the guided contemplative imagery opened various processing channels to the participants' supramodal space, and the potential of their fertile creativity online to unconscious intelligence appeared to ascend to consciousness. Stressful conditions and demanding tasks and deadlines blocked this potential, reduced the complexity of consciousness to a narrow focus on exams and gave rise to doubts and worries.

The cybernetic psychology approach was a helpful mediating means for the reflections shared by course participants. This approach was helpful for reflecting on participants' personal experiences with, and ideas about, various forms of thought and knowledge. In the final evaluation, some participants emphasised that it was important for them to join the class every time, simply to participate in the contemplative activities and to be a part of this community, even if they had not managed to read and prepare the theoretical material. Some emphasised that, during the course, it was as though they were suddenly inspired or remembered something interesting for their exam project. After reading and assessing the exam projects, I was impressed by the variety of topics and, in several cases, the very high quality of the exam paper. As usual, I sent every participant my comments and reflections to explain my assessment, and several participants responded to this that the course had been valuable to them:

> It has been a terrifically inspiring class, addressing our entire life and spreading to every corner, professionally as well as privately.
> [P]articipating in that kind of unusual teaching was an incredibly valuable experience. I am sure I will bring a lot of that with me in terms of both theory and practice in my future work, especially if I am going to teach.
> (Examples of emails from course participants, 2020)

As a teacher, I found it very satisfying to find students deeply engaged in learning activities that involved not only the sophisticated application of theories and methods, but also personal reflection and the exploration of topics and experiences that mattered to them.

Academia and the Consciousness

The term 'academia' can be traced back to the olive groves of Akademeia, north of Athens in Greece, where Plato founded his school of philosophy in 388 bc (Skjerbekk & Gilje, 1995). Today, academia refers to the global community of researchers at institutes of higher learning and comprises various disciplines, schools and ideas about 'knowledge' and 'science'. Academic knowledge is developed and taught at universities through educational practices that are organised very differently from the ancient 'walks and talks' in the gardens of philosophy. Contemporary universities usually organise education in theatres, classrooms and laboratories, perhaps with opportunities for students to participate in experiments, fieldwork, discussions and reflection. At DPU, where I teach educational psychology, the major focus of education is on reflection.

I had several reasons for suggesting the above-mentioned course and teaching it in the experimental education lab. I wanted to address questions of consciousness as an important aspect of educational psychology, to include theories of consciousness and practices related to consciousness as experiential approaches for students to understand and reflect on, and to offer students an educational space that addressed their personal interests, intentions and creativity. Questions and theories of consciousness are the basics of psychology and paved the way for most of the theories of human learning and development and, in turn, educational theories – for example, Freud's (1974), Jung's (1993), Tart's (1975), Vedfelt's (2002, 2007, 2014) and Vygotsky's (1987). In recent years, a social and discursive turn has strongly influenced research and education (Lave & Wenger, 1997; Ergas, 2014) and overshadowed phenomena of consciousness. Consciousness studies have had a revival with the 'subjective turn', an increasing interest in subjectivity, contemplation and mindfulness in educational practice and research (Ergas, 2014; Forbes, 2016; Hart,

2004; Jennings, 2011; Napoli, 2004; Weare, 2013; Zahavi, 2003), which includes an expanding interest in the experience of consciousness (Bitbol, 2019; Nielsen, 2018; Petitmengin & Bitbol, 2009; Vedfelt, 2017; Winther-Lindqvist, 2018). This paved the way for my course to be recognised as part of the academic programme at the university, and theories in this field were included in the course literature.

Academia: Science and Passion

A well-established idea of academia as a domain focused on rationales, results and merits is illustrated in this statement by a junior researcher: "Emotionality is disapproved of in the academic world, where people are preoccupied with intellectual arguments, and the number of articles they have published" (Trøstrup, 2016, p. 56). This idea relates well to philosophical and science-based aims of developing true knowledge, the affiliated criteria for approving such knowledge, and ideas of rational research processes and procedures, which are more myth than reality according to Gregersen and Køppe (1985). In their book *Science and Passion* (1985), they analyse philosophical ontologies in the domains of the natural sciences and the humanities, the social and institutional contexts of the development of these domains, and historical ideas of science. They suggest we define a science as based on conditions that include a specific subject area and a part of reality viewed with a certain approach, an empirical-methodical tradition with limits for acceptable conclusions, and a historical system of concepts with some degree of consensus, which does not exclude contradictions and is often divided into smaller units, without contradictions. Also, a science may be in a developmental phase in which the fundamental concepts are established and its transition from a pre-scientific ideology to a science is evident, succeeded by the constitution of the science as an institution with distinction between research, education and application, and the determination of regulatory rules and rituals – that is, an exchange of results (such as publication rates, as mentioned by Trøstrup; Gregersen & Køppe, 1985).

The foregoing appears quite rational. However, Gregersen and Køppe (1985) also suggest a general model for studying science, including that a *researcher* must study a specific *object* by applying *methods*, and that the result is a certain *product*. Therefore, they analyse the constitution of science at three levels: (1) A personal level that includes the researchers' biographies – that is, diaries; (2) the level of the science, which includes works and manuscripts; and (3) an institutional level that includes laws, rules, articles of association and so forth. In their analysis, it appears that some researchers' personal characteristics and social, societal and institutional situations and conditions influenced existing scientific knowledge, theories, methods and practices (Gregersen & Køppe, 1985). Their analysis of the institutional level (3) demonstrates how the personal or financial preferences of those who have the power to employ have had implications in terms of who (at the personal level, 1) and what kinds of theories and methods (the science level, 2) had access to the institutionalised positions. Such an analysis of power does not exclude ideas of scientific knowledge, but it is illuminating to understand that the academic field is complex and includes rational and conscious forces as well as emotional, value-based, ideological and unconscious forces.

> It is as though we have to believe in a certain theory or theoretical approach, and team up with co-believers, to be met with interest – is that specific to psychological research, or is it like that in other domains as well?

A junior researcher posed this question at a meeting where we reflected on how to include valuable knowledge, conceptualised in a dominant theory and applied in often unethical ways, to further develop a better theoretical understanding of a given field of psychology. The question above illustrates the experience of science as divided into units without contradictory theories and methods and with, accordingly, low complexity, which blocks opportunities for fuller knowledge and understanding that demand higher levels of complexity. In academia, knowledge development and scientific analysis tend to reduce the scope of study, and therefore scientific knowledge is reductive (Gregersen & Køppe, 1985, p. 55). Through the lenses of cybernetic psychology and creativity theory, such reduction provides mediating means for focusing consciousness and contemplating and offers insights into science through intimation and deliberate symbolic practices that open multidimensional processing channels to the supramodal space of unconscious intelligence. Verification of new insights depends on the mediating means, levels of complexity and potential for integrative approaches of the domain stakeholders' theories and methods.

Cybernetic Psychology and Creativity in Academia

Theories, concepts and other mediating means provide certain symbolic resources for participants in academic domains.

> [A] domain can be defined as cultural and symbolic systems of rules and behaviours, it is the mastery of the domain that enables Preparation, the first creativity stage, and the symbolic resources of a domain determine what is intellectually and creatively possible.
>
> (Sadler-Smith, 2015, p. 16 of online article)

Through a cultural-psychology lens, mediating means, artefacts and practices provide participants in research domains with knowledge and experience developed through sociocultural practices and history (Edwards, 2005; Leontjev, 1983; Vygotsky, 1978, 1987). A domain's symbolic resources include theories and methods and practices of doing-with and relating-to data and experiences. Smaller units of the domain may constitute specific practices and approaches without contradictions, which accordingly appear impossible to question (Gregersen & Køppe, 1985). While rigidity prevents new and creative developments of knowledge, the mastery of the symbolic resources of a domain together with openness towards manifestations of intimation facilitates creativity through specific foci and approaches to new preparation, incubation, intimation, illumination and verification of new knowledge. In light of the various stages of creativity in research and in Gregersen and Køppe's analysis (1985), it is not possible to understand science and academia as results of only rational and conscious processes and modes of thought.

Some studies have explored how dominating theories in a research domain acted as mediating means that alienated knowledge of unconscious intelligence: Whiteman (2010) argues that strong emotional reactions to research material, which she calls "heartbreak", indicate important information that is often inaccessible through established theoretical discourse, which generalises and objectifies and thereby tends to alienate the researcher's personal experience of compassion and suffering related to general patterns of injustice (Whiteman, 2010). Dutton and Morhart add to Whiteman's contribution that 'heart-warming' experiences are also important to research-based knowledge and personal growth:

> Witnessing powerful moments and sensing underlying emotions that transpire from everyday moments inside organisations offer insights into phenomena often blinded by the quest for "objectivity," helping us to learn from data and research experiences in more meaningful and long-lasting ways.
>
> (Dutton & Morhart, 2010, p. 344)

Simovska, Lagermann, Abduljalil, Mørck and Kousholt (2019) support the idea that this emphasis on affectivity and emotions reveals meaningful information during research, often experienced as 'eureka moments', and they note that, in many research environments, working conditions leave little space for such exploration of data and research experiences.

Through the lens of cybernetic psychology, consciousness is a multilayered system of information processes with various levels of complexity, in which everyday experiences and theories are integrated by the unconscious intelligence. In this view, the domains of academia include mediating means such as theories, terminologies, visual signs and other symbolising practices to access various processing channels and potentially a complex supramodal space for further exploration and creative development of knowledge, and working conditions stressing effective productivity and rigid theories and methods therefore counteract creativity.

In contrast to many symbolic mediating means in academic domains, symbols in cybernetic psychology express something not-yet-known (Vedel, 2001). Such symbols may express intense meaning, and they cannot be fully translated into other forms of expression or modes of thought. In that sense, a symbol may express an opening to the unconscious intelligence experienced as intimation of a numinous calling, magical insight, wisdom or emerging creative knowledge. Cybernetic psychology and the conceptualisation of a supramodal consciousness offer a coherent theory for understanding and explaining dynamic changes in experienced states of consciousness and how they are nested in personal history and values, current life situation, expectations and potentialities for the future, and mediating means

(Fuchs, 2011; Hansen, 2015; Køster & Winther-Lindqvist, 2018; Vedfelt, 1996, 2001, 2017). Cybernetic psychology offers a terminology and therapeutic practices for analysing, understanding and transforming experiences, online to the unconscious intelligence, and potentially changing persons' conscious understanding of difficult situations and, accordingly, their agency in the situation.

In academia, the lens of cybernetic psychology provides us with a mediating means for reducing a focus on the environment in order to make us focus on the potential of the unfocused, highly complex supramodal space, various processing channels and unconscious intelligence as resources for well-being and creativity, personally, in education and in research.

Note

1 The Musée du Jeu de Paume housed many important impressionist works now housed in the Musée d'Orsay.

References

Bitbol, M. (2019). Consciousness, Being and Life: Phenomenological approaches to mindfulness. *Journal of Phenomenological Psychology 50*, 127–161.

Cassirer, E. (1999). *Et essay om mennesket*. Copenhagen: Hans Reitzels Forlag.

Dutton, J. & Morhart, F. (2010). Heartwarming as the Other Side of Heartbreaking Experiences in Research. *Journal of Management Inquiry 19(4)*, 342–344. DOI:10.1177/1056492610370285

Edwards, A. (2005). Relational Agency: Learning to be a resourceful practitioner. *International Journal of Educational Research 43*, 168–182. DOI:10.1016/j.ijer.2006.06.010

Ergas, O. (2014). Mindfulness in Education at the Intersection of Science, Religion, and Healing. *Critical Studies in Education 55(1)*, 58–72. http://dx.doi.org/10.1080/17508487.2014.858643

Ethelberg, E. (1985). Kvindelighedens modsigelse. *Kvinnovetenskapligt Tidsskrift 1*, Stockholm.

Forbes, D. (2016). *Modes of Mindfulness: Prophetic critique and integral emergence*. City University of New York (CUNY), CUNY Academic Works.

Freud, S. (1974). *Drømmetydning I–II*. Copenhagen: Hans Reitzel.

Fuchs, T. (2011). Body Memory and the Unconscious. In D. Lomar & J. Brudzinska (Eds.), *Founding Psychoanalysis Phenomenologically – Phenomenological Theory of Subjectivity and the Psychoanalytical Experience*. New York: Springer.

Fuchs, T. (2017). Intercorporeality and Interaffectivity. *Phenomenology and Mind (11)*, 194–209.

Gitz-Johansen, T. (2016). Jung in Education: A review of historical and contemporary contributions from analytical psychology to the field of education. *Journal of Analytical Psychology, 61(3)*, 365–384.

Goodnow, J. (1978). *Børn tegner*. Copenhagen: Hans Reitzel.

Gregersen, F. & Køppe, S. (1985). *Videnskab og Lidenskab*. Copenhagen: Tiderne Skifter.

Haavind, H. (1987). *Liten og stor*. Oslo: Universitetsforlaget.

Hansen, T. (2015). *Det ubevidstes potentiale*. Copenhagen: Frydenlund.

Hansson, H., Nordström, G. Z., Pedersen, K. & Stafseng, O. (1991). *Children's Pictorial Language*. Stockholm: Carlssons.

Hart, T. (2004). Opening the Contemplative Mind in the Classroom. *Journal of Transformative Education*. https://doi.org/10.1177/1541344603259311

Jennings, P.A. (2011). Promoting Teachers' Social and Emotional Competencies to Support Performance and Reduce Burnout. In A. Cohan & A. Honigsfeld (Eds.), *Breaking the Mold of Preservice and Inservice Teacher Education: Innovative and successful practices for the 21st century* (133–143). Lanham, MD: Rowman & Littlefield.

Jung, C.G. (1993). *Den analytiske psykologis grundlag og praksis*. Copenhagen: Gyldendal.

Karpatschof, B. (1989). Psykologien og kulturen. In P. Berliner & B Karpatschof (Eds.), *Psykologi og kultur*, Psykologisk laboratorium. University of Copenhagen.

Keller, E.F. (1985). *Reflections on Gender and Science*. New Haven, CT: Yale University Press.

Køster, A. & Winther-Lindqvist, D.W. (2018). Personal History and Historical Selfhood – the Embodied and Pre-reflective Dimension. In J. Valsiner & A. Rosa (Eds.), *Cambridge Handbook of Sociocultural Psychology*. Cambridge: Cambridge University Press. https://doi.org/10.1017/9781316662229

Larsen, H.H. (1979). *Tegneterapi I neurosebehandling*. Copenhagen: Dansk Psykologisk Forlag.

Larsen, H.H. (1989). *Tegneterapi*. Copenhagen: Dansk Psykologisk Forlag.

Lave, J. & Wenger, E. (1997). *Situated Learning – Legitimate Peripheral Participation*. Cambridge: Cambridge University Press.

Leontjev, A. (1983). *Virksomhed, bevidsthed, personlighed* [Activity, Consciousness, Personality, translated from Russian to Danish]. USSR: Forlaget Progres.

Leontjev, A. (1994). The Development of Voluntary Attention in the Child. In R.v.d. Veer & J. Valsiner (Eds.), *The Vygotsky Reader* (289–312). Oxford: Blackwell.

McDermott, R.P. (2001). The Acquisition of a Child by a Learning Disability. In S. Chaiklin (Ed.), *The Theory and Practice of Cultural–Historical Psychology* (15–34). Aarhus, Denmark: Aarhus University Press.

Miller, A. (1989). *Den skjulte nøgle*. Copenhagen: Hans Reitzels Forlag.

Mortensen, K.V. (1971). *Børnetegning – udvikling og udtryk*. Copenhagen: Munksgaard.

Napoli, M. (2004). Mindfulness Training for Teachers: A pilot program. *Complementary Health Practice Review 9(31)*, 31–42. DOI:10.1177/1076167503253435

Nielsen, A.M. (1992). Køn og symbollag i børns billeder. PhD thesis, Copenhagen: Royal Danish School of Educational Studies.

Nielsen, A.M. (1995), Boys' and Girls' Pictures: A study of gender-marking in aesthetics-based subjects. In Arnesen, A.-L. (Ed.), *Apostrof*, special edition, A/1995.

Nielsen, A.M. (2012a). Børnetegninger som orienteringsspor og forskningsdata. *Psyke & Logos 33(2)*, 385–408.

Nielsen, A.M. (2012b). Forskeres arbejde med oplevelser af børns tegninger som forskningsmetode. *Psyke & Logos 33(2)*, 343–360.

Nielsen, A.M. (2018). Artikulationsanalyse i fænomenologisk perspektiv. In L. Bøttcher, D. Kousholt & D. Winther-Lindqvist (Eds.), *Kvalitative analyseprocesser* (63–88). Copenhagen: Samfundslitteratur.

Nielsen, A. M. & Petersen, F.F. (2021). Affectivity and Relational Awareness in Pedagogy and Education – Moments of Hesitation in Intersubjective Encounters. *International Review of Theoretical Psychologies 1(2)*. https://doi.org/10.7146/irtp.v1i2.128018

Petitmengin, C. & Bitbol, M. (2009). The Validity of First-Person Descriptions as Authenticity and Coherence. *Journal of Consciousness Studies 16(10–12)*, 363–404.

Sadler-Smith, E. (2015). Wallas' Four-Stage Model of the Creative Process: More than meets the eye? *Creativity Research Journal 27(4)*, 342–352. DOI:10.1080/10400419.2015.1087277

Simovska, V., Lagermann, L.C., Abduljalil, H.S., Mørck, L.L., & Kousholt, D (2019). Inside Out: What we (don't) talk about when we talk about research. *Qualitative Research 19(2)*, 113–130. https://doi.org/10.1177/1468794117749165

Skjerbekk, G. & Gilje, N. (1995). *Filosofiens historie, 1.* Copenhagen: Gyldendals Bogklubber.

Tart, C.T. (1975). *States of Consciousness*. New York: E.P. Dutton.

Thielst, P. (1990). *Kønnet, kroppen og selvet*. Copenhagen: Gyldendal.

Trøstrup, C. (2016). I Aggerbeck, A.: Arbejdsgiverne vil have de robuste, men hvad så med de sensitive? *Magisterbladet (9)*.

Vedel, V. (2001). Nøglen til det ubevidste. In P. Skogemann (Ed.), *Symbol analyse, virkelighed – Jungiansk teori og praksis i Danmark* (13–28). København: Lindhardt & Ringhof.

Vedfelt, O. (1996). *Bevidsthed – bevidsthedens niveauer*. Copenhagen: Gyldendal.

Vedfelt, O. (2001). Fra Jung til kybernetisk psykologi. In P. Skogemann (Ed.), *Symbol analyse, virkelighed – Jungiansk teori og praksis i Danmark* (288–314). Copenhagen: Lindhardt & Ringhof.

Vedfelt, O. (2002). *Ubevidst intelligens*. Copenhagen: Gyldendals Bogklubber.

Vedfelt, O. (2007). Religiøse højdepunktsoplevelser i transpersonligt, psykodynamisk og kybernetisk perspektiv. *Psyke & Logos 28*, 675–705.

Vedfelt, O. (2014). Cultivating Feelings through Working with Dreams. *Jung Journal: Culture & Psyche 3(4)*, 88–102. DOI:10.1525/jung.2009.3.4.88

Vedfelt, O. (2017). *A Guide to the World of Dreams. An integrative approach to dreamwork*. London: Routledge.

Vedfelt, O. (2020). Integration versus Conflict between Schools of Dream Theory and Dreamwork: Integrating the psychological core qualities of dreams with the contemporary knowledge of the dreaming brain. *Journal of Analytical Psychology 65(1)*, 88–115.

Vygotsky, L.S. (1978). *Mind in Society – The Development of Higher Psychological Processes*. London: Harvard University Press.

Vygotsky, L.S. (1987). Thinking and Speech. In R.W. Rieber & A.S. Carton (Eds.), N. Minick (Trans.), *The Collected Works of L. S. Vygotsky, Vol 1*. New York: Plenum Press. (Original work published in 1934.)

Weare, K. (2013). Developing Mindfulness with Children and Young People: A review of the evidence and policy context. *Journal of Children's Services 8(2)*, 141–153. DOI:10.1111/camh.12040

Whiteman, G. (2010). Management Studies That Break Your Heart. *Journal of Management Inquiry 19(4)*, 328–337. DOI:10.1177/1056492610370282

Winther-Lindqvist, D. (2018). Analyse af personperspektiver. In L. Bøttcher, D. Kousholt & D. Winther-Lindqvist (Eds.), *Kvalitative analyseprocesser* (41–62). Copenhagen: Samfundslitteratur.

Zahavi, D. (2003). *Fænomenologi*. Frederiksberg: Roskilde Universitetsforlag.

3

Cybernetic Psychology and Systemic Coaching

Mikkel Anthonisen

The world needs decision-making and action. The greatest untapped resources we possess are good intentions never turned into action. There is also, however, a need for reflection and consciousness of the inner human processes that create the necessary conditions for the actions we finally bring to life. In this chapter, I explain how cybernetic psychology can help us obtain a deeper contact with ourselves as a point of departure for reaching the correct and most creative decisions and how this, combined with systemic coaching, can make us more proactive. The chapter argues that true change must commence in an open and trusting state of calm acceptance interacting and combined with a focused aim.

Psychotherapy and Coaching – Connecting the Inner and the Outer

When a person decides to start therapy or coaching, it comes as a wish to take conscious responsibility for problems or life situations. This is an expression of personal leadership. Leadership means sensing, understanding inner and outer correlations, being able to have meaningful relationships and making good decisions as well as performing appropriate actions for oneself and others (Whitmore, 1997). Combining psychotherapy and coaching is fruitful for both processes. The inner consciousness-expanding work of psychotherapy will have an influence on the extrovert activity of coaching, and, vice versa, the outer activity of coaching will nourish psychotherapeutic work.

Later in the chapter I will give examples, from my practice, of the coaching aspects of cybernetic psychotherapy. In my experience, psychotherapy and coaching can be combined advantageously. In the case studies, I demonstrate that a psychotherapeutic process can have the effect of coaching. I commence by mapping out the theoretical basis for a methodical combination of cybernetic psychotherapy and systemic coaching and proceed to argue that systemic coaching can advantageously be integrated into cybernetic psychotherapy. The point is not about methodology but about a way of meeting and being with oneself and others, that we understand how to expand our area of consciousness, thus enabling ourselves to create greater capacity for ourselves as well as others, whereby our inner resources interact with the world around us.

DOI: 10.4324/9781003360247-4

Dorthe

Dorthe is a 36-year-old, well-educated and successful woman, happily married with two children. Dorthe has always searched for meaning in her work but, until recently, only with frustration as a consequence. Paradoxically, she is a trained coach herself and daily works in education and career guidance. In the psycho-therapeutic process, she senses a powerful life force of almost spiritual dimensions. With this inner connection, we can integrate a coaching approach. Thus, she can begin making important decisions about her professional life. In therapy, consciousness is focused on inner as well as outer processes, creating interaction between the two. This interaction gives Dorthe insight into the reciprocal connection between the processes. Added to this insight is an acknowledgement of the irrational, circular and creative intelligence being equal to the logically rational and linear intelligence.

When we are in touch with both introvert and extrovert aspects of ourselves, we expand our range of consciousness. We gain access to larger parts of the mental system, understood as the unified body and intellectual information capacity in both conscious and unconscious mental processes. The aim and practice of cyber-netic psychology are to create a dialogue with unconscious intelligence in order to release greater information capacity and thereby activate and widen the client's consciousness. Innate self-healing powers are thus stimulated, and frozen patterns are unblocked. This creates a potential for personal development. In cybernetic psychology, the personality is seen as a multilayered, purposeful, self-optimising and hyper-complex information system. According to Vedfelt's cybernetic psy-chology, the system organises itself spontaneously in a network of subsystems with greater or smaller levels of consciousness and various overlapping memories (Ved-felt, 2002). The system is open but rhythmically swings between states of lesser or greater contact with its surroundings – like pulse beats through life.

Sleep is a good example of this interaction. Outer stimuli and activities are cut off. At the same time, brain activity during sleep is exceedingly large, and parts of the brain, which during waking hours digest outer stimuli and motor activity, are integrated into inner processes with very large information capacity as a result. This rhythm is also present while we are awake – for example, when we succumb to our own thoughts during daytime. Recordings of brain activity suggest that we are in a dreamlike, vegetative state for 25% of our waking hours (Vedfelt, 2007).

Our breathing, with its inhalation and exhalation, is a very basic example of interaction. It is the only bodily function that both works unconsciously, by itself, as well as within our conscious control. As such, it is a link between the uncon-scious, autonomic functions and the conscious functions governed by willpower. Our breathing is controlled by the autonomic nervous system and happens by it-self, even without the interference of our will. As we inhale, the sympathetic part of the autonomic system is stimulated, and the parasympathetic part is stimulated on exhalation (Sjaastad, 2004). Apart from its physiological function, breathing also creates a psychological interaction between focused and determined attention during inhalation and an open and trusting calm during exhalation. This happens subtly and automatically. We are all acquainted with tense, shallow breathing in stressful situations – we inhale rapidly and hold our breath when frightened and exhale with relief once the danger is over. Breathing creates a natural shift between extrovert openness and a less social introversion. By knowing our natural exchange between inward and outward consciousness, we gain access to an understanding of our resources and motives. Our actions in life can become more meaningful and purposeful.

Today, there is much focus on personal development through psychotherapy and coaching. Critical voices speak of a tendency to be oversensitive and of navel-gazing. That may, at times, be the case. But I see it as a very positive development in our society. The physicist Albert Einstein is quoted as saying:

> The intuitive mind is a sacred gift and the rational mind is a faithful servant. We have created a society that honours the servant and has forgotten the gift.

I sense a change in our part of the world, where "the sacred gift" is increasingly recognised. But you have to crawl before you walk. I believe a combination of cybernetic psychotherapy and systemic coaching is an example of a way to learn to walk. Here, intuition, the irrational, the body and creativity are connected with rational linear logic. With an expanded contact with our inner resources, we will be able to act with greater purpose in our outer life, in harmony with the needs of society.

There is a need for decision-making and action in the world. The British advertising consultant Cindy Gallop (n.d.) is very precise when she says that the greatest untapped resources we possess are good intentions never turned into action. But an understanding of the internal processes in the mental system – and in social systems – is a necessary precondition for us to be able to make the right decisions as a starting point for our actions. Without this insight, we risk drawing hasty, incomplete conclusions based on fear and lack of empathy.

Today, the world faces challenges with population growth, resource scarcity, social inequality and climate change. We work more than ever before and have a hard time making ends meet between family and professional life. We need decision-making and action to create sustainable societies for ourselves and for future generations. But we cannot solve the challenges of the present and the future with the solutions of the past. It is a frustrating realisation, and what unfortunately often happens in such situations is that we still try old solutions to new problems in the desperate hope that, if we just add a little more of the old medicine and pull ourselves a little more together, then everything will work out in the end.

When I mention these conditions in a chapter on psychotherapy and coaching, it is because these realisations start with the individual. Most of us recognise the experience of having plans for change that never materialise. We observe ourselves making the same mistakes, exhibiting the same inappropriate behaviour or ending up in the same types of conflicts. If we want to create real change, it must begin in an open and trusting state of calm and acceptance in combination and interaction with a determined focus. A methodological combination of cybernetic psychotherapy and systemic coaching is an example of the possibility in achieving such an expanded field of consciousness.

Coaching traditionally deals with decision-making, focus, action and improvement in performance. It is about deciding where you want to go and laying out a plan to get there. Clients need to identify their resources and motives and, from there, devise a plan of action. This approach is very sympathetic and meaningful. Interesting movements are taking place in our time in relation to recognising resources in people and social networks that have not been noted before. Information technology contributes to this process, where people across cultures and borders can enter into relationships and collaborations at the click of a button. In this movement, however, I will argue that there is a need to spend more time on the deep motivation and the inner resources of the individual (or group) as a necessary prerequisite for coaching. This is precisely what psychotherapy offers. Conversely, the coach's focus on action will nurture the psychotherapeutic work regarding personal development. Thus, a synergy – an interaction – between the two ways of working will be established.

Personal Leadership and Personality Development

In coaching, we talk about personal leadership – that is, being able to lead oneself. It requires insight into one's own inner motives and driving forces. This is essential in order to set realistic goals for oneself and others and, thereby, sustainable solutions for the individual and society. It is about taking responsibility for one's own life, one's personal development and one's interpersonal relationships. We talk of following one's heart in one's decisions and actions – a way of thinking which emphasises that we make better use of our resources, not only for ourselves but also for the benefit of society as a whole, by making an effort with what we are good at and passionate about. The challenge is to find out both what we are passionate about and good at as well as what society needs. In psychotherapy, you meet highly educated and gifted people in good positions who still have not found what they are passionate about. An exclusive coaching course would not make sense to these people. They would be just as doubtful and insecure about the big decisions in their lives as before. Dorthe, from the initial case, seems to be an example of this when it comes to her professional life.

Personality development goes hand in hand with decision-making and action. This is part of the individuation process: The individual's inner resources are released and developed in harmony with the needs of the surrounding society. It is this synergy to which a methodological combination of cybernetic psychotherapy and systemic coaching contributes. In the following, I will show examples of the synergy effect between cybernetic psychotherapy and systemic coaching through cases from my practice. First, I will give a brief introduction to the common theoretical and conceptual basis for cybernetic psychotherapy and systemic coaching.

Here, no adequate account is given of either theory, but hopefully the reader will become curious enough to try working along the same track.

Background Theory

Cybernetic psychology and systemic coaching can both be understood as systems theory and cybernetics. Cybernetics explains how living systems, as opposed to mechanical ones, are able to both create and resist change. Living systems are adaptive, they can adapt and enter into relationships with other systems. Systems theory is an interdisciplinary meta-theory according to which all subject areas can be seen as systems or subsystems. In a systems theory perspective, matter, life, psyche and society will be seen as equal and correct levels in an interdisciplinary framework of understanding (Køppe, 1990). Systems theory is synthesis-creating and claims that the whole is more than the sum of its parts. Properties can arise out of the system that are not inherent in the individual parts, such as consciousness and life. This is called *emergence*. A system is seen as a complex of elements that are connected and communicative, both internally and with its ecological niche. When one system observes another system, both systems change because of this mere observation (Bertalanffy, 1968).

Similarly, the relationship between a client/focus person and a psychotherapist/coach is seen as the overall systemic unit consisting of two subsystems in the form of the two individuals. The two subsystems change when they meet. This has implications for the relationship between the two, which in psychotherapy is traditionally explained as *transference* and *countertransference*. Transference is the phenomenon where the client, in relation to the therapist, experiences feelings and thoughts that spring from his or her previous experiences and context. Countertransference is the therapist's primary response to the client and his or her transference.

Cybernetic psychotherapy systematically combines methods from different therapeutic directions and brings them together in one overall meta-theoretical systemic framework. Cybernetic psychology offers a unifying theory of personality. One can somewhat popularly say that cybernetic psychotherapy offers a practical apprenticeship in becoming the master of one's own house – with all its many rooms, nooks and crannies, skeletons in the closets and shadows in the basement and – more importantly – goldmines of resources, enthusiasm and love.

As a cybernetic psychotherapist, the art is to change the so-called process channel at the right time, when there are signs that the level of consciousness you are communicating with has met its limitation to solve or regulate a given problem. A change of process channel at the right time will activate higher levels of consciousness and control systems of a higher complexity and thus lead to greater information capacity. This change of process channel corresponds, in systemic coaching, to the term *structural coupling that triggers the system* and creates the appropriate interference, which means that the system can change and alter its approach to the problem in a constructive way. The point is, if the system is not challenged, it will not change. An overly overwhelming disorder will, conversely, lead to blockage of the change, which is often experienced by the individual as fear, anger or confusion – perhaps even shame. The appropriate interference, or disturbance, on the other hand, will arouse curiosity and a desire for change in an experience of meaningful development towards greater vitality.

The system gains practical knowledge of the world by recognising patterns and developing schemata. Schemata are coherent patterns of concepts created in the interplay between a person's innate potential and the individual's experienced life. The individual's schemata serve to deal with the numerous events of daily life. Schemata are activated by pattern recognition in a specific context that creates the necessary *goodness of fit* – that is, that something is recognised meaning-fully. In systemic understanding, no system is able to include all information in a given situation. Our pattern recognition, and thus the activation of a schema, will always take place on the basis of incomplete blocks of information. How much information a system can hold depends on the complexity of the schema. A simple schema is activated on the basis of a few blocks of information, and hasty conclu-sions are often drawn. It is said that the schema is rigid and causes very one-track behaviour. More complex schemata hold larger amounts of information and al-low the person smoother action in accordance with the current context. Schema thinking points out the role of previous experiences through pattern recognition. One could say that schema thinking offers a concrete method for understanding how past experiences define the perception of present-day events. Awareness of one's own schemata thus becomes important for the individual's behaviour in a new situation. One sees the world sharper with new eyes and not only through the prism of the past.

The realisation that we always draw our conclusions from incomplete blocks of information provides an understanding that two systems (individuals) will never understand the same situation in the same way. No systems can take in the full complexity of the contexts in which they are involved. We continually attribute purpose and intention, cause and effect to all inputs from the external and inter-nal world to create meaning for ourselves. Within systems theory, systems are self-creating, and there can never be two identical versions of reality; reality is a multiverse. There is, naturally, an acknowledgement of the objective presence of the physical world, independent of us, but also a recognition that everyone will understand and act in the world based on her or his own unique interpretation of reality. The perfection hypothesis points out that all systems always act perfectly in accordance with logics that constitute the system. This does not imply that, on that basis, one may abdicate responsibility for one's actions, on the contrary. It means that we must strive to meet our fellow human beings with an open, curi-ous and open-minded approach, as we will never be able to fully understand an-other human being – let alone ourselves. In cybernetic psychotherapy, the therapist should, based on this realisation, be irreverent towards his or her own hypotheses.

One may form hypotheses, but one must be prepared to reject them. In systemic coaching, this is known as the coach being prepared to wonder. As a consequence of this understanding, a very appreciative and open form of dialogue is used, in both cybernetic psychotherapy and systemic coaching, with reflection and curiosity as means of prologue.

Cybernetic psychotherapy is a method of creating dialogue with the higher control systems of the unconscious intelligence and of creating development in the personality, among other things, through an expansion of the complexity of the schemata. Cybernetic psychotherapy is not, from the outset, solution-focused but process-oriented. Systemic coaching, by contrast, does not consciously deal with unconscious processes. Despite the overlapping way of understanding the mental system and its schemata, systemic coaching is significantly concerned with external processes.

In systemic coaching, the coach helps the focus person see different perspectives of the relationship between him or her and an issue. It is about changing one's attitude to one's own challenges. It is a help-oriented form of conversation, where the coach, with an inquisitive attitude, inspires the focus person to become wiser about her or his own resources and options for action. In this process, systemic coaching is solution-focused. The so-called performative, creative property of the language used plays a major role. The language helps create a reality through speech acts. How we position ourselves and others in our communication is crucial to the outcome. The same goes for what we say and the way we ask questions. Before we move on to the cases, I will elaborate on three key concepts in the systemic coaching understanding of the performative properties of language through speech acts, namely:

- Communicative positions.
- Questions types.
- Coordinated management of meaning (CMM).

The concepts are recognisable from therapeutic practice, but, in systemic coaching, one works more consciously and purposefully with them. Since systemic coaching is solution-focused, the coach is trained as a so-called *gamemaster* who creates a specific movement and direction in the dialogue. We look closer at this below in the description of types of questions and Karl Tomm's U-Model.

Communicative Positions

Communicative positions describe how, through speech actions, one positions oneself in relation to those with whom one communicates. Is the intention open and clear? Or does it close off the other party? Does the communication expand the other party's room for manoeuvring answers and reflections? Or is the room for manoeuvre reduced? One can place oneself or the other party in four different positions, which in practice, however, mutually overlap (Moltke & Molly 2009):

Strategic/Manipulation Position

The purpose of the communication is closed, and the scope for the recipient's an-swers is limited. For example, one wants to confirm a hypothesis which is kept hidden; one wants a specific answer from the other party. This could have the char-acter of "Guess what I'm thinking" and seem manipulative. It does not develop problem-solving in the other party and creates a hierarchy in the dialogue between the conversers.

Helping/Succorance Position

The intention here is also closed, but the room for manoeuvre for the other party is large – for example, if one has a hidden hypothesis, where the aim of the ques-tion is to 'make the penny drop' in confirmation of the hypothesis. It may position the other party as a non-expert and thereby create a relationship of dependence. Conversely, in building a relationship, it can be reassuring for the focus person or client that it is possible to get help from a knowledgeable person. However, neither the succorance nor the manipulation position respects the principles of irreverence towards one's own hypotheses or preparedness to wonder.

Instructive/Confrontation Position

The purpose of the communication is open, but the room for manoeuvre is limited. An example of this is focusing on a specific theme and openly communicating why. It can be experienced as a help towards structure, in confidence that the sender knows best. It can be perceived positively, as a trustworthy means to get help and guidance. However, there is the risk (as in the succorance position) that the recipi-ent has the experience of being talked down to or positioned as a non-expert.

Authorising/Empowerment Position

There is an open intent with communication and a large margin of manoeuvre for answers. Such empowerment of a person strengthens her or his confidence in her or his own ability and is, in most cases, appropriate in coaching and psychotherapy. However, one must be aware that, in some situations, it can seem challenging and anxiety-provoking for the focus person or the client if he or she does not feel that he or she has sufficient resources to solve his or her problems.

Question Models

Karl Tomm's U-Model poses four different types of questions (see Figure 3.1). The starting point is the assumption and intention lying behind and whether the questions are informative or influential: What is the background to my question? What is the intention? And how will it affect the other party? A linear assumption

Detective Linear **Captain**
assumptions

| | Linear and simple questions related to the past:
 ▪ clarifying,
 ▪ defining
 ▪ investigating | Strategic and simple questions pointing to the future:
 ▪ directing
 ▪ confronting
 ▪ inspiring | |

Background *Solutions*

Inquiring questions related to the past ◀ ────── Influencing questions pointing to the future ▶

Anthro-pologist

| | Circular and complex questions concerning:
 ▪ relations
 ▪ patterns
 ▪ different positions and perspectives | Reflective and complex questions pointing to the future:
 ▪ hypotheses
 ▪ possibilities
 ▪ scenarios
 ▪ "miracles" | |

Futurist

Relations/patterns Circular *Possibilities*
assumptions

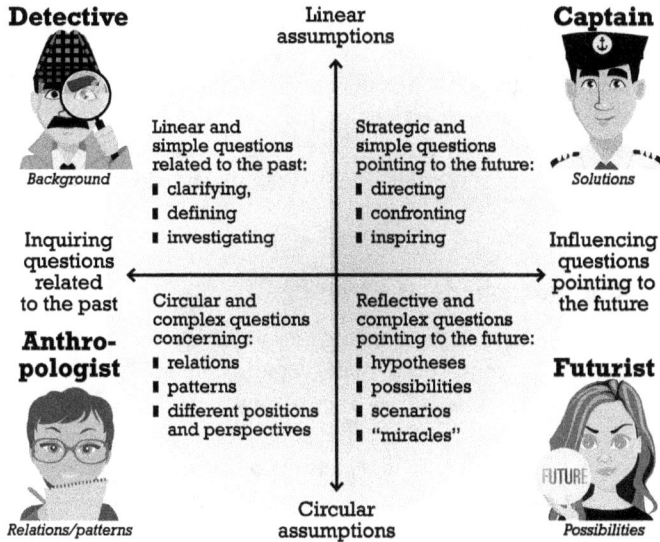

Figure 3.1 Question Models

is based on a cause–effect logic. A circular assumption, on the other hand, is based on a systemic way of thinking about the unpredictability of complex interactions. The question models are perceived as a continuum between the various extremes. By being aware of positioning and types of questions, the coach or therapist can take on a role as a gamemaster, consciously guiding the process through a specific movement with a solution-focused goal.

The figure sets out these four types of questions:

- *The detective*: Asks simple, linear, informative questions; is processing, defining and investigative: "Then what happened?"
- *The anthropologist*: Asks complex, circular, informative questions; examines patterns, relationships, different positions and perspectives: "What did your colleague think?"
- *The futurist* (*the fortune teller*): Asks complex, circular, influential questions: is future-oriented and tests hypotheses and possibilities: "What if?", "What would he do if you said that?"
- *The captain*: Asks simple, linear, influential questions; is leading, confrontational and inspiring, strategic, action-oriented: "What are you going to do to get to harbour (goal)?"

The U in the model draws the movement that a conversation can take in a coaching session from defining the problem (the detective), through inquisitive and open-minded examination of the background (the anthropologist) and possibilities (the futurist), to deciding on action (the captain). Knowledge and training in the use of postures, question models and understanding of the movement proposed by Karl Tomm's U-model can strengthen the therapist's or coach's awareness of the influence of her or his own speech actions on the course of the therapy or coaching. One can choose to be solution-focused or, through postures and question models, consider it appropriate to stay in the more systemic and circular ways of leading the conversation.

Coordinated Management of Meaning

CMM is a context model for categorising and understanding given episodes and speech acts that take place in social contexts (see Figure 3.2) – for example, in a company or a family. The model tries to create awareness of what each one takes for granted as implied (implicit forces) in the given context (contextual forces). In the specific situation, each individual has his or her own understanding of what culture prevails, and each has his or her own self-narrative about who he or she is in that culture and what types of relationships he or she has. This constitutes the contextual forces in the organisation – that is, the context in which the given episode is understood. This has an impact on which speech acts are expressed and by whom. These speech acts will, in turn, be interpreted and assessed on the basis of an implicit perception of the organisation of those involved. This is called the implicit forces.

For me, the understanding of positions, question types and the CMM context model as a whole creates a conscious approach to working with external processes and is a useful contribution to understanding the movement of conversation in a coaching or therapy session.

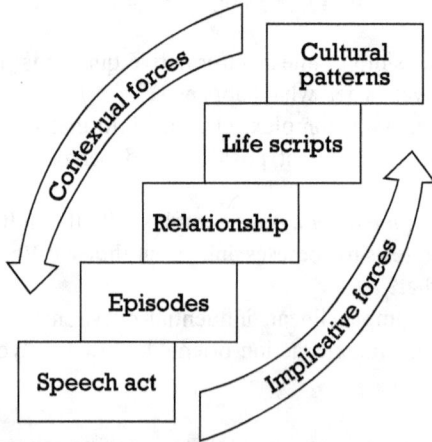

Figure 3.2 Coordinated Management of Meaning

Cases

The cases below serve to show some coaching aspects of cybernetic psychotherapy, where there are process and conceptual parallels to systemic coaching. However, there is the significant addition that cybernetic psychotherapy is also conscious of transference and countertransference in the relationship between therapist and client and, furthermore, consciously enters into dialogue with unconscious intelligence through integration of dreamwork, bodily sensations and drawing therapy, for example. I believe a cybernetic psychotherapeutic course is a good starting point for fruitful coaching work and I also believe most psychotherapists recognise coaching aspects in their work.

In addition to providing an insight into how cybernetic therapeutic work can unfold, the cases serve to show parallels to systemic coaching.

The coaching aspects are highlighted in the text based on the concepts in cybernetic psychotherapy and systemic coaching, respectively, as reviewed above. Subsequently, the cases are put into perspective from a cybernetic psychotherapeutic and a systemic coaching perspective, respectively. The following keywords from coaching will be highlighted in italics the first time they appear in the text in each case:

- Curiosity/inquisitiveness (readiness to wonder/principle of irreverence).
- Question models – Karl Tomm's U-Model (1992).
- Communicative positions.
- Appropriate interference/structural coupling (corresponds to change of process channel).
- Coordinated meaning of management (CMM).
- Perspective on the issue.

In all three cases, the clients commenced therapy through a desire for help to deal with a concrete and current challenge in their lives. They had a desire to improve performance or change old-fashioned and inappropriate behaviour. In both the therapeutic and coaching sense, they wanted to take responsibility for releasing resources within themselves and change their attitude to habitual patterns. The schemata of these habit patterns needed to become more complex and flexible. The clients' blocking of impulses from the self-regulating higher levels of consciousness and control systems ideally had to be turned into acceptance so that the same impulses could be included. In this way, larger parts of the mental system could be activated with much greater information capacity as a result.

As we shall see in Case 3, this can be a very lengthy therapeutic process. The point is that such therapeutic work can form the basis of a more coaching-like approach when necessary trust has been established, both in the relationship and in the client's inner judgement and impulse control. In Case 1, we see that initial good transference and countertransference in exclusively cybernetic psychotherapeutic work, without focus on a concrete solution, may yet have a coaching effect and actually solve the client's experience of the problem. In Case 1, in contrast to Cases 2 and 3, coaching was not directly applied to external processes, only work with internal ones. The method was to enter into dialogue with unconscious intelligence and thereby free up self-regulating resources and potentials. Finally, Case 2 is an example of a process where both therapeutic and coaching approaches have been used more consciously and openly.

Case 1: Peter

This case is an example of a therapeutic relationship established over few sessions, with strong, positive transference and countertransference contributing to a powerful effect on the central goal of the client. It is worth noticing that at no point has the work been consciously coaching- and solution-focused. The focus has predominantly been on the therapeutic aspect.

Peter is 35 years old and a writer. He suffers from multiple sclerosis (MS).

I first meet Peter, in my capacity as doctor, in a neurology department. He has no visible injuries from his illness, and the neurological examination is normal. But he feels bothered by so-called MS fatigue and dizziness. During the conversation, his experience is mirrored and acknowledged, while the positive in the normal neurological examination is emphasised. He is instilled with realistic hope of having the benign version of the disease. We talk about existential aspects of the disease as possible competing causes for his fatigue and dizziness. Peter feels understood, and finds that co-responsibility is taken for his situation.

MS is an inflammation-like disease of the central nervous system (CNS), which typically occurs in so-called attacks. These attacks can cause all sorts of CNS outcome symptoms, such as sensory disturbances, visual disturbances, loss of strength, dizziness and balance and coordination problems. Not least 'invisible' symptoms, with cognitive difficulties and mental and physical exhaustion, are extremely disabling.

Two weeks later, we meet again. Since our last meeting, Peter has not felt MS fatigue or dizziness, for the first time since the MS diagnosis was made. We agree that he will continue as a client in my psychotherapy practice. Peter and I have a shared experience of his situation. His positive transference on my person is a very resourceful starting point for our collaboration in psychotherapy. Peter is also motivated to use himself and his own situation in his creative work as a writer.

MS fatigue greatly disturbs Peter up to a deadline with a manuscript. He has previously experienced the fatigue disappear after one of our sessions and is strongly motivated for this to happen again. The manuscript deals, on a symbolic level, with his own experience of having MS.

Peter is overwhelmed by MS fatigue and cannot work. He has an impending deadline and wants help to make it. This is the coaching perspective to the session. The cybernetic therapeutic perspective is that the fatigue is only partly due to the MS illness, as it disappeared for a few days after our first meeting. The fatigue can be understood as information from the unconscious intelligence and the psyche's self-regulating control systems, which normal consciousness perceives as irrelevant and disturbing and therefore spends large amounts of energy pushing into the background – blocking instead of accepting. A dialogue with these processes may prove beneficial in relation to Peter's desire to write a manuscript which, on a symbolic level, exactly deals with his illness.

In the session, Peter talks about his frustration. I mirror and acknowledge his story and show empathy and open *curiosity* towards his experience. With open and circular *question models*, Peter's ability to reflect expands on the current level of consciousness, which revolves around the attempt of normal consciousness to create meaning and a rational solution. With this form of dialogue, Peter's way of expression changes to being more freely associative, and we can look with *curiosity* at, among other things, relationships with parties involved in his life. The parties' respective *communicative positions* in the specific context are examined (*CMM*).

Gradually, his bodily expression and voice conduct reflect a more fluid state in which input from the unconscious intelligence begins to emerge more clearly. The fatigue is examined through guided introspection: How does it feel? Where in the body? What does he come in contact with regarding thoughts, feelings, images? As he halts, I ask him to reinforce the feeling and sit with his eyes closed. He now recounts a dream he had during the previous night. I ask him to draw the dream. I try, with a sensitive consciousness approach, to follow Peter and, at the same time, notice the resources in the process and follow them in the drawing work. With this change in process channel, positive feedback is given to the self-regulating systems. Parallel processing levels of consciousness, or control systems, are activated with the release of greater information capacity in the overall mental system. Peter's understanding of the fatigue as purely MS fatigue was a simple, and thus rigid, schema that drew the hasty conclusion that these impulses should be blocked. Changing the process channel and thus welcoming impulses from overall control systems is equivalent, in systemic understanding, to disturbing the system by *structural coupling* in order to create change and thus expand the complexity of the schema. An appropriate interference is in that sense a disturbance that is precisely appropriate for the system to meet it with acceptance and not block it. In cybernetic psychotherapy, the therapist tries to be open to signals from the unconscious intelligence of the overall control systems in order to be able to change the process channel at the right moment.

The work ends with a drawing, which Peter calls the "stock cube" regarding his situation. He describes an "aha" experience and senses calm and intense meaning. The stock cube is the essence of his problem. Peter describes it as a bodily experience that cannot be immediately described in words. The experience involves the whole mental system, understood as the total bodily and intellectual information capacity in both conscious and unconscious processes. The session was conducted as cybernetic psychotherapy, but in the approach to external processes there were aspects that are recognisable from systemic coaching.

A week later, Peter enthusiastically recounts he had felt strangely invigorated and had completed his manuscript in just four days. This does not necessarily confirm the correctness of the above theoretical considerations, but it supports that appropriate resources were released in Peter during the process.

Case 2: Laura

The client in this session changes her attitude towards a simple and rigid inner schema that tells her she is stupid. This change gives her better ability to concentrate as well as executive functions while reading for exams. This is an example of a therapeutic process where the duration of the relationship is not so crucial and where there is a large element of both coaching and therapeutic approach in the working method.

Laura is 33 years old and a student, but has difficulties with concentration and sustained attention. She is easily distracted and impulsive. She benefits from external structure and regularity and has difficulty managing time on her own. In primary school, she was bullied and had a hard time keeping up. She felt stupid despite the fact that she – judging by our meeting and her current ability to study – is very gifted. Laura also has much self-blame over things she would have done differently if only she had not acted so impulsively. She wants specific help to be able to concentrate on reading for exams.

The coaching aspect here is a concrete, solution-focused desire for help to concentrate on and structure exam reading. The cybernetic therapeutic perspective is the client's perception of herself as stupid and wrong. She confirms her perception with self-blame and is angry at herself. A simple, rigid schema in her mental system plays in a loop.

Laura talks about her frustrations, self-blame and anger with great pressure of speech. It is important for her to get all the details in. She speaks quickly, goes off on a tangent and does not always return to the subject she has just left. I help Laura with structure and overview. Based on the *communicative positions* in systemic coaching, I position her as someone who needs help and who creates a relationship of dependency in her transference to me. This is both good and bad. In the long run, she should ideally internalise my role. Conversely, she finds it is actually possible to get help. In the beginning, I ask linear clarifying and influential *question models* to keep together the large amount of information and not open too much up at once. You could say that I, alternately, take on the role of detective and captain. This way, we arrive at a structure for the session with a specific issue: To investigate what happens when she sits down to read. This concerns Point A, the physical environment, such as time, light, sound, mobile phone, email and so on; and Point B, emotions, thoughts, images and so on, which she comes in contact with along the way.

After clarifying Point A, I can, together with Laura, examine Point B using more circular clarifying questions. Through this process channel, Laura comes into contact with her anger and self-blame. The feelings emerge, in this context, in the form of the simple, rigid schema mentioned earlier – that Laura is stupid.

The schema was created at an early stage in her childhood, when the complexity of her system could not regulate more nuanced interpretations. In the safe therapeutic space, Laura dares to look at the schema, which I suggest be external-ised in the form of a drawing. This shift in the process channel corresponds to an *appropriate interference* or *structural coupling* of the system in order to solve the problem at a higher level and thereby increase the complexity and flexibility of the schema. We invite Laura's adult, more complex system along to examine, in a more emotionally neutral way, what the motives for the schema might be and what it might need. At the end of the session, at my request, Laura takes the drawing of the psychic schema in her arms and comforts it, as if it were a small child.

At the next session, Laura explains that the anger and self-blame now show up to a lesser extent during her exam reading than before. She has been able to look at these emotions with greater acceptance and care, which has strengthened her reading concentration.

Laura's *perspective on the issue* regarding the schema has thus changed from blocking to acceptance. The "love, which the system directs towards itself" (Ved-felt 1996, p. 141) has increased Laura's ability for reflection, concentration and executive functions – to quote Ole Vedfelt on the core of all wisdom. As shown, the sessions with Laura have a structure that initially works through external pro-cesses, drawing on aspects known from systemic coaching, after which we work therapeutically with internal processes.

Case 3: Liselotte

This case shows how long-term psychotherapeutic work with internal schema can lead to a stronger impact in work contexts and changes in external behaviour. The psychotherapeutic space creates a safe laboratory for experimenting with repressed energy, for example – energy that, in the case of uncontrolled discharge, may cre-ate problems for the client and activate strong feelings of guilt, shame and anger, for example. After spending time processing, one can assist the client in trying out new behavioural patterns in real life through a more coaching-like approach. The long-term psychotherapy and the sound relationship between client and therapist are in this case a safe base and strengthen the client's judgement.

Liselotte is 38 years old and a school teacher. She grew up with a tyrannical father, which left her marked in adulthood with an alert sense of guilt and shame as well as a fear of exclusion from social contexts should she make a wrong move. For a year and a half, we have been working with the feeling of shame and her repressed anger. The therapeutic space has been a laboratory to test emotions and possibilities for action before they can be carried out in real life.

In this selected session, Liselotte wants to work on an upcoming meeting at her workplace, where the classes for the next school year will be allocated. Two colleagues have created an alliance to get a certain well-functioning class, where Liselotte otherwise teaches. She has previously had difficulty standing up for her rights and wants help with this.

The coaching perspective is the competition at work for an attractive working space. Liselotte wants help to stand firm and remain as teacher for a particular class. The cybernetic therapeutic perspective points to a failing belief in one's own judgement in relation to one's own needs and their justification and legitimacy. This may, in a dynamic sense, be due to a tyrannical father who disavowed her opinions and feelings and punished her arbitrarily. Liselotte now fears she cannot stand firm on a legitimate desire to retain a job that colleagues plan to take over.

As in the first two cases, the point of departure is the client speaking freely, and I, as therapist, mirroring and acknowledging in a state of *inquisitive* empathy and sensitive attention. Earlier, Liselotte has shared her most shameful experiences and she seems safe and free in our relationship. I still experience very good transference. In the session, we focus mainly on the external processes, to begin with, through linear, clarifying *question models* (the detective) to understand the problem, followed by lengthy work on the relationships in her workplace, with *circular, clarifying questions* (the anthropologist). Finally, *circular questions of an influential nature* (the futurist) are asked to test the different possibilities for reactions in the group and the outcome of the meeting. We also work with the culture of the workplace, the self-narrative (*CMM*) of management and individual employees. We look at Liselotte's proposals for the significance of certain speech acts for the colleagues' perceived *communicative positioning*. Along the way, various shifts are made in process channels to ensure that we do not overlook important information from higher controlling systems. But there is more focus on the external processes, at least on the surface, for our form of collaboration on the session's theme could not have taken place without our lengthy prior psychotherapeutic work. Previously receiving her experience of shame with acceptance, I see it as crucial for her daring to be completely open to me in our experimental approach. This sincerity, as well as my recognition and acceptance in the therapy room, I see as an important factor for her daring to rely on her own judgement at the actual planning meeting at the school.

Liselotte meets up with enthusiasm at our next session and proudly recounts that she stood firm and thus kept her class. She mischievously adds, "I felt like a man". Our long-term cybernetic psychotherapeutic work forms the basis, and is a prerequisite, for the pronounced systemic coaching aspect of the working method in the given session. I would argue that a purely coaching approach, at worst, could have led to a violent physical reaction in the situation, as great energy from lower control levels could have been released without the possibility of higher control levels to regulate it.

Summary

Cybernetic psychotherapy and systemic coaching have overlapping meta-theoretical foundations (systems theory and cybernetics) and several corresponding working concepts and explanatory models. In practice, systemic coaching mainly focuses on external processes, with many methods for understanding processes between people in social contexts, such as CMM, communicative positioning and question models. Question models from systemic coaching are recognised in cybernetic psychotherapy, but systemic coaching uses them more concretely and purposefully. In systemic coaching, there is a recognition of the importance of internal processes without them being described or attempted to be understood on a deeper level. Cybernetic psychotherapy has both a theory for, and a practical approach to, the inner psychic processes and involves unconscious intelligence in the client's work towards understanding the outer processes in, for example, interpersonal relationships.

All three cases express a desire for help with a specific problem. They wish to mobilise internal resources to perform better according to their needs and potential in the given situation. That is the coaching and solution-focused perspective. The case sessions have been performed as cybernetic psychotherapy with the inclusion of concepts from systemic coaching. By marking these in the text, I have wanted to show that the two ways of working, cybernetic psychotherapy and systemic coaching, are two sides of the same coin, with respect for, and understanding of, the human mental system being in constant interaction between introverted and extroverted awareness. The psychotherapeutic approach promotes a secure opening of the many layers of the mental system and provides space for the self-regulatory properties of the higher control systems, while the coaching approach creates focus and purpose and can thereby facilitate a decision-making process towards action.

Conscious and simultaneous contact with both internal and external processes – in a mutually dependent, interactive pulse – is essential for personality development and thus also for deeply felt decision-making and subsequent actions. What takes place on an individual level is reflected in the collective, and vice versa. The same conflicts take place on a micro as well as a macro level. This is a central point in my desire to work with a combination of cybernetic psychology and systemic coaching: A prerequisite for personal development and the individuation processes is harmony between the individual's awareness of his or her own inner motivation and potential along with these being lived out in accordance with the opportunities and needs of the outside world.

Cybernetic psychotherapy and systemic coaching are methods that share common ground, with opportunities for mutual synergy in both personal development work and creating communities that may afford us tools to address present and future challenges. Both methods are both theoretical knowledge and practical apprenticeship. When approaching the systemic circular way of thinking, one approaches an experience-oriented domain. The systemic way of understanding the world can accommodate the complexity of the world and allows otherwise incomparable quantities to enter into a meaningful context – such as the recognition of the irrational, circular and creative intelligence on an equal footing with the logically rational and linear as two relevant sides of the same issue, the interaction between the inward-looking, calm, open and secure and the outward-looking, focused and purposeful.

In practice, both cybernetic psychotherapy and systemic coaching are about a way to listen to ourselves and each other and a way to be with ourselves and our fellow human beings; that we practise – and dare – to meet ourselves and the world with an open heart, an open mind and an open will; and that we thereby contribute to releasing resources to bring good intentions into action.

References

Bertalanffy, L. von (1968) *General System Theory*. George Braziller.
Gallop, C. (n.d.) http://ifwerantheworld.com
Køppe, Simo (1990) *Virkelighedens niveauer*. Gyldendal.
Moltke, H.V. & Molly, A. (Eds.) (2009) *Systemisk coaching. En grundbog*. Dansk Psykologisk Forlag.
Sjaastad, Øv et al. (2004) *Fysiologi. En grundbog*. Gyldendals Akademiske.
Tomm, K. (1992) *Interviewet som intervention*. Forum.
Vedfelt, Ole (1996) *Bevidsthed. Bevidsthedens niveauer*. Gyldendal.
Vedfelt, Ole (2002) *Ubevidst intelligens – du ved mere, end du tror, du gør* (2nd ed.). Gyldendal.
Vedfelt, Ole (2007) *Drømmenes Dimensioner*. Gyldendal.
Whitmore, J. (1997) *Coaching for Performance*. Nicholas Brealey.

4

Three Dilemmas in Dreamwork

Anders Vogt

Dreamwork is an amazing therapeutic tool but not without its challenges. When working with dreams in therapy, we want to find answers, draw conclusions and move forward. But, if we reach for the conclusion too soon, there is a risk we will close the creative exploration of the dream and miss out on important insights. First, using the Danish therapist and author Ole Vedfelt's model for dreamwork, I will look at how we can keep the dream open while we move forward with the therapeutic process. Second, as therapists, we train for years to become experts in dream interpretation, and our clients seek us out because of that expertise. But there is a risk that expertise and authority can get in the way of an open, creative exploration of dreams. Based on thoughts from Michael White, founder of Narrative Therapy, I will describe how some approaches to dream interpretation can inadvertently result in an asymmetrical power dynamic and discuss how we can mitigate this. Finally, when we interpret dreams, we put them into words, and this in itself can contribute to closing the dreamwork process. From the perspective of cybernetic psychology and with the help of Gregory Bateson, Daniel Stern and James Hillman, I will be looking at problems that can result from prematurely attempting to translate dream symbolism into conventional language. Along the way, I hope to offer a peek into the amazing world of wisdom and creativity offered by dreams and perhaps inspire readers to start working with dreams themselves.

Dream Interpretation in Cybernetic Psychotherapy

According to Ole Vedfelt's cybernetic psychology, when we are awake, our consciousness is constantly busy processing the enormous amounts of information we are subjected to through our experience of the world. But, when we sleep at night, consciousness is relieved of the burden of processing this information. Vedfelt explains dreams as a result of the surplus of capacity with regard to information processing thus arising and as a result of activity in higher-level psychological operating systems, which are able to process more information with higher complexity than the awake consciousness. When we dream, consciousness starts processing information which has come in during the day. New material is compared with existing

DOI: 10.4324/9781003360247-5

material, and new associations and possibilities of meaning are formed. Simultaneously, dreams produce model simulations, creatively synthesising different aspects of experience and experimenting with problem-solving in a risk-free environment (Vedfelt 2007, p. 503 f.).

Cybernetic psychology sees the psyche as a network where associations between clusters of information are constantly created and adjusted while the system dynamically responds to outside influences and the state of consciousness. When we are awake and deal with tasks that require special attention, the psyche will utilise particular sub-networks in the consciousness. But, in dreams, these constraints are loosened, and we get freer access to unconscious parts of the psyche. Thus, the whole psychic network and all modes of consciousness are accessible to variable degrees in the so-called supramodal space – a type of conscious experience combining all modes of experience – that is, thoughts, sights, sounds, scents, bodily sensations, kinetic experiences and atmospheric moods (Vedfelt 2007, p. 504).

Hermeneutics of Dream Interpretation

The cybernetic psychology approach to dreamwork has many facets and utilises techniques and interpretation methods originating in a range of psychological theories. A dreamwork session usually starts with the dreamer recounting the dream. The therapist listens and mirrors the story back to the dreamer, while sometimes pausing to ask questions or offer reflections. The process then goes on to explore the associations in the dream, and a great deal of attention is given to the thoughts, bodily feelings and emotions arising in both the client and therapist as a result of working with the dream. Sometimes, meditation-like contemplations are used (so-called guided introspection) to go deeper into feelings and associations resulting from the dream. To further open up the process to the bodily, visual and kinetic aspects of the dream, body therapy may be used, or the client may be asked to draw scenes from the dream, which can then be explored in conversation.

As a matter of principle, the cybernetic therapist will not offer definite interpretations of dreams, and it is seen as important not to commit to any particular interpretation. On the contrary, it is recommended to test out different interpretation perspectives to see how they resonate with the dreamer, while looking out for new interpretive insights emerging from the process. Vedfelt recommends that the interpretation process toggles between two positions, (a) the dreamer's own subjective interpretation and (b) the co-interpretation and offering of perspectives by the expert. By shifting between these positions, the dreamer's own interpretation and the expert's co-interpretation can creatively inspire each other. In this way, new layers of understanding of the dream and its significance for the dreamer's life can be continuously uncovered (Vedfelt 2007, p. 511).

Vedfelt bases this approach on the hermeneutics of Hans-Georg Gadamer. Gadamer saw it as unavoidable that we have prejudices or preconceptions when we start reading a text. As soon as we grasp an initial meaning in the text, we will project a meaning on to the whole text. This is because we read the text with certain expectations of meaning. The aim is to become as aware as possible of one's own prejudices and always be prepared to revise the meaning. If we understand dream interpretation from this perspective, it has a number of implications (Vedfelt 2007, p. 185 f.):

- It is impossible to avoid interpreting. One will always articulate a tentative meaning or understanding, even if one chooses not to express it.
- Interpretations can never be neutral or objective, because the interpretation will always be based on one's prejudices
- It is not possible to reach an exhaustive interpretation, because new possibilities of interpretation emerge as the meaning is revised.

Alternating between Openings and Closures

Seen from the hermeneutic perspective, dream interpretations must in a sense always be tentative, and the psychotherapist must remain open to the possibility that new, surprisingly different interpretations, which could be helpful to the client, may later emerge. Of course, this should not be understood to mean that we can never conclude anything. On the contrary, some form of interpretation and conclusion is important for the client as well as the therapist to feel that the process moves forward. But knowing that all interpretation is tentative means that dreamwork requires a special attitude, where we always remain prepared to alternate between small closures of meaning and openness towards new interpretations. It is not desirable for a dream interpretation to be perceived as a final or unambiguous explanation, because this is likely to close down the creative exploration of the dream.

Dreamwork as a Therapeutic Tool

Because dreams expend most of their energy organising experiences and coming up with possible solutions to problems, they will naturally concern themselves with that which is important to the dreamer and will therefore, directly or indirectly, point to topics and issues of great relevance to the therapeutic process. By paying attention to their dreams, we can learn a lot about our clients and their particular attitudes towards the world. Such insights into the network of meaning in the psyche can be very profound, not least because the problem-solving model simulations in dreams can point out issues and suggest solutions that the dreamer would never have noticed in the waking state.

In the following, we shall look at how the work with a specific dream provided a new perspective for a client on his life and developmental outlook.

Anton's Dream: About the Inner Life of the Dreamer

At the start of his therapy, one of my clients, Anton, dreams that he is a woman who is owed money by a man. After various complications, the woman manages to get the man to pay her the money.

We look at the dream from different angles. There are many possible interpretations. A psychodynamic interpretation, for example, may choose to focus on the dreamer's childhood and try to tease out similarities between the relationship of the woman and man in the dream and that between his mother and father. A more pragmatic interpretation may instead focus on events the day before – so-called day residues. Yet others may choose to see the dream as a comment on the dreamer's gender identity.

After looking at several possibilities, we choose to focus on the dream as a depiction of Anton's inner life, so that characters in the dream are seen as representing aspects of himself. The dream in a sense offers Anton a chance of seeing himself from a completely different perspective, as if through a different consciousness. Working with the dream from this perspective, he sees his own compassionate and empathic qualities – which he feels he has not paid enough attention to or managed to sufficiently integrate in the past. The 'feminine' qualities of compassion and empathy stand in contrast to his usual understanding of himself as sensible, direct and pragmatic – qualities all of which he sees as 'masculine'. He now understands his dream to say that the masculine side of his personality should yield or surrender something to his feminine side and, so to speak, 'finance' it in a psychological sense. The revaluation of feminine aspects of his personality becomes a central theme in his therapy. Gradually, more nuances appear in subsequent dreams, and this perspective turns out to be very helpful to him in his self-development.

When dreams are used in psychotherapy, they often seem to suggest new perspectives and potentials for development. And, when clients progress in their personal development, the dreams appear to comment on this and suggest adjustments to the course. Thus, dreams can become kinds of creative collaborators in the therapeutic process (Vedfelt 2007, p. 512).

Keeping the Dreamwork Process Open

In order to use dreams in psychotherapy, we must understand that they are complex and always open to a multitude of interpretations. But this may conflict with a client's desire to find meaningful and instructional advice in dreams. By virtue of their metaphorical fusion of everyday experiences and deeper memories, dreams can process much more information and a much higher degree of complexity than the awake consciousness. Therefore, the potential meaning of dreams is equally extensive, nuanced and complex, and it is rarely possible to reduce it to simple advice or instructions. If we try to force out a simple and easy to understand conclusion from a complex and nuanced dream, it can lead to a vulgarisation of the dream's message and a diminishment of its insights. For dreamwork to really lead somewhere, we must try to adopt the perspectives of the dream and open ourselves to its many possible meanings. And we must give the process time. We should allow the dreamer to learn from the process and gradually become more familiar with the language and themes contained in their dreams.

But the endless possibilities of interpretation and the fantastical imagery of dreams challenge most of us and leave us yearning for some kind of closure. The vast potential of meaning makes us ask ourselves: How can I understand this and make sense of it in the context of my life? If we consider, at the same time, the fact that people who seek psychotherapy typically long to find solutions to deeply personal, complex and painful problems, it becomes obvious that the desire for closure – to be able to conclude something significant – will be of central concern to them. But, if we progress too quickly, without paying attention to how our interpretations can affect the therapeutic alliance and, not least, our clients' understanding of themselves, the dreamwork may be less fruitful. An experienced therapist will often be able to recognise important psychological patterns and problems based on a few dreams long before the client becomes aware of those problems. And, because the therapist has practical and theoretical training and experience, he or she would easily be able to come up with complex and far-reaching conclusions about what the dream means. But it is often a better choice for the therapist to hold back and not share his or her insights with the client too early in the process. Even if the interpretation is offered with the best intentions, it can be problematic if the client is not able to keep up and take in the interpretation.

In Anton's example above, it is by no means certain that he would have been able to benefit from a far-reaching theoretical interpretation explaining the so-called male and female aspects of the psyche. If we present such interpretations to our clients too soon, before they have started to develop their own insights, there is a risk that the essence of the interpretation, even if it is wise and insightful, will escape them. The interpretation may be understood cognitively and logically but will not be felt in the body – not experienced emotionally. Therefore, it will not resonate with the client to the same extent as would have been the case if she or he had had time to acquire her or his therapeutic insights from inside the process her- or himself. And, without this quality of insight, the client will not gain much from the process, and it will at least partially have failed. When dreamwork works best, it offers a very rare opportunity to establish a therapeutic alliance on a deep level, enabling the therapist and client to understand the client's inner world through a unique and personal metaphorical language. To begin with, the dream images may only appear as vague inklings of meaning, but gradually those meanings become clearer and clearer. When a dreamwork process goes on over a longer period of time, the therapist and the client can develop their own special language, where the secret codes of dreams become an important shorthand for understanding the client's unique way of experiencing the world. This can lead to profound emotional attunement between client and therapist as they learn to understand subtle nuances in the client's emotional and cognitive experience of the world, which may otherwise have gone unnoticed. Such a connection can give the client a feeling of being understood on a very deep level and a feeling of not being alone with his or her problems – and this will help the healing process move forward.

Asymmetrical Relations

In the following, I will examine how perceptions of expertise and authority can result in an asymmetrical power dynamic, which can get in the way of an open and creative dreamwork process. Based on thoughts from Vedfelt and Michael White, I will describe the problem and suggest ways to mitigate it.

Vedfelt explains that the different types of interpretations put forward by the various schools of dream interpretation often turn out to be constrained by the theoretical contexts in which they were conceived (Vedfelt 2007, p. 211). It should come as no surprise that Jungian dreamworkers produce Jungian interpretations, and that Freudian dreamworkers produce Freudian ones. But this is not without its problems, because a specific theoretical perspective can turn out to exclude other perspectives. However, as Vedfelt points out, a theory-less approach to dreamwork is not the solution either, because anti-theoretical attitudes often result in the interpreter unconsciously projecting their personal value systems on to the dreams of their clients (Vedfelt 2007, p. 184).

Theory-based interpretations can be problematic insofar as the interpretation can only be done by someone who has familiarised themselves with the theory. The typical client in psychotherapy will rarely be as well versed in the theory as the therapist and may therefore have trouble understanding the exact premises behind an interpretation. This, in turn, makes it more difficult for the client to keep a critical mind. Vedfelt warns against so-called "theoretical abuse", in which a therapist pushes ready-made interpretation down the dreamer's throat (Vedfelt 2007, pp. 512, 518). Thus, theory-based interpretations can put unnecessary constraints on the dreamwork process and make a creative hermeneutic exploration difficult, even when the therapist does not insist on being right. As an example, archetypal interpretations in the Jungian tradition can be very hard to understand without prior knowledge of the theory. C.G. Jung himself discusses this in *The Structure and Dynamics of the Psyche*, explaining that he considers it "impossible for anyone without knowledge of mythology and folklore and without some understanding of the psychology of primitives and of comparative religion to grasp the essence of the individuation process" (Jung 2014, p. 290). If archetypal interpretation requires this level of knowledge, it seems reasonable to assume that the average client could have trouble following the premises of the interpretation. Even if an interpretation is actually in accordance with its theory and is both precise and relevant to the client's situation, it may still be problematic if the client does not (yet) have the skills and knowledge required to understand it.

A trained therapist, with good communication skills, knowledge of the client and an empathic attitude, will be able to make the interpretation relevant and helpful for the client. But, if the therapist does not have the necessary pedagogical skills, and the client is not able to take in the interpretation and assimilate its meaning, it may be lost on the client, like the cryptic answer from an oracle with which the receiver is not able to argue or have a dialogue.

This can result in an unequal dynamic, where we risk the client being alienated towards the therapeutic process. The therapist can end up appearing as a knowledgeable authority and the client as a mere recipient of information – a situation which is likely to put an end to the free and open exploration of the dream's meaning.

Discursive Power in Therapy

Today, very few people in therapy would be happy with a therapist behaving like an old-fashioned professor facing a young student. Most people expect more equal, respectful relationships with a higher degree of symmetry. But less overt asymmetries can easily slip into the therapist's office.

Using the concept of *discourses* as coined by French philosopher Michel Foucault, it can be explained how ideas about authority and power may inadvertently come into play in the relationship between therapist and client on a very fundamental level. Discourses can be understood as types of unspoken rules and practices that help constitute areas of knowledge such as medicine, psychiatry, economics, sociology or biology and make them appear coherent. A discourse works by defining which types of language and knowledge are viewed as meaningful within a certain area and what is acceptable to do and say at a certain time and in a certain context (Nilsson 2009, p. 52 f.). Different groupings in society thereby acquire speaking rights in certain contexts by virtue of their ability to master the relevant discourses.

Michael White, an Australian therapist, social worker and founder of narrative therapy, has brought Foucault's thinking into the field of psychotherapy. He points out that it is a problem that discourses "encourage persons in the belief that the members of these disciplines have access to an objective and unbiased account of reality, and of human nature" (White 1991, p. 29).

Considering this statement, we may wonder how it affects the therapeutic relationship when we meet clients who have such discourse-based expectations towards the division of roles, competency and authority, whether conscious of them or not. This could, for instance, manifest as a belief that it is only the therapist who has the knowledge required to analyse the client, interpret dreams, give the right answers, evaluate the process, diagnose the client and so on. This would also entail that the client does not have the same authority to interpret, evaluate the process, give answers and so on.

At the beginning of his therapy, one of my clients always used to pause after telling me his latest dream. He would sit back, smile at me and then ask: "So then, what can you make of this?" Something in the way he said it made it clear that I was supposed to act as the expert interpreter who would come up with the answers, while he would sit back and listen. In such a situation, it is easy to be caught off guard and difficult to resist the temptation to take on the role of the expert. Who does not like to be seen as wise and insightful? But, if I had chosen to play along, it might have reinforced a problematic power dynamic. If the client believes that the therapist has access to unique knowledge that gives him or her special abilities and authority to interpret dreams, the client may see the therapist's dream interpretations as more authoritative and definite than would be ideal. As a result, the client could become less likely to contribute her or his own interpretations to the process and instead either choose to hold back her or his own ideas or try to mimic the therapist's interpretations.

But there are strategies that can be used to mitigate this problem. Michael White describes a number of techniques to counteract preconceptions about the therapist as someone who has privileged access to knowledge. He recommends addressing one's own preconceptions up front, making them known both to oneself and to the client. White very much strives to redefine his own role, from that of an authority figure to a kind of co-author in the therapeutic process, while also encouraging the client to take a more active role in the therapeutic search for knowledge (White p. 31 f.). As therapists working with dreams, we can try to do the same. We can explicitly tell our clients that we see the client and therapist as equal interpreters, and we can make an effort to actively encourage our clients to engage in the process as co-interpreters and evaluators, thereby giving the right to interpret (back) to them. This seems important, not least because many people still imagine a dream interpreter to be a person in possession of special esoteric knowledge that is not accessible to normal people, like a fortune-teller able to extract mystical messages from the reading of tea leaves or hand lines.

Jung described how he always aspired to be tactful when interpreting a dream to avoid violating the dreamer's self-respect unnecessarily: "I have made it a rule, when someone tells me a dream and asks for my opinion, to say first of all to myself: 'I have no idea what this dream means'" (Jung 2014, p. 283). By reminding himself of this, Jung was trying to keep his mind open towards the contents of the dream. It sounds like he mostly kept this reminder to himself and did not say it out loud. Perhaps he wanted to guard his reputation with his clients as an expert dream interpreter. But, as modern psychotherapists, we may choose to share this insight with our clients up front, making it a prerequisite that we really do not know what a dream could mean, but that we can explore its meaning together. By reminding the client that the therapist does not have a natural authority as a dream interpreter, we can frame the dreamwork process in an understanding that both the client and the therapist are entitled and able to find meaning in dreams.

Authority in Cybernetic Psychotherapy

Cybernetic psychotherapy addresses the problem of the dream interpreter's authority in several ways. As mentioned above, Vedfelt sees dream interpretation as a process alternating between the dreamer's own interpretation of the material and the expert's co-interpretation and theoretical contextualisation. This approach makes the interpretation process a joint effort between dreamer and expert. This process requires that the therapist make an effort to become aware of his or her own preconceptions. For this reason, Vedfelt criticises Medard Boss, founder of existential-phenomenological psychotherapy, for not making his theoretical frame of reference clear. Vedfelt finds built-in phenomenological preconceptions on which Boss's interpretations are based but which are not made visible. He directs a similar criticism towards Fritz Perls, founder of gestalt therapy, for ignoring his existentialist preconceptions (Vedfelt 2007, pp. 174, 181, 193).

According to Vedfelt, becoming aware of our preconceptions consists of two steps. First, we must become aware of the theoretical foundation on which we base our interpretations and, second, we must be aware of *when* we start interpreting. He recognises that it is democratic and tactful when some dreamworkers insist that the dreamer must acknowledge the interpretation. But the experienced dreamworker will often be able to see tendencies and motifs in dreams which the dreamer is not yet aware of or willing to recognise, but which may provide valuable insights to the interpreter (Vedfelt 2007, p. 510 f.).

He also discusses how we can best respond to the situation when the therapist presents an interpretation which the client is not ready to accept. In classic psychoanalysis, this would be seen as resistance, which, put simply, means that the client resists the healing process. Cybernetic psychotherapy does not subscribe to this view. Instead, the dismissal of an interpretation by the client is seen as the result of self-regulating processes trying to establish communication on a different level. When a client is reluctant to accept an interpretation, the psychotherapist should therefore not persist or try to reinforce it but should instead shift attention to how the proposed interpretation makes the client feel, and what could be helpful for them in that moment. This can spark a creative process, which enriches the interpretation and helps strengthen the therapeutic alliance (Vedfelt 2007, p. 513).

When Vedfelt uses the client's reluctance to accept the interpretation as a springboard to new levels in the process, it shows that interpretations which the client does not accept can sometimes, nonetheless, become helpful. But he also stresses that it is important to always stay aware of the power dynamic between therapist and client and avoid pushing the client into situations where he or she does not want to be (Vedfelt 2007, p. 516).

Vedfelt and White make it clear how important our preconceptions are to our work as therapists. In order to keep the dreamwork process open, we must strive towards an equal, respectful and democratic relationship between client and therapist, where co-interpretation, co-authoring and dialogue are key concepts. And we must avoid the risks connected to the therapist becoming a theoretical authority, resulting in an asymmetrical power dynamic.

Reductionist Language

As I described above, theoretical interpretations and preconceptions of authority can affect the dreamwork process negatively by creating an unbalanced relationship between therapist and client. It is, perhaps, less obvious that language itself – the process of putting the dream into words – can also contribute to closing the process of exploration.

The problem is inherent in the process of verbalisation, which can have a tendency to reduce highly ambiguous dream symbols to more literal and unambiguous concepts. We will examine this dilemma from three angles. First, we review Gregory Bateson's understanding of dream language as metaphorical, kinetic and paralinguistic. Second, we examine Daniel Sterns concept of emotional attunement as an example of how paralanguage is essential to progress in therapy. And finally, we look at James Hillman's suggestion for what could be called a 'kinetic vocabulary' in therapy.

Metaphors, Relations and Feelings

In his book *Steps to an Ecology of Mind*, Gregory Bateson, anthropologist and cyberneticist among many other titles, discusses the challenges involved when trying to translate the largely non-verbal language of the unconscious into conventional verbal language. Bateson explains that not only are the contents of the unconscious difficult to access, but the information we are able to extract can be very difficult to translate into words. This is because the unconscious material, as found in dreams, is almost entirely metaphorical in nature (Bateson 2000, p. 139).

The metaphorical language of dreams and other unconscious activities has certain limitations compared with conventional language. Everyday language has particular words denoting particular things, persons, events and so on. It has adjectives characterising the things. It has predicates describing what someone or something does, and adverbs describing how this is done. And, in addition, conventional language has negatives to describe those things that are not there or do not happen.

The metaphorical language of the unconscious does not have any of that – it must instead make do with metaphorical images. Metaphors describe relationships between things, Bateson explains. "A metaphor retains unchanged the relationship which it illustrates while substituting other things for the persona or relata", and the particular relationships that dreams deal with are the relationships between self and others. Another way of saying this is that the metaphors of dreams are primarily concerned with feelings (Bateson 2000, pp. 139–140).

Let us look at an example of how metaphors describe relationships and feelings. For example, I may choose to describe a participant in a meeting as 'a bull in a china shop'. Here, it is not the actual things mentioned in the saying, the bull and the china shop, that are important, but the relationship between the person's presence or behaviour (bull-like, aggressive, insensitive) and the meeting situation (fragile or delicate, like pieces of china).

Dreams are abundant in such imagery describing relations and feelings in the life of the dreamer. And, by virtue of their metaphors, they are sophisticated and able to hold more nuances of meaning than conventional language. The image of the bull in the china shop could be understood to mean "this person was clumsy and insensitive towards the delicate situation in the meeting". But it could also quite adequately describe the feelings of a nervous bull trying to navigate the aisles of a china shop or simply the feeling of not fitting in. Likewise, the sounds of plates and vases shattering on the floor may be good analogies to the feelings that an insensitive or awkward remark could cause, and the china may well describe the sensitive nature of the meeting. Metaphors, by nature, are open to many interpretations.

Bateson points out that metaphor is uniquely suited to communicate the contents of the unconscious, which makes it a defining characteristic of both art, myth and dream. He quotes the American dancer Isadora Duncan as having said, "If I could tell you what it meant, there would be no point of dancing it". Bateson notes the ambiguity of the statement and goes on to discuss the nature of a message which must be danced to be communicated: "It is [...] the kind of message which would be falsified if communicated in words, because the use of words (other than poetry) would imply that this is a fully conscious and voluntary message" (Bateson 2000, pp. 137–138).

Kinesics and Paralinguistic Communication

Elsewhere, Bateson explains that a certain type of metaphorical communication is fundamental to animals. He describes a pack of wolves, where the leading male punishes a lower-ranking male for an insubordination by pressing its head down to the ground as if it was a puppy. By behaving the way adult animals normally do towards puppies, the pack leader communicates his own position clearly to the other but, through the visual metaphor achieved by his actions, he also manages to depict the lower-ranking wolf as a puppy (Bateson 2000, pp. 366–367).

Human language is predominantly verbal, based on conventional signs and meanings. But in parallel with this exists a non-verbal analogue language not entirely dissimilar to the communication of other mammals. This language is based on kinesics (facial expressions, postures, hand movements etc.) and paralanguage (intonation, rhythm, volume, as well as sounds such as gasps or sighs).

He suggests that this kind of iconic communication "serves functions totally different from those of (conventional) language and, indeed, performs functions which verbal language is unsuited to perform". Like metaphor, this type of language is very well suited for communicating relations and feelings. When a boy tells a girl that he loves her, she will be wise to pay more attention to his non-verbal communication in the form of intonation, facial expressions and body language than to the mere digital message of the words (Bateson 2000, pp. 374, 418). If the non-verbal part of the communication does not feel authentic, the words will not either. In a way, kinesics and paralanguage can be seen as essential communication channels for authenticity. Words by themselves can always be dismissed as 'just something you say', whereas kinesics and paralanguage communicate those unconscious aspects of the communication that cannot be put into words.

Bateson suggests that dreams can be seen as a kind of cross between the nonverbal, metaphorical communication of animals and conventional verbal language. They are a window into an archaic, prelinguistic way of experiencing the world that still operates in parallel with our modern language, involving understanding the world through feelings, relations and pattern recognition – and, although ancient, in no way obsolete (Bateson 2000, pp. 427–428).

The way I read Bateson, he tells us that dreams, by virtue of their metaphorical, kinetic and paralinguistic properties, are able to authentically communicate feelings, relations and unconscious patterns in a very information-dense form, and with a higher degree of complexity than conventional language. If this is true, it points to special challenges with regard to dream interpretation, namely the difficulty of translating dreams to verbal language without important meaning being lost. Paraphrasing Isadora Duncan, we could ask: "If I could tell you what it meant, what would be the point of dreaming it?"

Paralanguage in Psychotherapy

The developmental psychologist Daniel Stern explains how paralanguage plays a key role in connection to affective attunement. Affective attunement is defined as a way in which we show that we understand someone and that we are able to put ourselves in their place. This is done by imitating "the temporal dynamics of the intensity, form, or rhythm of the other's behavior but in a different modality or at a different scale" (Stern 2004, p. 241) In other words, this is about catching the intonation, the rhythm or the mood of what is said or done and showing that we have understood this by using the same intonation, rhythm and mood, although not necessarily the same words.

According to Stern, affective attunement is essential for the relationship between therapist and client, especially with regard to how authentic the relationship is going to feel. He describes the authentic connection between therapist and client as more important for the effectiveness of therapy than any interpretation in itself. Without affective attunement, there is a risk that the therapist's interpretations will simply be seen as a "technical maneuver from a neutral professional", which may alter "the patient's explicit understanding of herself, but not the intersubjective field between her and the therapist" (Stern 2004, p. 189). He even goes as far as saying that it can be problematic to verbally address the attunement. The drawback can be that this kind of interpretation "makes the implicit explicit, which necessarily pulls the process away from the ongoing here and now to a different here and now in which the stance is more abstracted and removed" (Stern 2004, p. 170).

Stern is talking about psychotherapy in general, but, assuming that what he describes is also true for dreamwork, it would mean that it is more important for therapist and client to be able to tune into the emotional dynamics of the dream than it is to make any kind of interpretation.

A Vocabulary of Kinesics

The psychologist James Hillman is famous for his work in the tradition of C.G. Jung and for his radical approach to dreamwork in which he argued that we should "[s]tick to the image" of the dream and ideally avoid interpretations altogether (Hillman 1991, pp. 74–76). He was a proponent of experiencing the dream images directly and feeling what they do to us, as well as "spreading the dream out" and disclosing the many associations to what the dream is like (Hillman 1991, pp. 244–245). Hillman wanted to avoid conclusions in terms of conceptual and especially clinical language.

In a lecture given in 1977 (Hillman 2010), he argued for the use of metaphorical rather than theoretic language in psychotherapy. He advocated seeking inspiration in the language of alchemy, which C.G. Jung had introduced to modern psychology. Jung showed how the alchemists of the Middle Ages had been engaged in extensive processes of refining themselves spiritually in parallel with their attempts to refine chemical substances into gold and other precious metals, and he found that the processes described by the alchemists very much resembled those he could observe in his modern-day therapeutic clients.

The language of alchemy describes psychological states and processes as if they were a cross between chemical processes and mythological tales. As an example, alchemist language borrows many of its terms from metallurgy, fabric dyeing, embalming, perfume production and pharmacy. In their descriptions of inner processes, alchemists use terms such as digging, melting, forging, soaking, colouring and drying. They dissect, clean, preserve, grind, mix, distil, dissolve, powder and so on. The personality is described as consisting of chemical compounds such as salt, sulphur, mercury and lead. Development requires corrosive acids, heat and cold, and man is seen as an alchemical flask, an alembic, which must be kept closed and at constant temperature for the process to progress. The chemical processes are accompanied by symbolic signs and visions – for example, rising birds or suns, sweating kings or living trees.

The advantage of alchemical language over that of modern psychology, according to Hillman, is that it is entirely metaphorical. We know that, in a concrete sense, there is no fire burning in our stomachs, birds do not hatch in our chest, and we do not consist of sulphur or mercury. Therefore, the alchemical language cannot be taken literally, and we are forced to understand the psyche metaphorically – in a sense, more on its own terms. Another obvious advantage of alchemical language is that its metaphors, such as melting, forging, soaking, drying and so on, are clearly kinetic by nature. They refer to processes in motion and development and are therefore well suited to describe emotional and psychological processes (Hillman 2010, pp. 9–19).

The Delicate Language of Dreams

The examples above illustrate that verbal language has certain limitations compared with the 'language' of the unconscious, including that of dreams.

Bateson helps us understand dreams as metaphor, kinesics and paralanguage uniquely suited to communicating about relations, feelings, authenticity and unconscious experience. The language of dreams shows us things which are difficult, sometimes impossible, to put into words. Therefore, we must be careful, when we talk about our dreams, that we do not reduce them to simplified concepts.

But Stern and Hillman offers hints to how we can work with dreams without reducing their meaning. We can try to tune into the emotional dynamic of the dream, we can focus on experiencing the dream directly as image and we can pay attention to the kinetic and paralanguage aspects of dreams.

This points to the need for a dreamwork method that can focus on the dream as an image, while paying attention to the paralinguistics and kinetic aspects of the experience. I believe cybernetic dreamwork offers such a method.

Cybernetic Dreamwork

According to Vedfelt, dreams are supramodal, holistic experiences in which emotions, thoughts, imagery, bodily sensations and impulses of movement are experienced not separately but as aspects of a unified whole (Vedfelt 2007, p. 297). Supramodality is characterised by a high capacity for information and is well suited for reflection and creative transformations (Vedfelt 2002, p. 103). Moreover, it is capable of synthesising important themes governing the person's experience and actions in extensive ways (Vedfelt 2002, p. 105).

In cybernetic dreamwork, the therapist therefore helps the client explore supramodal associations arising from the dream. Together, they examine what is happening in the various modes of experience – for example, which sensations arise in the body, which thoughts and emotions appear and which patterns of movement, postures or body language emerge during the conversation. Sometimes, the therapist will ask the client to draw a symbol from the dream, which then may evoke certain bodily feelings that, when focused on, can be amplified and cause emotions, which may then again lead to inner imagery, memories or other associations. Vedfelt sees these chains of association as Ariadne's threads, leading to higher and more essential levels of organisation in the psyche (Vedfelt 2007, p. 298). Supramodal associations also involve the therapist, who will continually attempt to discreetly mirror the client's body language, expressions, intonation and so on using so-called vicarious introspection – observing what happens in his or her own realm of experience, trying to pick up on feelings and associations of which the client may not be aware, but which may nonetheless be sensed supramodally (Vedfelt 2007, p. 49).

Through the supramodal method, Vedfelt promotes a high degree of awareness of kinetic and paralinguistic communication. Supramodal ability is explained as a natural, intuitive expertise which has its origin in the emotional attunement between mother and infant (Vedfelt 2002, p. 120).

The supramodal method makes it easier to stay in touch with the paralinguistic and kinetic experiences in the dream while exploring its symbolic metaphors. Vedfelt notes that supramodal chains of association should not be interrupted, because this tends to draw attention away from the authentic contact with the self (Vedfelt 2007, p. 299 f.). When done successfully, the emotional attunement achieved through vicarious introspection will let the client and therapist experience a deep level of mutual understanding without the need for any interpretation.

Michael's Dream: A Supramodal Exploration

In a dream, one of my clients, Michael, finds himself in a primitive cave with a beautiful woman. The floor is covered by a mix of slate and shredded bicycle tubes. This is where she sleeps, and he wonders why her home is so primitive.

In the session, I suggest we explore the scene supramodally and ask him how he experiences each dream symbol in terms of bodily sensations and emotions, while paying attention to any associations that arise. While picturing the cave floor in his mind and paying attention to the feelings and associations arising, he discovers that the floor, which at first had seemed hard and rugged, actually feels surprisingly soft, as if he was laying himself down on a tongue. This reminds him of a childhood fantasy which involved being swallowed by a whale; a fantasy which had been scary, pleasant and mysterious at the same time. As we proceed, the cave appears more inviting to him, and, the more he gets into the mood of the setting, the more he feels that he and the woman become one. At the end of our exploration, he explains that it feels like disappearing into a dark, soft and peaceful space.

The supramodal exploration takes around 15 minutes and has a considerable effect on Michael, making him gradually more relaxed and grounded. I avoid offering interpretations but focus instead on exploring the various elements of the dream through supramodal associations. The dream symbols, the dark cave, the association with being swallowed by a whale and the melting together with a person of the opposite sex are, of course, all open to interpretation. We could interpret this as a classic dream about 'the dark night of the soul'. The whale theme is known from the biblical tale of Jonas and the fairy tale about Pinocchio, in both cases an indication of a personal and spiritual crisis. The woman in the dream may suggest that aspects of the opposite sex may be emerging in the personality and may indicate the potential of transformation through integration of male and female aspects of the psyche. But, as the description of the therapy session suggests, it is not necessary to verbalise any interpretation for the client to experience a result. Feeling the supramodal associations emerging from the dream symbols has a profound effect in itself.

However, later in the session, we circle back to the dream and start discussing how it could be interpreted. But this makes Michael lose some of the newly achieved grounding and instead makes him focus mentally on the fascinating ideas emerging from the interpretation.

Understanding patterns, connection and possible interpretations of course has its place in therapy, but, as the example shows, there is a risk that sudden shifts away from supramodal exploration to verbal interpretation can make us lose touch with important emotional and bodily aspects of the experience. Often, it will be a better choice to remain in authentic contact with the self and benefit from the emotional attunement made possible by the supramodal approach.

Dreamwork Is High-Level Communication

In this chapter, I have tried to illustrate some of the dilemmas I see in psychotherapeutic dreamwork.

Taking a starting point in Ole Vedfelt's cybernetic psychology, I have examined the basic dilemma of wanting to keep the dreamwork process open to further interpretation while simultaneously responding to the urge to reach closure and conclusions. I have tried to show how dreamwork has the ability to provide profoundly new perspectives and I have emphasised the value of sometimes slowing down the process and holding back interpretations so that the client can keep up.

With help from Michael White, I have gone on to examine the dilemma of expertise versus co-interpretation and the risk of creating unhealthy power dynamics. I have explained how a theoretical, authoritative attitude on the part of the therapist can negatively affect the relationship, but also how the client's preconceptions and expectations regarding competence and authority can play into this. And I have suggested strategies to counter these problems.

I have also examined the inherent dilemma of verbal interpretation's potential to reduce the complexity of dream symbols. With the help of Bateson, I have shown why dreams are sensitive to verbal interpretation and, with Stern and Hillman, I have suggested ways in which we can work with dreams without providing conventional verbal or psychological interpretations.

Finally, I have suggested cybernetic dreamwork as a unique approach capable of addressing all three of the dilemmas. With its hermeneutic approach to dreamwork, it aims at keeping the client and therapist on the same level and the dream interpretation process open. The method also emphasises an egalitarian perspective, where the therapist is not seen as having more direct access to the truth than the client, and both are equally entitled to interpret the dream. Lastly, the supramodal exploration method enables a multifaceted exploration of the dream in which the dream is experienced through body and thought associations, emotions, drawing exercises and so on, while close attention is paid to the kinesics and paralinguistic aspects of the experience.

References

Bateson, Gregory (2000) *Steps to an Ecology of Mind*. University of Chicago Press, Chicago.

Hillman, James (1991) *A Blue Fire: Selected writings by James Hillman*. Introduced and edited by Thomas Moore in collaboration with the author. HarperPerennial, New York

Hillman, James (2010) *The Therapeutic Value of Alchemical Language: A heated introduction in James Hillman*, Alchemical Psychology. Spring Publications, Putnam, CT.

Jung, C.G. (2014) *The Structure and Dynamics of the Psyche*. Routledge, Hove, UK.

Nilsson, Roddy (2009) *Michel Foucault. En introduktion*. Hans Reitzels Forlag, Copenhagen.

Stern, Daniel N. (2004) *The Present Moment in Psychotherapy and Everyday Life*. W.W. Norton, New York.

Vedfelt, Ole (2002) *Ubevidst intelligens – du ved mere end du tror*. Gyldendal, Copenhagen.

Vedfelt, Ole (2007) *Drømmenes dimensioner*. Gyldendal, Copenhagen.

White, Michael (1991) Deconstruction and Therapy [Article]. Dulwich Centre, Adelaide.

5

The Narcissistic Wound

Theoretical and Therapeutic Approaches

Solveig Thorborg

The topic of this chapter is the concept of narcissism, with special focus on the injury that by many is termed the narcissistic wound. As used, the term encompasses a wide variety of meanings, so threads are drawn through the development of the concept of narcissism and selected therapeutic approaches are presented, from Kathrin Asper's Jungian approach to the more esoteric understanding of A.H. Almaas. The relevance of the term is investigated within the framework of Ole and Lene Vedfelt's cybernetic psychology, thereby observing how Vedfelt integrates experiences from narcissism theories remodelled within the framework of their resource-oriented psychotherapy.

Introduction

In Ancient Greece, according to classical myth, lived a young hunter named Narcissus, son of the nymph Liriope and the river god Cephissus. Aged 16, he was handsome and loved by many, but he was proud, and everyone was disappointed in their love for him. A rejected youth sent out a prayer in pain that Narcissus himself might experience unrequited love. The goddess Nemesis heard the prayer, and one day, while Narcissus was bending over a forest lake, he fell in love with his own reflection. It took time for him to realise that it was not another human being he beheld. And then it was too late.

Some 2000 years ago, the Roman poet Ovid described Narcissus's bitter realisation in his *Metamorphoses*:

> It is my self I love, my self I see;
> The gay delusion is a part of me.
> I kindle up the fires by which I burn,
> And my own beauties from the well return.
> … How gladly would I from my self remove!
> And at a distance set the thing I love.
> My breast is warm'd with such unusual fire,
> I wish him absent whom I most desire.

Garth 2017, p. 161)

DOI: 10.4324/9781003360247-6

Life seeped out of Narcissus. When the time came to bury him, no corpse was found, only a white flower, yellow in its centre (Berg 2001, p. 138).

Ovid recounts that Narcissus was the result of a rape. Greek mythology contains many violent conceptions, but the punishing start to life must be regarded as a central theme, seen in the light of later developed concepts of narcissism. From this perspective, the myth seems to tell us of a person that grew up with *a wounded mother*, who had difficulty both *seeing* and *mirroring* the boy with loving eyes owing to her own problems, and an apparently *authoritarian father*, who was not supportive of the mother or of the son throughout his upbringing.

The Concept of Narcissism Arises in Psychoanalysis

The first reference to the myth of Narcissus in relation to a description of the psyche was in 1898, when the English physician Havelock Ellis (1859–1939) used the myth to describe women preoccupied with their own self-admiration. The following year, the German psychiatrist Paul Adolf Näcke (1851–1913) used the term narcissism about people who were preoccupied by sex with their own bodies – that is, masturbation. The German psychoanalyst Karl Abraham (1877–1925) introduced the concept into psychoanalysis in 1908, when he used it to describe certain schizophrenic states in which sexual instincts are directed towards the individual's own person. Sigmund Freud (1856–1939) first used the term in 1910 about homosexuals, whom he believed were *narcissistically* seeking love with someone who resembled themselves, one of their own gender (Møhl in Andkjær Olsen 2002, p. 498). The concept of narcissism had emerged, but suffered from the beginning with conceptual ambiguity. Freud was never satisfied with the concept but distinguished between *primary narcissism*, inherent in the natural development of the infant when it "experiences being at one with everything good, imbuing it with an oceanic feeling of oneness and connectivity with the world" (Møhl in Andkjær Olsen 2002, p. 409), and *secondary narcissism*, where the adult has not developed a balanced *reality-self* – the *ultimate real self*.

The Polish psychoanalyst and neurologist Herman Nunberg (1884–1979) believed that the myth of Narcissus, better than any theory, explained the essence of narcissism, which for him was "arrogance and self-obsession, grandiosity" and an "uncertain body image", as well as an "inability for deep object relations and psychological substance" (Møhl in Andkjær Olsen 2002, p. 498).

Narcissism Entails Investing in an Image

The lack of capacity for deeper relationships in the Narcissus myth is further understood through the nymph Echo, who worships Narcissus. When he flees from her with the words "Rather death than I give you power over me", she answers with the fatal echo: "I give you power over me" (Berg 2001, p. 137). Echo is worn away by unrequited love. In mythological contexts, as in dreams, different aspects of the same subject are often introduced through various images. As we shall see, the pair can be said to illustrate two seemingly opposing, narcissistic reaction patterns, which nevertheless are connected and alternately appear in the individual: Narcissus clings to his experience of his own excellence and cannot detach himself from his mirror image, which, all the same, cannot answer his love (Dahl & Dalsegg 2001, p. 102). Echo represents low self-esteem, as she self-destructively invests all her energy in a loveless relationship and, in the end, can be neither seen nor heard. The theme for both can be said to be *visibility*: They are not lovingly mirrored, seen, loved or recognised for who they are, which, according to the Danish Jungian Misser Berg (b. 1948), is largely owing to both parents being consumed by mutual conflicts filled with "aggression, jealousy, mistrust and force" (Berg 2001, p. 138).

The bioenergetic body therapist Alexander Lowen (1910–2008) highlighted Narcissus's rejection of Echo in the narrative. Had Narcissus said, "I love you", the echo would have been just as loving, and Narcissus would have known love, Lowen writes (Lowen 1985, p. 44). For Lowen, the most fundamental thing about the narcissistic structure is that "Narcissists are more concerned with how they appear than what they feel. Indeed, they deny feelings that contradict the image they seek" (Lowen 1985, p. 11). "What happens is that the narcissist identifies with the idealised image. The actual self-image is lost" (Lowen 1985, p. 23).

> Narcissists love their image, not their real self. They have a poor sense of self; they are not self-directed. Instead, their activities are directed toward the enhancement of their image, often at the expense of the self.
>
> Lowen 1985, p. 42)

In the bioenergetic method, work is done with bodily release of emotional blocking of life currents and energies, including a release of the voice, which is so central to the myth of Narcissus and Echo (Lowen 1985, p. 44).

Narcissistic Personality Disorder

Research on the development of the young child has provided a comprehensive understanding of the development of narcissistic challenges, as it has become clear that these mainly stem from problematic conditions in early childhood. This period of human life has, in particular, been dealt with by infant research, developmental psychology and the neo-Freudians' object relation theories. These studies of children and their development in their immediate environment, with carers, from the fetal state to approximately 12 years, have changed the concept of narcissism over the past 50 years.

The term *narcissistic personality disorder* was first used by Heinz Kohut (an Austrian-American psychoanalyst, 1913–1981). Kohut and his colleague and compatriot Otto Kernberg (b. 1928) have both dedicated a large part of their work to narcissistic disorders, based on their own respective types of patient groups. Narcissistic personality disorder can, according to both, despite their differences, be characterised by a deficit[1] personality structure,

[w]hich manifests itself primarily in fluctuating self-esteem, extreme self-obsession and the need for the admiration and love of others ... a grandiose self-image, fantasy of unlimited success, power, beauty and the like ... [Unable to] engage in mutual relationships and will often try to exploit others to meet their own needs ... interpersonal relationships alternate between idealisation and devaluation. Self-esteem is extremely fragile.

(Møhl in Andkjær Olsen 2002, p. 504)

Kernberg developed transference-focused psychotherapy based on his work with *borderline* patients. They were people with personality disorders (Diderichsen 1998, p. 52), and Kernberg considered them *patients*. Kohut, for his part, worked with less severely affected clients and developed so-called self psychology based on his type of patient. His hypothesis was that one can rebuild the damaged self through therapy, and that malfunctioning structures will fall apart when a well-functioning self is formed (Diderichsen 1998, p. 57). The two modalities of experience created different theories and varying therapeutic approaches to narcissistic disorders, which is also an expression of the very different degrees of suffering and self-impairment covered by the concept of narcissism: For some, it is difficult to establish both a well-functioning love life and an everyday life, while others can work their way through the condition and experience a degree of healing of their challenges. For others still, it is mostly in connection with vulnerable periods and life crises that the traumatic experiences of the past break out into emotional states and reactions so violent they can be described as narcissistic.

The Child's Development and Dream Symbols for Early Injuries

Relational disorders in early childhood with profound consequences for the adult's emotional life and relationships are also the focus of the German Jungian Erich Neumann (1905–1960), who divided the child's development into five phases. In *Mandens og hans indre kvinder* [Man and His Inner Women] from 2003, Ole Vedfelt, who is head of the Danish Vedfelt Institute of Integrative Psychotherapy (founded in 1995) has taken inspiration from Neumann's phases and linked them to his understanding of his clients' nightly dreams.

Vedfelt finds that painful experiences in clients' early upbringing correspond to frequently recurring symbols in adult clients' dreams, which thus constitute part of many reactions to conditions in childhood. Dreams can recount *early injuries* – injuries and wounds that can challenge adult life in ways which, as already established, by some are called narcissistic conditions or disorders.

"If children are betrayed, abandoned, rendered helpless or abused by their loved ones", Vedfelt writes, "the ability to regulate their emotional states diminishes and their attachment patterns are disrupted" (Vedfelt 2002, p. 235). Contact with the immediate environment, which Vedfelt also calls *the ecological niche*, is so crucial because the child, from birth, actively tries to "create contact with his ecological niche of carers ... with whom it is an apprentice human being" (Vedfelt 2002, p. 153). Especially in the first years, writes Vedfelt, the mother serves as *door-keeper* to the child's experience of the world. It is primarily from her being and way of relating to the child that the child receives its most basic experience of what it is like to be in life. These experiences are stored as unconscious experiences or *tacit knowledge*, as Vedfelt calls it, inspired by the Hungarian physicist Michael Polanyi (1891–1976). This tacit knowledge largely forms the background for what the adult will expect from life and from relationships based on a premise that Vedfelt calls *pattern recognition* (Vedfelt 2002, pp. 202–203, 2017, 39). Problems in adulthood arise, among other things, when the individual's emotional response to events in the present is amplified by unconscious "echoes of much earlier stages" and assumes seemingly disproportionate strength (Vedfelt 2003, p. 151).

Since many of the child's early experiences are established before it has learned a spoken language and rationally understands what is going on, the therapist must seek information about the prior experiences in the client's unconscious layers. Vedfelt has many years of experience in searching for these – for example, through body language and the language of our dreams. When we dream, we receive images, stories and sensations that can express observations and experiences that we are not consciously aware of. It can therefore be highly informative to examine a client's dreams when working with early disorders.

The following briefly introduces Neumann's phases and the signs of suffering and disorders in the clients caused by disturbances or abuse in the given phases as explained by Vedfelt.

Neumann's *cosmic and vegetative phases* correspond to the developmental stages of the young child, from fetal state to approximate walking age. "The ego/self experience/sense of self", Vedfelt writes,

> is shaped by touch from the carers and by contact with substances, different textures, heat and cold, pain and pleasure. All such experiences after birth, contribute to the child's consciousness being rooted, so to speak, in its own as well as its mother's body.
>
> (Vedfelt 2003, p. 158)

Signs of serious disturbances in the *cosmic phase* manifest themselves symbolically and emotionally as abandonment, the doom of the world, the experience of being sucked into a hole in the universe or of a glass wall between oneself and the surrounding world, alienation from life and worldly realities. Allergies that restrict opportunities for contact are other symptoms or effects. They can also manifest themselves in a prematurely awakened spirituality as escapism, or as an escape into the intellectual sphere at the expense of the emotional (Vedfelt 2003, p. 159).

The *vegetative phase* is roughly similar to Freud's *oral phase*, with focus on the mouth and the ability to taste, suck, feel and eat. For Neumann, positive associations with this phase are through lush landscapes, fertile meadows, protective trees and sparkling springs (Vedfelt 2003, p. 162). This phase is essential for whether the child builds trust or distrust in the world. Vedfelt asks whether it learns to head into life relaxed and confident or tense and ready to battle.

If the child experiences betrayal in this phase, disturbances occur in deep layers of what Vedfelt calls the *mother network* and the child's experience, as well as pattern formation. The child finds difficulty in regulating its inner emotional states, and the person might, throughout life, have difficulty with what Vedfelt calls *emotional self-regulation*. This means the child, and later on the adult, is easily frightened or stressed and has difficulty returning to inner reassurance, fullness of being and peace. If, as a child, you have not been nurtured, supported and encouraged in an age-appropriate way, the dream symbols associated with this phase will typically be drought-stricken or scorched landscapes, ruins, radioactive or otherwise polluted areas (Vedfelt 2003, p. 162).

A gradual socialisation begins between 2 and 4 years of age. During this period, which Neumann terms the *animal phase*, the child travels between the experience of being "in love with the world" (as Vedfelt quotes the child psychiatrist Margaret Mahler; Vedfelt 2003, p. 174) and what Freud called the *anal phase*, in which the child must learn to control itself. In the gradual unloosing from the mother, the father, correspondingly, becomes more visible; the likewise-called *father network* takes over to some extent, Vedfelt writes, and shows the child qualities such as impulse control, rationality and purpose. The *mother network* descends and becomes unconscious or *tacit knowledge* (Vedfelt 2003, p. 178). Children often dream of animals in this phase and react more instinctively and with far less self-control than adults. When adults thus dream of animals, it can be a positive sign that they are taking time to turn their consciousness inwards, letting go of self-control and allowing themselves a certain amount of immediacy and spontaneity. It allows space for the internal experience, only partly consciously, to begin to express itself and open up to bodily and intuitive knowledge.

In Neumann's *magical phallic phase* (3–4 years of age) and *magic warlike phase* (6–12 years of age), the earlier phases remain active but now constitute the emotional and social knowledge of the child on a more unconscious and automatic level. This leaves space for other forms of learning in the consciousness of the child (Vedfelt 2003, p. 183). What used to feel safe with the mother can now be perceived as overprotectiveness. It is a period when the child experiences imagination and creativity, and it is essential for the later adult's creativity and desire to act in the world that the mother supports the child in this phase of self-reliance.

> It is with her the child can stock up on joy and playfulness, it is she whose absence makes the child irritable and depressed. Her love and admiration are a sparkling source of life, and her condemnation can turn the world barren.
>
> (Vedfelt 2003, p. 183)

Later on, at 6–12 years of age, the child is socialised in relation to peers, schooling and specific societal demands. A 'linguisticised' memory of the child will normally be growing; the narcissistic wounded person, however, might still have difficulty remembering large parts of childhood experiences and finding expression for them.

Narcissism and Early Abandonment

Both Neumann's developmental psychology and Kohut's analyses are a starting point for the Jungian psychotherapist Kathrin Asper when describing her clients' response to the *experience of abandonment* perceived in early childhood. In the book *The Abandoned Child Within*, translated from German in 1993, she describes her therapeutic work with what she calls *narcissistic disorders* (Asper 1993, p. 2).

The narcissistic wounded person is characterised by not having a strong *Self*, Asper writes. At first glance, the person may appear strong, but behind the apparent strength lies a weak connection between what in Jung's terminology constitutes the ego and the Self and a rigid perception of oneself. Asper identified this as the clients' inability to "affirm themselves and had little self-confidence; their self-esteem was unsteady, they yearned for acknowledgement and approval, and were inclined to invest a great deal of energy in developing their personas" (Asper 1993, p. 9).

> Uprooted and unsheltered too early, the narcissist knows little about his own nature. He is estranged from his own sense of himself and does not have, in Neumann's terms, a stable "ego–Self-axis".
>
> (Asper 1993, p. 62)

To feel cohesiveness as a person and make an everyday life function, the narcissistic wounded individual must distance her/himself specifically from the wound, Asper writes, yet thereby also loses contact with other parts of the Self:

> All protective attitudes serve to ward off suffering. They should be assessed as creative ego accomplishments that contribute to the individual's survival, and they ensure the fragile coherence of the narcissistic personality. The discerning eye sees that distance from suffering means a considerable detachment from the emotional aspects of the narcissistic wound, such as abandonment, emptiness, sadness, helplessness, fear, rage, envy, and hatred. Beyond that, this distance also includes distance from one Self, and ultimately in addition, this distance also includes a removal from the self, which ultimately means self-estrangement. Thus, there exists a double dissociation: from the narcissistic wound, and from the Self as the individual's most basic nature.
>
> (Asper 1993, pp. 216–217)

According to Asper, the therapeutic work lies in particular in examining and seeking to release what she calls *behavior in abandonment* and *gestures of longing*.

As characteristics of abandonment behaviour, she describes over-adaptation, renouncing one's own feelings, extensive childhood amnesia, narcissistic rage and narcissistic depression with emptiness, paralysis and lifelessness (Asper 1993, pp. 159–185). This is where we probably find Echo, I believe. We are more likely to encounter Narcissus in the gesture of longing, because here, writes Asper, the desire to love and be loved "appears in the form of striving both to mirror one's own grandiosity as well as for ideal people and relationships" (Asper 1993, p. 185).

> In narcissistic wounded people we very often see the fantasy of being the center of attention and of being admired; equally often appears the fantasy of having pure bliss in harmonious unity with another, unspoiled by any kind of disturbance.
>
> (Asper 1993, p. 184)

In the understanding of Kohut, Asper states, the abandonment "means frustration and alienation from the person's own life pattern", often resulting in longing for paradise (Asper 1993, pp. 92–93).

> They are striving to be esteemed and viewed as important, and striving for ideal people and relationships that provide absolute security.
>
> (Asper 1993, p. 93)

Since the client does not have good contact with his or her *being*, he or she will typically try to perform and seek respect in the therapy room. The person in question thus seeks what Asper calls the *student attitude*, which she attaches to another concept, the *paternal attitude*. This, Asper writes, typically lends itself to action and performance, and the client can angle for the therapist's explanations, interpretations and assessments. But Asper's, as well as Vedfelt's, therapeutic approach emphasises that a safe environment must be established where clients do not have to perform but can learn to sense their selves and experience the inclusiveness and care of the *maternal attitude* (Asper 1993, p. 227).

In order for a therapist to meet the client with this maternal attitude, it is very important to "explore the narcissistic analysand as nonjudgmentally as possible. He needs to learn to accept, and enjoy exploring, the space and freedom he now has to reflect on his life" (Asper 1993, 237).

> For the narcissistically disturbed analysand, it is important that the child in her emerges from her overshadowed existence; this child imparts vitality and rootedness in her own history.
>
> (Asper 1993, p. 265)

This corresponds to what Vedfelt also emphasises as an inspiration from Kohut: "Kohut observed how important it was for the therapeutic process, especially in connection with narcissistic problems, that the therapist was supportive, appreciative and contributed to the client's feelings of self-esteem" (Vedfelt 2000, p. 547).

Almaas and the Wound of Emptiness and Everyday Narcissism

Used as an insult, the term *narcissist* can cut deep. Most people acquainted with the word will typically have an understanding that it refers to a ruthless self-preoccupation. However, if you meet the injured client in a joint examination of the client's own experiences, instead of dwelling on the hurtful term *narcissist*, you can delve into deeper work with inner personality aspects that the client has not been in contact with since early childhood. This open and appreciative approach to the client's inner wound is in line with the work of both Vedfelt and Asper. I have furthermore been inspired in my work by Kuwaiti-American psychotherapist A. Hameed Ali Almaas and his concept of *everyday narcissism*, contrasting a deeper, culturally imposed *emptiness*.

Almaas was born in Kuwait in 1944 and is the founder of the Ridhwan School of Spiritual Development in the United States. He is a psychologist and physician in the Western tradition and links psychotherapy with his goal of spiritual self-realisation in the Sufi tradition, the mystery religion of Islam. Almaas uses the term *everyday narcissism* to explain the condition he believes we pretty much all seem to live as a *normal condition* for people in the West (Almaas 2001, p. 27). He argues for this in his book *The Point of Existence – Transformations of Narcissism in Self-realisation* from 2001. Here, he deals with the individual's narcissistic disorders both in the psychological sense and within his spiritual goal of *self-realisation.*

Almaas, like Asper, uses the theories of both Kernberg and Kohut as foundation for his description of *narcissistic conditions.* However, he contrasts their perception of *the ego and the self.* Kohut speaks of recalling the past and childhood memories as a requisite condition for establishing a *cohesive identity* and describes the goal of *strengthening the self's coherence* so that "the patient's core self is consolidated, and his abilities and skills revived" (Diderichsen 1998, p. 57; author's translation). The aim of Almaas is different, as he, in line with Sufism and, among other traditions, Buddhism, believes that we must abolish the ego and our perception of what our *personality* is. Ultimately, writes Almaas, the *ego identity* (*self-concept*) constitutes one of the most significant blockages for us to enter into *self-realised states* (Almaas 1998, p. 259). He asserts that our actual state of being is living in what he calls *Essence*, which he describes as "a certain presence, very definite, very clear, very precise, very palpable" (Almaas 1998, p. 36).

Essence is neither a thought nor an idea a person has about himself. It is not self-image. In fact, the self-image, the collection of concepts one has of oneself, is one of the main barriers to the recognition and development of essence.

(Almaas 1998, p. 32)

Even with good conditions for growing up, he claims that, if their personality is the centre of the parents' lives, this will also apply to their children. The children cannot remain in their essential qualities unless there is resonance for them in the immediate environment in support of them. "They will end up with the personality at the centre and the essence being buried", he writes (Almaas 1998, p. 154).

> The lives of most people involve a constant effort to "prop up," defend, promote and improve this identity, whose status as a mental construct is never challenged. Thus the liberation and joy of knowing our true identity is lost.
>
> (Almaas 1998, p. 10)

Almaas links some of Kohut's and Kernberg's narcissistic concepts to layers in the psyche, which he believes the individual must examine for self-realisation, and he "describes the importance of working through narcissistic abandonment, emptiness and grandiosity", Vedfelt notes (Vedfelt 2007, p. 700).

The journey leads through experiences of falseness, both of oneself and of one's surroundings, including the feeling of being like an empty shell, as well as experiences of narcissistic meaninglessness and uselessness. The work provides a period of loss of orientation and self-perception, depression, hopelessness and rejection of some of one's prior relationships. For Almaas, one now begins to dismantle the personality and open to the experience of non-doing, inner fullness, trust and keeping the *loving light* (Almaas 2001, p. 303). Experiences of essential qualities arise, and *Essential Identity*, as Almaas calls it, is sensed. Almaas speaks of an essential self-recognition, as opposed to the mirror metaphor of self-reflection or self-representation (Almaas 2001, p. 130). The dismissal of ego-structure is, according to Almaas, connected to the individuation of the soul and the experience of "personhood" independent of personal history (Almaas 2001, p. 363). To Almaas, narcissism is not necessarily tied to early childhood experiences of abandonment, harassment or abuse. In his terms, narcissism is an innate result of the upbringing into a personality remote from our true inner essence.

> We are capable of living a personal life as a human being, with competence, dignity, and maturity, but our inner center and source is the timeless preciousness of true nature. We are in the world, but we never leave the transcendent depths of Being.
>
> (Almaas 2001, p. 370)

The narcissistic wound specifically is, for Almaas, the greatest of the narcissistic challenges, as the wound, according to him, is experienced when one touches on the bearing notions of oneself, the *narcissistic supplies* (Almaas 2001, p. 310). He describes the wound often being experienced as a physical pain caused by blocked energy currents in the chest (Almaas 2001, p. 312). Fantasies of catastrophe and disease as well as nightmares will often occur (Almaas 2001, p. 309). Feelings of embarrassment and shame, he writes, are a common experience when entering the narcissistic wound, also called the *wound of emptiness* (Almaas 2001, p. 315).

This is where Almaas finds the opportunity to get behind the shell or mask that he believes we, unconsciously, have hidden behind (Almaas 2001, p. 314).

The narcissistic layer, he believes, covers the *horror* that a discovery of emptiness generally creates. Only when we pass through the horror and experience the emptiness do we open up to completely different states and ways of being present in life (Almaas 2001, p. 315).

> We recognise that the hurt is due to losing sight of what is genuine in us, of our precious nature, because we are not supported and mirrored in our early years. We feel hurt that the people in our environment did not see us, did not appreciate our truth, and were not attuned to our true nature.
>
> (Almaas 2001, p. 317)

Similarly, for Vedfelt, the more one enters states of inner emptiness with a strong enough self – the more one can enter into a deeper being and spiritual experience.[2]

Cybernetic Psychotherapy and Narcissistic Conditions

Ole Vedfelt works with all the conditions and patterns of reaction described so far. Unlike Asper and Almaas, however, he generally chooses to avoid the term *narcissism*, which he believes may seem judgemental and prove inhibiting. By avoiding the troubled term, Vedfelt seeks a more open encounter with the challenges the client experiences.[3]

> From this perspective, it is possible to redefine central psychoanalytic concepts so they acquire a more universal character and can be seen as constructive attempts at self-regulation and adaptation.
>
> (Vedfelt 2002, p. 194)

Vedfelt deals with what is termed *self-regulating* and *self-healing forces* in the personality and with the healing and developmental possibilities that lie in interpersonal relationships.

> The concepts of self-organisation and self-regulation have been developed within modern systems theory and cybernetics. They refer to the ability of living organisms to regulate, organise and renew themselves.
>
> (Vedfelt 2003, p. 31)

With his approach, based on innate health in the *doctrine of salutogenic approach*, Vedfelt challenges the concepts of *narcissist* and *narcissism*, which, as shown, originate from pathology and diagnosis.

> In cybernetic theory, the overall interest shifts from what is wrong inside the person to what resources can be developed in relation to the environment. This movement from "troubleshooter" to "resource scout" is far more healing (and constructive) than the human perception of past reductionist theories.
>
> (Vedfelt 2002 p. 35)

This corresponds with Vedfelt's cybernetic personality model, where we understand "personality as an appropriate system for processing complex information, a system constantly working to optimise itself" (Vedfelt 2012, p. 52). As cybernetic integrative therapists, we consider the psyche to be composed of many different levels and forms of consciousness, also called *systems* and *modalities* (Vedfelt 1996, p. 113). The system seeks "an optimal internal balance in relation to the pressure and development opportunities of the surrounding environment" (Hass 2015, p. 88). It also means that perceptions and reactions that seem inappropriate for the adult's current life usually prove to have had an *important function* in protecting the individual earlier in life.

A simple example clarifies this: If you were accustomed to getting slapped in the face in your childhood, it is still a natural reaction for you, as an adult, to duck your head instinctively if someone quickly raises a hand close to your face.

> [In] the unconscious, positive and negative fragments of memory float about and, under certain conditions, [they] can be activated and affect consciousness and behavior in a drastic way.
>
> (Vedfelt 2002, p. 248)

This also occurs on physical levels of a smaller scale. A mother's quick frown at the presentation of a planned project by her adult son can cause him, instantly and unconsciously, to lose interest in his project (Vedfelt 2003, p. 190). Or a partner's innocent flirtation can ignite jealousy and rage. If a therapist yawns, it can provoke powerful reactions in the client, who may interpret it as a personal offence and feel rejection, or somehow feel maltreated, with great anger and disappointment as a consequence.

As presented, the *narcissistic vulnerability* of the exemplified reactions consists of entering emotional states that are far more violent than the actual situation would otherwise evoke. This happens because the experience points inwards to far deeper layers of the psyche. Vedfelt uses the terms *pointed peaks* and *soft hills* (Vedfelt 2002, p. 200) about the moods and emotional fluctuations that most of us can experience, but which can be quite violent for some.

Vedfelt highlights several features from the narcissism theories,[4] which for him too are important points of attention in working with clients: They are excessive self-preoccupation and fluctuating self-esteem shifting between inferiority and grandiosity. One can, for example, have big dreams that do not correspond to reality, and the slightest criticism can cause the house of cards to collapse. In addition, it can be difficult to set a course and pursue one's goals. One typically finds it difficult to accept ambivalence and will likely understand situations as black or white and people as either good or evil. Emotional impulsivity is often visible – for example, high fits of *narcissistic rage* or deep plunges into inertia and depression – as neutralising strong emotions proves difficult. Vedfelt talks of the *narcissistic defence*, where the person separates from his/her experiences and feelings through *splitting*, *projections* and *dissociation* (Vedfelt 2002, pp. 212–214).

The therapist, Vedfelt explains, should pay special attention to his/her own moods and feelings in connection with narcissistic conditions as, owing to the client's lack of contact with him/herself, the therapist will often feel a certain level of boredom, impatience, irritation, emptiness and stagnation, as well as become drowsy. One can then easily succumb to throwing oneself, impulsively, into interpretations, which, as Asper described, the client angles for, and try to stimulate the process forward with good advice or admonitions.[5] If the therapist does not act on this momentary inner response, he/she can merely note this as a hint that his/her client has difficulty sensing him- or herself owing to a *narcissistic state*.

In line with Kohut's and Asper's work, Vedfelt believes the goal is to *strengthen the self's coherence*, and the therapist helps to gather the threads of life which the client may find incoherent. Recalling the past and childhood memories is a part of establishing a coherent identity (Diderichsen 1998, p. 57). As a therapist, Vedfelt writes, one constitutes the external overview, but one should, at the same time, use the client's own words in repetition, in a *reflection* of them, in order to strengthen the client's sense of being able to feel and describe his/her own emotions and experiences (Vedfelt 2002, p. 246).

The construction of the individual's personal strength takes place in accordance with the self-organising mechanisms and messages from, what Vedfelt calls, *unconscious intelligence*. His main thesis is that unconscious intelligence "is superior to rational consciousness" (Vedfelt 2003, p. 31). The unconscious, according to Vedfelt, has far greater information capacity and complexity than normal consciousness. Furthermore, extensive regulation of personality through therapy – that is, regulation of painful or redundant patterns – only takes place in cooperation with the *unconscious intelligence*, as it is:

> different in form and expression to rational consciousness and processes information in a more holistic way. It manifests itself in dreams, body language, emotions, free associations and in the way we relate to each other. The unconscious intelligence is a creative force that is constantly pushing from within, for us to use our resources optimally and stay in balance with our surroundings.
>
> (Vedfelt 2003, p. 31)

In the therapeutic room, this is translated into presence and methods that ensure that what emerges for the client is received, recognised and unfolded.

Thus, for Vedfelt as for Almaas, there is no contradiction between working with *religious peak experiences* and the *personal story* of hurt. The two processes can take place at the same time or in processes close to each other and support one another (Vedfelt 2007, p. 702), contrary to Asper, who believes that narcissistically wounded people generally have too weak an *ego* to be part of the Jungian *individuation process* (Asper 1988, p. 11). However, all three agree that working with early injuries is a lengthy process that requires time. And, as Vedfelt writes, one should, as a general rule, "first let go of the old negative patterns as the positive [self-realisation] is awakened and starts to grow" (Vedfelt 2003, p. 169).

Supramodality and Subpersonalities

As cybernetic psychotherapists, we work actively in what we call the *supramodal space*. This means that, in principle, all levels of consciousness and various modes of experience and forms of expression are recognised in a holistic perception of the client and the therapist, of the space and of the relationship between them.

With our normal, rational, awake consciousness, we can only contain a certain amount of information. But this part of our consciousness is only a very small part of our overall modes of experience. In Sanskrit, there are no less than 80 words for consciousness, in acknowledgement of the variety of human states of experience. With the systemic thinking of cybernetics, *we transport information* in many ways, also called *modalities*, and via many different tracks, called *processing channels* (Vedfelt 2002, p. 96). In the rational, awake state, we can only relate to information on one level at a time but, in the *supramodal space*, we make use of our *supramodal abilities*, which means we relate to many inputs at the same time and get behind the understanding of rational thought by finding "the small gaps in consciousness that we can learn to become aware of" (Vedfelt 2002, p. 96).

The starting procedure of a cybernetic therapist will typically involve asking the client to tell about a specific situation in his or her everyday life or an experience that he or she finds difficult. From there, we typically enquire about the experience evoked by the client's bodily sensations and associations while talking about the chosen situation. By offering time and peace for the client to sense him- or herself, glimpses of associations from previous experiences or sensations might occur as discomfort in the body, which the therapist will then explore with the client by enquiring more deeply into the sensations. In cybernetics, we call that *changing* processing channels. We help the client to go from the interpretation of the actual occurrence on the normal level of consciousness, *one process channel*, to another, far more subtle level of consciousness, an awareness of the body's sensations and the *information* that comes through there.

"The body remembers", and "unconscious body experiences are stored in this memory for a long time", writes Vedfelt (2002, p. 60). By tuning into the language of the body, we can get in touch with other layers of what is happening. The therapeutic room thus forms a framework for a *vegetative and contemplative* state, where the client can access a hidden layer of the psyche, possibly a *subpersonality*, with which the client has not had conscious contact for a long time – for example, since a certain age – the *inner child* in the client's upbringing.

The work with *subpersonalities*, in particular, is one of the focal points in Vedfelt's method. Vedfelt concludes that we mostly sense subpersonalities in vulnerable parts of our mind. We do not notice them under normal circumstances but, under pressure, they emerge more clearly, to the extent of being insistent (Vedfelt 2002, p. 259). This is precisely where traces of narcissistic conditions can be found.

When we have been traumatised, abandoned or understimulated in the ecological niche, [subpersonalities] can live a hidden or detached life, which creates conflicts in the personality.

(Vedfelt 2002, p. 259)

The subpersonalities are typically those parts of ourselves for which there was no room in our ecological niche. We adapt to the demands, expectations and aspirations the niche has set for us. But that which we thus learn to experience *as our true self* is far from *our whole self.*

> The child's first and foremost task is to develop its experience of being a particular person in a particular body. This coherent, subjectively experienced unity does not include all the child's characteristics, experiences and possibilities, but is a personification of a particular self-perception.
>
> (Vedfelt 2002, p. 314)

Dream- and bodywork, as well as other sources of association such as drawing, give us insight into inner states, unconscious reactions and subpersonalities at play in a given situation. The therapist supports the client in finding the old patterns, shedding conscious light on them and healing the old patterns so that new ones can emerge, a process Vedfelt describes in his book *Unconscious Intelligence* from 2002:

> [Self-]regulating forces in a wounded personality [may] have gone into hibernation and lived a relatively unspoiled life on their own. The overwintering emotions can be brought out of this state and enrich the personality.
>
> (Vedfelt 2002, p. 116)

Just as Echo disappeared, parts of us give up when not enough loving care has been offered to them. With the guidance of a therapist, the client can experience the abandonment of his or her inner subpersonality and then experience a redemptive relief of connecting to it anew, many years later. *Mirroring* will then become an instrument for evoking and confirming this vital part of the client.

> [T]he subpersonalities ultimately always have a constructive potential that can enrich the personality when met correctly.
>
> (Vedfelt 2002, p. 259)

When contact is thus re-established, and several threads of the individual pull together interactively, creating something *new* and *more* than the individual parts, *emergence* occurs, according to cybernetics and systems theory (Vedfelt 2002, p. 35). Expansion of consciousness and changes of attitude go hand in hand, Vedfelt writes (2002, p. 112). In therapeutic processes, extending over several years, a gradual opening takes place to ever deeper layers of the psyche.

> In this process, consciousness changes perspective, other layers of personality emerge, memories of childhood change, self-perception becomes different and life history changes retroactively.
>
> (Vedfelt 2002, p. 112)

Vedfelt thus, as far as I can perceive, goes further than Asper, who writes that we cannot "give the analysand what she once lacked. But we can help her become aware of her longings and understand them" (Asper 1988, p. 161). Vedfelt believes that one *can* regain what was once lost and what was never there (sufficiently), in cooperation with the *higher control systems* of the psyche. The unconscious intelligence can, when set in motion, create awareness and *regulate* the *lower*, more unconscious, levels where the "conflict unfolds" (Vedfelt 2002, p. 34).

The Narcissistic Wound: A Summary

I have outlined the origins and development of the concepts of narcissism in line with contemporary research regarding child development. First, I have described a Jungian and subsequently a spiritual teacher's approach to narcissism and their formulated characteristics of narcissism.

I have presented a number of typical conditions and reactions from the narcissism theories and therapies mentioned, which the therapist can use for his or her own overview, without disclosing them to the client.

Referring to Asper, the narcissistic wound is a collective term for many emotional reactions based specifically on the experience of early abandonment.

Turning to Almaas, stepping through the *narcissistic wound* will mean an existential realisation of the falsehood of one's own personality or one's world, thereby opening oneself to greater spiritual depth (Almaas 2001, p. 315). What the chapter otherwise deals with is called, in Almaas's own words, *everyday narcissism*.

Within Vedfelt's understanding, we have seen how we can re-establish contact with wounded subpersonalities. The lack of contact and the wound can to a large extent be understood through the theories of developmental psychology and object relations. They *may* well be called *narcissistic*, but this is not *necessary*, either for the healing process or for understanding.

Although Vedfelt rarely uses the term, I have shown that many of the theories that narcissism theorists draw on also underlie several of his insights. Emotional states are thus described that form part of his theory and experience based on many years of therapeutic practice. It does not seem *necessary* to use the term *narcissism* to comprehend these conditions, but I must conclude that Vedfelt does use the term occasionally, and that I myself find it rewarding, for my understanding of human processes, to have knowledge of both the concept and the extensive work done by therapists and researchers in what are called *narcissistic conditions*.

The chapter's study of the concept of narcissism has led to insight into the child's development and psychotherapeutic work with injuries from childhood in the adult client. It is necessary to know the developmental psychology of the child in order to be supportive in working with the client's early material. The therapist's own ability to be present and offer gentle attention, at all times, is essential, as is the extra caution required when we want to strengthen a very injured client's personal self and individuation process. Another central aspect is the importance of the cybernetic psychotherapist being able to sense symbolic language and bodily information in a creative and open encounter with the client's subpersonalities, understood as structures for inner processes.

Narcissism touches, as shown, on eternal questions in human life: Am I loved and wanted? Am I seen, heard and understood as I am? Can I join communities – or will I be rejected? Can I love others, can I enter into deep relationships and feel safe among people? It is probably in these questions that we should seek the strength of the old myth and the continuous search to unfold the concept.

Notes

1 The term deficit comes from Heinz Kohut's self-psychology and refers to "a mental deficiency as a result of early traumatization" (Andkjær Olsen 2002, p. 152).
2 Insights passed on by Ole Vedfelt at his spoken lecture on "Narcissism and Psychosomatics" at the Vedfelt Institute of Psychotherapeutic Education on 27 September 2016.
3 See note 3.
4 See note 3.
5 See note 3.

References

Almaas, A.H. (1998) *Essence with the Elixir of Enlightenment.* Samuel Weiser, York Beach, ME.

Almaas, A.H. (2001) *The Point of Existence – Transformations of Narcissism in Self-realisation.* Shambala, Boston, MA.

Andkjær Olsen, Ole (Ed.). (2002) *Psykodynamisk leksikon.* Gyldendal, Copenhagen.

Asper, Kathrin (1988) *Ravnen i glasbjerget – følelsesmæssig forladthed og ny terapi.* Gyldendal, Århus.

Asper, Kathrin (1993) *The Abandoned Child Within.* Fromm International, New York.

Berg, Misser (2001) En myte om afhængighed: Ekko og Narcissus, in Pia Skogemann (Ed.), *Symbol, analyse, virkelighed – Jungiansk teori og praksis i Danmark*, pp. 133–156. Lindhardt & Ringholf, Randers.

Dahl, Alv A. & Dalsegg, Aud (2001) *Charmør og tyran – Et indblik i psykopaternes og ofrenes verden.* Munkgaard Bogklubber, Copenhagen.

Diderichsen, Birgitte (1998) Psykoanalytisk psykoterapi, in Esben Hougaard, Birgitte Diderichsen & Thomas Nielsen (Eds.), *Psykoterapiens hovedtraditioner. En indføring i psykoanalytisk, oplevelsesorienteret, kognitiv, systemorienteret og integrativ psykoterapi*, pp. 17–71. Dansk Psykologisk Forlag, Gylling.

Garth, Samuel (Trans.). (2017) *Ovid's Metamorphoses* (1st digital ed.), Book the Third. Anna Ruggieri.

Hass, Henrik (2015) Den nødvendige kompleksitet, in T. Hansen, T. (Ed.), *Det ubevidstes potentiale*, Frydenlund, Copenhagen DK

Lasch, Christopher (1982) *Narcissismens kultur – En analyse af et samfund i opløsning.* Gyldendal, Copenhagen.

Lowen, Alexander (1985) *Narcissism – Denial of the True Self.* Touchstone, New York.

Solms, Mark & Turnbull, Oliver (2004) *Hjernen & den indre verden. De subjektive erfaringers neurovidenskabelige grundlag.* Akademisk forlag,

Vedfelt, Ole (1996) *Bevidsthed*. Gyldendal, Haslev.

Vedfelt, Ole (2000) Delpersonligheder, objektrelationer og kybernetisk netværksteori. *Psyke og Logos*, *21(2)*, 542–563.

Vedfelt, Ole (2002) *Ubevidst intelligens* (2nd ed.), Gyldendals Bogklubber, Viborg.

Vedfelt, Ole (2003) *Mandens og hans indre kvinder*. Gyldendal, Copenhagen.

Vedfelt, Ole (2007) Bevidsthedens klare lys og sjælens dunkle dybder. Religiøs højdepunktsoplevelsers psykologi. *Psyke og logos*, *28(2)*, 675–705.

Vedfelt, Ole (2012) *Din guide til drømmenes verden*. Gyldendal, Riga.

Vedfelt, Ole (2017) *A Guide to the World of Dreams*. Routledge, New York.

6

Mindfulness and Cybernetic Psychology

Torben Hansen

Studies have documented that people who practise mindfulness benefit more from psychotherapy and, vice versa, that people who go into psychotherapy more easily make progress in mindfulness practice. The aim of this chapter is to show how cybernetic psychology and psychotherapy can be fruitfully involved in this dual process. Cybernetic psychology is the study of the creative complexity of the mind. The theory of cybernetic psychology is presented in the second part of the chapter, with particular emphasis on two key concepts: *unconscious intelligence* and *the supramodal ability*. The concept of *unconscious intelligence* describes the unconscious as an intelligent and purposeful self-optimising information system. The concept of *supramodal ability* in cybernetic psychology denotes the natural function of the psyche that underlies mindfulness practice. Against this background, the chapter shows that cybernetic psychotherapy can advantageously and naturally supplement a mindfulness meditation practice.

Paradoxically

Many years ago, I attended a week-long meditation course. On the last day of the course, the end was to be marked with a group dinner. Food, wine and beer came to the table, not in excessive quantities, but enough to make the mood light and for people to become somewhat more talkative than they otherwise would have been. At dessert, a conversation at one of the tables developed into a discussion. The dessert ended abruptly with the course leader giving a woman a stinging slap. The woman was a slightly older lady. Maybe she had gotten drunk, maybe she was troublesome. I do not remember. But I clearly remember the sight of the meditation teacher's arm and hand moving through the air. Now, no one is infallible – neither the pope nor a meditation teacher. One can certainly not demand that the teacher should not have been annoyed or even felt angry in the situation. But what one could rightly expect was probably that he would have been able to accommodate these feelings and, at the very least, could refrain from slapping someone. We who witnessed the situation were filled with wonder. In our minds, a meditation teacher should be able to exhibit more balanced behaviour.

DOI: 10.4324/9781003360247-7

A balanced personality and a high ethic were also what I expected from an Eastern so-called master of meditation. For a while, I was very close to him. The reason was that, after taking some courses, I had started working for him. I soon joined more private contexts where there were only a few people present. He had obvious so-called spiritual qualities. He attracted people, and many enrolled in his courses. But what I also, even very clearly, got to see was the dim side of the bright light – a dominant person who did not eschew manipulation. Both at meetings held in connection with the planning of the work and in other contexts, there was, among those of us who were close to him, consensus that it was far beyond what is generally considered appropriate behaviour. Situations arose where he, with charm, anger and attempts to activate feelings of guilt, tried to persuade someone to do this or that. I could not help but perceive this as manipulation and, thus, abuse of power. In my mind, the experiences triggered wonder, but also curiosity at this apparent paradox.

The above examples are, of course, not objective, but they serve the purpose of pointing out the fact that the ability to excel in mindfulness meditation does not in itself necessarily lead to personal maturity and empathy. Even many years of training seem not to guarantee a personality development that lifts the practitioner out of basic psychological, existential and character difficulties. The intention is to use these examples as a starting point for general research-based considerations arguing that mindfulness practice can generally gain from increasing awareness of psychological conditions and psychotherapeutic possibilities.[1]

In the following, I will examine these considerations using cybernetic psychology developed over the last 30 years at the Copenhagen-based Vedfelt Institute founded by Danish psychotherapists Lene and Ole Vedfelt, research by Danish philosopher and meditation teacher Jes Bertelsen, and the views of British psychologist Jack Engler.

Mindfulness

In the first part of the last century, psychiatry was the dominant body in the treatment of mental disorders. Around the mid-century, worries voiced over some rather inhumane methods gave rise to the so-called anti-psychiatry movement, which challenged the basic hypotheses of biomedical psychiatry and its way of practising treatment. This led to a wave of new treatment methods merging psychotherapy and psychiatry. New, more humanistic-oriented psychological theories and methods emerged as a counter-reaction to this form of psychiatry (Laing 1985). In the 1960s, as a reaction to reductionistic psychiatry, the *Human Potential Movement* emerged as a new wave, with American psychologist Abraham Maslow as a key proponent. Out of this new wave emerged a long line of therapies and treatment methods including gestalt therapy, body therapies, transactional analysis, and neo-Freudian and neo-Jungian lines of therapy. Simultaneously, another great movement was under way, with an unprecedented mutual influence between East and West taking place. Eastern meditation practices such as mindfulness went very well hand in hand with the Human Potential Movement, and, especially throughout the 1960s, Eastern currents flowed into the West. Masters of ancient Eastern practices such as meditation, yoga and *dai ji* began teaching in the West, opening up new concepts of consciousness and daily life. Westerners travelled to the East and came home with Buddha in their suitcase.

One profoundly influenced by this inspiration from the East and especially the ancient Eastern techniques of wisdom is the American professor and molecular biologist Jon Kabat-Zinn. Based at the MIT School of Medicine from the early 1970s, he developed ways to integrate mindfulness meditation from Buddhist traditions for use in Western hospitals and clinics, with the goal of helping patients with depression, anxiety, stress and somatic disorders. As part of documenting the benefits from the techniques and in order to get scientific approval for the Eastern methods in a Western clinical context, a number of research projects were launched. Kabat-Zinn's efforts led to the widely recognized and globally applied MBSR (mindfulness-based stress reduction) and MBCT (mindfulness-based cognitive therapy) programmes.

One challenge around mindfulness's Western adaptation is that it apparently is a multifaceted phenomenon. There is no consensus on what to understand and expect. (Hecksher, Nielsen & Piet 2010, p. 192). Yet, despite the fact that mindfulness is a multifaceted phenomenon, according to the American psychologist and founder of the Center for Mindful Self-Compassion Christopher Germer, there are three elements that recur in the vast majority of descriptions of mindfulness:

- Awareness
- Of the present
- With an accepting attitude.

These elements also apply to Kabat-Zinn's programmes. Though one cannot say that he invented mindfulness, one cannot escape the fact that he has had a formative influence on the spread and recognition of the methods. Kabat-Zinn's success in producing clinical evidence for the benefits of MBSR led to the fact that it has been his version of mindfulness that has found its way to practitioners around the world. Therefore, it seems relevant to introduce mindfulness based on Kabat-Zinn.

He originally studied with the Zen Buddhist master Seung Sahn, and he transferred the meditation experiences from here to the aforementioned stress treatment programmes. The inspiration from Seung Sahn and Buddhism philosophy shines through in Kabat-Zinn's writing. For example, he makes use of a classical Buddhist analogy for the human mind: "Water is in its essence always pure and clear" (Kabat-Zinn 1990, p. 165). Consciousness is described as the water of a lake. The waves or ripples on the surface are an analogy to the movements in the currents and forms of our thoughts and feelings. In depth and as part of the whole, the water – and thus consciousness – is always clear and calm.

According to Kabat-Zinn, the core of mindfulness is that the practitioner builds an ability that, over time, allows the meditator to observe moods, thoughts and bodily sensations from an inner, neutral point of view – an inner mild awareness of the present moment. He also calls this mindset an *impartial witness* – that is, an observer that does not take part in what is experienced. Elsewhere, he calls it disidentification with one's own thoughts and feelings (Kabat-Zinn 1990, p. 33). In this light, suffering would consist of a misunderstood identification with a particular thought or emotion content. For example, one may completely identify with a feeling of anger or grief so that one almost *is* the anger or the grief. Mindfulness training thus aims at loosening this unnecessary identification, and this defines the healing function of mindfulness (Kabat-Zinn 1990, p. 282).

Kabat-Zinn's descriptions of mindfulness are thus, according to the aforementioned, similar to those found in a large number of other authors. But what in particular can be said to have succeeded for Kabat-Zinn is to speak to a very wide audience, including atheistic, scientifically minded and more spiritually oriented people.

In much mindfulness teaching and literature, it may from time to time seem unclear when the view is clinical scientific and when the mindfulness teaching is seen as one among many elements in spiritual consciousness training. This also applies to Kabat-Zinn, and maybe just that makes his reach so wide. In some quotes, he speaks in clinical, scientific, non-religious terms, claiming that the MBSR programme is spiritually neutral. Elsewhere, as mentioned, language and message are characterised by the Buddhist paradigm, as when he writes, for example, about "the great quiet reservoir of consciousness beneath the surface of the mind" (Kabat-Zinn 1990, p. 165).

Mindfulness and the Neutral Observer

According to the Danish author and meditation teacher Jes Bertelsen, mindfulness is considered to be one training piece in a larger consciousness puzzle. He sees it as one training step on a ladder of consciousness and development that will, in principle, be able to lead the practitioner towards a decidedly higher consciousness[2] – and ultimately what is called enlightenment in Buddhism.

Neutral observation is the term Bertelsen uses, which is equivalent to the concept of the *impartial witness* in Kabat-Zinn's mindfulness. Neutral observation is considered by Bertelsen to be an intermediate step between the ordinary consciousness and what he calls a higher consciousness. The description of neutral observation seems only rhetorically to differ from Kabat-Zinn's concept of mindfulness. Bertelsen defines mindfulness in the following way: "It is to know of what is and what happens while it is and while it is happening" (Højsgaard 2013). Bertelsen writes that

> if neutral observation is to be effective, it is important that it is truly neutral. Like a mirror. Without comment, without sorting, a mirror shows what is in front of it. Neutral observation is a mirror-like function of consciousness, clear, objective and immediate.
>
> (Bertelsen 1999, p. 32)

Bertelsen operates with a hierarchy of consciousness that simply considers the phenomenon of consciousness as a continuum with a myriad of levels. To this hierarchy of consciousness belongs the ordinary and, in its content, 'lost' and dual (dividing) consciousness, which, with training, can learn

> to distinguish between being separated, neutral observing, and being like we are usually distracted, in the sense of being identical with the contents of the mind, without distance from its moods and considerations [...] This mind set is achieved by repeatedly distinguishing between neutral observation and distraction.
>
> (Ibid., p. 31)

When neutral observation is practised, it is to promote a detachment from identification with the ordinary busy mind and the associated feelings and body sensations. In other words, the same attitude as with Kabat-Zinn. When neutral observation is really functioning – which, according to Bertelsen, is not often the case, even for the experienced – it can be experienced as a relief or as a certain degree of freedom. The meditator discovers that he or she *is not* the pain in the knee, for example, but rather is the one who *experiences* the pain in the knee. Then, instead of identifying with the content and rather moving the emphasis towards the detached or neutral observation of the currents and perceptions of the mind, some of the energy bound in the identification will be released. This can be experienced as more clarity and calm awareness.

This function of the psyche is the background for mindfulness to be used, for example, in clinical treatment of stress and anxiety and for relief of physical and mental symptoms, just as it has been documented that clinical use of mindfulness has a positive impact on the autonomic nervous system in the treatment of chronic pain and so on (Risom 2013).

The intellectual acquisition of what mindfulness is often precedes the true experience in practice.

> It may sound easy, but you should not have practiced for very long before you discover that it is actually not that easy at all. In the beginning, the neutral observation will only be possible for quite a few moments, one becomes distracted again and again, and again and again the alertness is lost.
>
> (Bertelsen, p. 30)

Being aware of the fact that it is not so straightforward must be said to be very important when one is practising or teaching mindfulness. The training requires great patience, and the intellectual understanding of the phenomenon changes as practical experience is gained. But, nonetheless, it is a natural function of the mind, and therefore it is a practice that many will be able to familiarise themselves with.

Empathy

Mindfulness is, somehow, a strange word. You would think that it only has to do with something mental (of the mind). However, this is by no means the case. There are many arguments for the importance of empathic qualities also being trained in the context of mindfulness practice, Kabat-Zinn himself being one key proponent of this. One can imagine, for example, a soldier who, through mindfulness exercises, perfects his or her calm concentration in order to better shoot the enemy, which most people will probably consider rather unempathetic.

Being mindful as the neutral witness, without empathy, is not as such all there is to mindfulness. Kabat-Zinn has devoted considerable space in his writing to empathy and the heart qualities of mindfulness practice (Kabat-Zinn 2005). Bertelsen consistently warns against mindfulness teaching that does not include empathy training (Kjems & Rasmussen 2011).

Kabat-Zinn's popular, evidence-based MBSR programmes have inspired other programmes where empathy and acceptance are central, which is also evident from the names: *compassion focused therapy* (CFT) and *acceptance and commitment therapy* (ACT). Compassionate mindfulness is the term used by the American professor Poul Gilbert (Gilbert 2010, p. 193).

Ole Vedfelt also sees the necessity of and the need for acceptance and love directed inward towards oneself. On empathy, he writes that "it is not a sentimental feeling, but an ability, from self-insight and life experience, to feel into others without being entangled in primitive emotions. It is a 'high' form of consciousness that can be developed on many levels" (Vedfelt 2002, p. 122). Based on altruism research, Vedfelt justifies the need for self-acceptance and argues that there is basically no contradiction between self-love and love for others.

Integration of Mindfulness and Psychology

Integration of psychology and mindfulness is widespread in clinical practice. It is primarily cognitive psychology that is found along with mindfulness. The aforementioned MBCT programmes (mindfulness-based cognitive therapy) have been successful in relation to specific target groups. Research seems to show good results in the treatment of certain limited disorders (Risom 2013).

Cognitive therapy works primarily on removing or at least reducing unwanted thoughts. Unpleasant thoughts need to be erased, corrected or replaced (Germer 2005). Sure, it has been documented that cognitive therapy can have an effect on certain disorders, but, when mindfulness and cognitive therapy are brought together, the consequence may be that an end is put to deeper personality processing. Symptoms such as anxiety and depression may be reduced through mental restructuring, but are the underlying traumas and causes of the problems actually addressed? The thing is that the original cognitive therapies do not operate with the unconscious. Thus, significant resources are overlooked. However, this view is predominantly theoretical. Studies have shown that therapists from all schools in practice work on a broader basis than their theoretical starting point dictates. By extension, Vedfelt explains that thoughts are only one of many parameters to be taken into account in treatment, and that they are by far the most powerful (Vedfelt 2002, p. 68). It should also be mentioned that newer directions of cognitive therapy have shifted the focus from changing the content of thought to rather promoting the acceptance of thoughts, feelings and the content of the psyche in general, which to a large extent seems to be compatible with mindfulness.

Just as it is important to understand mindfulness in the context of empathy, it is also important that mindfulness be coupled with psychotherapy. A meditative process never moves in a direct ascent to spiritual heights. What, on the contrary seems to be the case, is that the process has a spiral-like character, which means that one constantly returns to some basic problems, simply experienced on new levels (Washburn 1990; Vedfelt 2007a).

According to the Australian professor of psychology and neurology Roger Walsh, it is remarkable how little the original meditative texts underlying mindfulness have to say about the difficulties and discomfort of practising mindfulness. For example, try closing your eyes for an hour and try to focus your attention on one object, such as your breathing. Most people will then quickly discover that it is not all that easy. The confrontation with the interior in the form of thoughts, body sensations and emotions will seem quite provocative to many. Bertelsen believes that "the training of the neutral observation slowly but surely removes the repressions, whereby the repressed elements (shadow sides, trauma, shock, infantile sides) will emerge from the cellars of the mind" (Bertelsen 1999, p. 32). Furthermore, he writes that, if the therapeutic processing is not sufficiently in-depth, it will be difficult to be mindful/neutrally observant, and, as mentioned, he warns – like Vedfelt – against uncritically opening up to deeper layers without a continuous processing of the material that surfaces.

There can be many reasons to skip therapeutic processing and instead jump straight on board mindfulness training. It is new and is often portrayed as something extraordinarily positive, which can create vague, hopeful notions that it can bring happiness and well-being without the need to work with emotions and memories. Psychotherapy is rewarding, but it can also be time-consuming and sometimes challenging, not to mention the sheer cost of it. If something constructive is to come out of therapy, it is important that, once one has found a good therapist, one then stay with him or her for a period of time.

Kevin

Kevin is 44 years old when he comes to my practice because he has problems controlling his temper. He can get so furious about little things at home that he shouts and screams and sometimes pushes or hits his wife. One day, she is badly injured because he has become more violent than usual. Kevin has been going to mindfulness meditation for over a year when he starts therapy. He feels that mindfulness has helped his overall stress level and that it has done him much good, but he also feels that it has made him a bit selfish because he is now better in contact with the things *he* needs and would like to do. For example, he has realised that it is important for him to sleep for a long time and be allowed to be undisturbed for a few hours when he wakes up in the morning. And, despite the good things that have happened, he can see that the mindfulness training has not been enough to change the situations where he loses his self-control.

Only when Kevin gets to work with his relationship with his stepfather and the underlying traumatic experiences can he begin to take a step back in the situations where he gets angry and use some of what he has learned in his mindfulness training. In addition, working with the gender roles he experienced at home brings him into contact with an inner schema that has resulted in him generally looking down on women. As he becomes aware of this, it becomes a little easier for him to benefit from the mindfulness training, observing the emotions and eventually accommodating and witnessing them without acting them out in conflict – at least, easier than before. In this way, Kevin succeeds in profiting from mindfulness assisted by working with cybernetic psychotherapy.

Spiritual Bypass

In the article "Promises and Perils of the Spiritual Path" (2006), the British psychologist Jack Engler explains some of the issues that may be associated with treading a meditative path without, at the same time, relating to the personality in general. His overall theory is that, in spiritual processes, personal emotional layers are very often overlooked and repressed. He believes that the meditator can subconsciously be searching for perfection and invulnerability. This notion is, of course, distorted, in that this ideal is not fulfilled. One certainly becomes *neither* perfect *nor* invulnerable by practising mindfulness. Likewise, the practitioner may have a notion of having already realised selflessness. This is, of course, a delusion, and the ideal cannot be of use to the practitioner as a defence against taking responsibility for him- or herself and relating to his or her life as it actually is.

Engler also argues that it may be the case that a practitioner has problems with intimacy on the personal level, and that these problems are explained away from the theory of non-attachment, which is a Buddhist ideal, an ideal that perhaps also is sneaking into mindfulness circles. A final example that mindfulness and its underlying theory can be used as an explanation or armour against a more troublesome and deeper insight into the personality is that emotions can be observed from a safe distance. Emotions are (in part) seen in Buddhism as 'dirt' or unwelcome. The goal can therefore be, consciously or unconsciously, that these should be avoided, and it can even lead to guilt when they do show up anyway (Engler 2006, pp. 17–30).

It should be noted that, because a person practises mindfulness in clinical terms, it is not the same as he or she treading a spiritual path, but it is often seen that what is initiated with one intention (for example, clinical treatment) then unfolds into a deeper interest in self-development, as well as perhaps meditation and spirituality. Therefore, I believe that Jack Engler's views above support this chapter's assertion about the benefits of treating and relating to psychological and psychotherapeutic areas when practising mindfulness and, for that matter, teaching it.

Jack Engler's views above lead to the concept of *spiritual bypass*. It is a concept introduced by John Welwood and later described by Robert Augustus Masters (both American psychotherapists). The term covers what they think happens to many who practise meditation, namely that they fall victim to an unconscious bypass, which could be translated as skipping. A person can be highly skilled on one level – for example, meditative/spiritual – and at the same time, on another level – it could be in relation to personal relationships or ethics – be quite less mature. This was illustrated in the introduction with the example where a meditation teacher slapped a student.

Masters's experience is that there can be a more or less subtle separation of certain aspects of the personality (Wilber 2010; Masters 2010). For example, anger, fear, guilt and shame can be suppressed in favour of the so-called positive emotions. The consequence of this may be that the person is not in a sound relationship with him- or herself, and only those parts of the personality that are perceived as fine and right come to light, become conscious and connected to the self-image. From this could arise a personality split cemented by the repeated blocking of unwanted sides of the personality in the meditative practice.

Cybernetic Psychology

The aim of mindfulness can be in the form of treatment or management of stress, anxiety, depression and so on. Practice promotes better self-regulation and self-calming. Here, increased tenderness and acceptance in relation to oneself are trained. With mindfulness training, it may seem possible to make contact with untapped qualities and resources, and, at best, the training will open one up to essential life qualities, such as greater empathy, emotional depth, better body anchoring, and the ability for self-contemplation. The improved contact with oneself is optimally reflected on to other people in the form of greater acceptance and non-judgement.

Usually, however, such a process does not proceed without self-confrontation with the dim or darker sides of the personality. If this confrontation takes place in conscious harmony with the person's self-perception, a real integration will be possible. This is where psychotherapy comes into the picture, and, as suggested in the introduction, cybernetic psychology and psychotherapy have special opportunities to be fruitfully involved in this dual process.

Cybernetic psychology is a theory of consciousness and personality developed and described by the Danish author and psychotherapist Ole Vedfelt. It was developed around the science of the creative complexity of the mind. In broader terms, cybernetic psychology can be laid out as the science of how information is regulated and distributed in the psyche and between people. The theory draws inspiration from cybernetics, information and systems theory, with consciousness pictured as a dynamic and hyper-complex self-optimising information system that organises its elements into a network of subsystems. The psyche is thus divided into levels and manifests itself in a complex of different levels and states of consciousness. It is possible to differentiate and describe these levels and states.

A fundamental concept is that our 'normal, everyday, rational consciousness' constitutes only an infinitely small part of the totality of consciousness. In cybernetic psychology, the normal consciousness is called the *personal self*. It is the subjectively experienced personality or self-perception. The totality of consciousness is called the *cybernetic self*. The personal self is perceived as an important subpersonality but is thus functionally subject to the cybernetic self. That is, the overall network of consciousness holds far greater capacity and information than we generally assume. The ongoing regulation and structuring of this sea of information and the interplay between the cybernetic self and the everyday consciousness are controlled by what in cybernetic psychology is called the unconscious intelligence. In traditional psychologies – for example, in Freudian psychoanalysis – the unconscious is interpreted primarily as a container for unwanted and more or less chaotic impulses such as aggression and sexuality, whereas the existence of the unconscious as defined in the early cognitive schools is completely denied. In cybernetic psychology, it is quite the opposite. Here, the unconscious is considered to be superior to the normal consciousness. The unconscious is an intelligent and self-regulating system that constantly seeks to optimise personality. In cybernetic psychology, it is said that problems must be solved at a higher level than where they occur. If, for example, you have a problem with authorities in your workplace, the reasons for and processing of this can be done in completely different ways from just talking about the troublesome boss. Of course, one must try to solve the specific problem, but perhaps behind this hides a more comprehensive complex of self-development that only reveals itself in relations to authorities.

The unconscious is not something distant or something that only a few with special talent have access to. It is as close as the glasses you have sitting on your forehead, but you are looking everywhere else. The unconscious is not an empty postulate either. Substantial research documents that the unconscious psyche accumulates extensive information, and that this information is stored as tacit knowledge (Vedfelt 2002, Hass & Hansen 2022). This turns our familiar notions upside down. Bringing the personality into contact with the unconscious intelligence creates access to untapped potential. This is key to promoting personality development. Unconsciously, we are constantly drawing on vast areas of knowledge and features. An important point in cybernetic psychology is that it requires altered states of consciousness to make contact with and achieve the influence of the unconscious intelligence. In these altered states, which may be established through psychotherapy or meditation, it is possible to make contact with the unconscious intelligence and be fruitfully inspired (Vedfelt 2002). However, access to the unconscious can be qualified intentionally, but access is by no means an exclusive phenomenon. The fruitful altered state of consciousness can be established in two minutes of slumber in the bus on the way home from work, and suddenly you have had an idea or solved a small problem. If the contact with the unconscious is reduced, reduced along with it are important sources of life. There are constant context-dependent circularity and exchange between the consciousness and the unconscious, which rhythmically oscillates between inner states and contact with the outside world.

That access to the unconscious and thus memory systems is context-dependent becomes clear, for example, if you are in a therapeutic situation with a therapist you trust. In that context, you will remember more, feel more, say and show more. Conversely, with a therapist who moralises and judges, the system automatically shuts down. If the therapist is not aware of this, she or he may perceive the client as troublesome or defensive, but the reality is that the client's system responds appropriately.

Overthinking or Unconscious Intelligence?

When a person seeks help for problem-solving in relation to emotional challenges, it is often seen that he or she has sought to solve the problems for a long time by endless thinking. Often, it has not helped, and frequently the person gets caught up in excessive, fatiguing thought spirals that lead nowhere. In cybernetic psychology, such a theme is explained by the fact that there is simply disorder in the person's self-regulatory functions. The self-regulating functions are natural consciousness properties, but, when access to these does not work optimally, the person will not be able to bring him- or herself into contact with deeper layers of him- or herself – that is, the unconscious intelligence.

Cybernetic psychotherapy is thus a process where the client is helped to dialogue with more extensive areas of the personality. The unconscious intelligence manifests itself in fantasy material, nocturnal dreams, emotions, body sensations and movement impulses. At first glance, these expressions may be perceived as disturbing and meaningless. On closer inspection, however, they turn out to hold meaningful information that can create access to higher levels of organisation in the psyche. Imagination material, inner images, dreams, emotions, bodily sensations and movement impulses can be seen as process channels for information or symbolic codes that contain relevant information that is important for the personal whole. In cybernetic psychotherapy, the non-intellectual experience parameters are considered necessary to decisively create therapeutic processing and development.

When communicating appropriately with these seemingly irrational layers, one actually responds intelligently again. When psychotherapy is working optimally it can be considered high-level communication, because here there is an opportunity for communicating through a high degree of emotional and information complexity. Mastering this is done primarily through practice learning. It is not possible to learn alone from reading. How to work concretely with these signals of self-regulation is carefully described in the literature of cybernetic psychology, just as it is described in other chapters of this book. But, overall, one can say that a 'reconciliation' or dialogue between the goal-oriented, creative, non-rational layers of consciousness (the intelligence of the unconscious) and the everyday consciousness is the main intention.

The inner landscape with its infinite content is called, in cybernetic psychology, the supramodal space or the multidimensional psychic space. To an untrained person, it can seem confusing to orient oneself in this space. But, with training – for example, in psychotherapy – or by meditation, one can build confidence that it is actually possible to navigate the inner self. And not only can one discover that it is possible to orient oneself, one can also discover that the unconscious is like a never-failing helper or friend who is constantly trying to optimise and regulate the personal system.

Supramodal ability is the term Vedfelt uses for our ability to experience and decode information in the interior. It is the ability to rise above the individual experience modalities and instead, from a supramodal inner point of view, observe how the different discernable modalities – thoughts, feelings, inner bodily sensations, body movements and mental imagery – form a wholeness and thus actually also access a larger memory. This supramodal ability is an inherent quality we are all born with, but for most of us these windows of perception are blinded as we mature. An analogy could be the fact that children are born with a disposition to be immediately open in contact with others, but, as can be seen with great clarity, this ability is more or less frozen in adults. With training, however, the supramodal ability can be practised. This is desirable because the optimising capacity of a system potentially, according to one of the laws of cybernetics, increases relative to the greater information capacity and complexity it possesses. And this is where the co-herence between mindfulness and cybernetic psychology appears. The supramodal ability is like mental capacity at the base of the neutral observation or mindfulness setting. Only the supramodal ability as performed in cybernetic psychotherapy is an expanded and intensified awareness of the different experience modalities, also named *process channels*, that might actually be involved in the mental contents and has thus varying degrees of consciousness. In cybernetic psychotherapy, an open and fluid awareness of the inner processes is sought, which is also the core of the meditative methods – yet with a wider perspective.

> One of the mindfulness-incorrect discoveries was that the unconscious intel-ligence uses jumps between process channels as a general way of communicat-ing. Where this is often considered in meditation teaching as that which must be counteracted, it became for Vedfelt a very special discovery of the language of the unconscious. If there is no flow on one channel, the unconscious shifts to another channel. Leaps of consciousness are meaningful. And it's important to go with these shifts and see what comes up. Like when a linguistic metaphor turns into a picture that can be drawn, and a drawing gives memories to a dream. How languageless moods can be explored as early body states that can testify to events that happened before language came into the mind of the infant. Condi-tions that can now be given language that lies on the border between emotions and everyday rationality. If in this way neutral attention could be maintained simultaneously on several different channels over shifts, the total continuous current could run towards states of a higher level of complexity.
>
> (Hass & Hansen 2022, p. 82)

If we too soon try to find rational and logical answers to problems, we shut off a deeper process, even though, in the situation, we believe we have found a solu-tion. Vedfelt believes that, in the context of treatment and development, we are too judgemental and fault-finding instead of being exploratory and curious, and he believes this originates in Western culture's split between reflection and process.

> In successful therapy and meditation, reflection and process proceed simultane-ously. The reflection is used here to dispel the prejudices that block both the ability to observe and the flow of life. Because we constantly evaluate parts of our personality negatively and suppress them, they live a crumpled existence where we are unable to see their growth potentials. The opposite of this blocking

is acceptance. It is the core of all wisdom. One could also talk about a love the system directs towards itself.

(Vedfelt 1996, pp. 140–141)

Integration of Mindfulness and Cybernetic Psychotherapy

Vedfelt considers mindfulness to be a training of consciousness, which is very broadly defined with many dimensions, and which can be developed on many levels. He believes that the concept of mindfulness works best coupled with a perception of the mind that is based on modern Western psychology and psychotherapy and especially with the involvement of unconscious intelligence.

Mindfulness and cybernetic psychology have in common that it is assumed that a theory of consciousness that rests solely on an intellectual foundation, as is largely the case with Western philosophy, is far too one-sided. Instead, deconstructing the limitations of consciousness through meditation or by bringing the unconscious intelligence to the table opens an inner, never-failing creative space, a treasure trove of information and valuable states and levels of consciousness that cannot be brought to mind by thinking but to which we can open ourselves up. From the outside, it may seem that what is primarily aimed at in mindfulness is to create calm and achieve relaxation. But that is not (only) the case. What is (also) striven for is a clear and open awareness that enables one to lift oneself out of habitual thinking.

Occasionally, therapy and meditation are criticised for giving rise to navel-gazing. In our X Factor culture, we get points for being outgoing. Introverts are categorised as delicate, troublesome or perhaps even strange. But this criticism is based on prejudice. The fact is that, if the outer becomes everything, the inner becomes nothing. What must be sought is an alternation between many different, both inward-facing and outward-facing states and levels. Dreams, vegetative states, imagination, daydreaming and meditation are examples of inward-looking states that are essential to our well-being. As Vedfelt puts it: "The system withdraws and simulates problem-solving models, performs counterfactual thinking, and hereby compensates and complements the normal consciousness" (Vedfelt 2007a, p. 691).

Vedfelt argues that meditation methods can be advantageously complemented by cybernetic psychotherapy. He points out that, unfortunately, Western psychotherapy generally does not prioritise mindfulness training itself. Conversely, he criticises that the Eastern forms of meditation reject psychic material (Vedfelt 2002, p. 137).

Vedfelt notes that

a lack of processing of mental material can lead to recurrent disturbances in the mindfulness training, as certain mental structures keep appearing. If attention training is continued stubbornly, there is a risk that the content that spontaneously emerged will be split from consciousness

(Vedfelt 2002, p. 128)

An example of this could be that a meditator, in his or her practice, repeatedly encounters the same traumatic memory but more or less consciously chooses to forget it again. However, this does not make the complex or the trauma go away, and therefore the recommendation must be that, in parallel with mindfulness practice, you include therapeutic processing of the psychic material that you come into contact with in your practice.

Amanda

In mindfulness courses, so-called body scan exercises are often used. Different body areas are felt and experienced. It sounds very innocent but is not always so. On a course I held, we did such an exercise. A few minutes into the exercise, we managed to feel our throats and necks. Amanda, an otherwise very well-functioning and resourceful woman, subsequently described that she had experienced a physical pressure on her neck, and that this had given her a powerful flashback: Memories from the past had emerged. The emotions had immediately begun to flow through the body and manifest as physical discomfort. She had felt her ex-sboyfriend's hands around her neck and a feeling of not being able to breathe. She had seen his face and his eyes. Again, as then, thoughts revolved around the same thing: Would she die now? At first, she felt nothing, was overwhelmed by surprise, and all power of action had suddenly disappeared. Only when he had released his grip did the anxiety come rolling in over her, like muscular tremors and a gasp for oxygen. Then again, suddenly she was back in the meditation room. She tried to reassure herself that it was all in the past, but the emotions and the physical reactions kept hanging over her body like a dark, heavy cloud.

It was fortunate for Amanda that she was a participant in a smaller team where there was good understanding. We could subsequently relate constructively to her experience and suggest paths to further psychotherapeutic processing. Had she instead been an involuntary participant – for example, in a course at her workplace – and sat side by side with the boss or a colleague she did not trust, or had she been a participant in a course with a poorly trained instructor, the consequence could have easily been a very unwanted retraumatisation far from the promised 'calm and relaxation'.

Ethics

A qualified mindfulness educator should have so much psychological insight and education that she or he could, first, identify the interfaces with psychiatry and, second, have an eye for when and why it is appropriate to refer to psychotherapeutic processing. The teacher should have an insight into when contraindication is necessary – that is, when mindfulness practice should be advised against owing to mental instability or vulnerability.

Both as a teacher and as a student in mindfulness, there are important things to be clear about. In any therapist–client or teacher–student relationship, complex transference and countertransference processes arise and play out. The relationship is, by nature, asymmetric. It is appropriate that the teacher knows more about the topic than the student, but the asymmetry can easily become inappropriate. For example, it is often seen, perhaps even after a few hours of teaching, that the teacher is attributed all sorts of positive qualities. If the teacher now begins to feed on the admiration of the students, he or she will be drawn into grandiose and narcissistic notions of him- or herself. For example, in his marketing material, a mindfulness teacher described that his ability to be in mindful states was transmitted to the students. This might esoterically be true, but is probably more fantasy or wishful thinking than reality. These complex relationships belong to what cybernetic psychology calls supramodal relationships. From a cybernetic perspective, the parties enter a systemic relationship that should be made more conscious to avoid inappropriate structures such as the notion of the omniscient teacher and the ignorant student. The narcissistic teacher will point to him- or herself as the one who has the answers, whereas a more balanced teacher will help the student to become his or her own authority. A meditation teacher is very easily attributed unconscious 'wizard projections'. If she or he mindlessly jumps on to the energy of these projections, she or he is likely to form unconscious notions of her- or himself as a bit of a magician and, in special and unhealthy cases, as a saviour.

Once one has trained in mindfulness for some years, or perhaps even teaches it, one can quickly forget how much inner pressure can actually be generated and how much unprocessed mental material can manifest as a consequence of the training. Therefore, it must be a requirement that a teacher has a relatively comprehensive psychological insight and has him- or herself been in therapy. In therapy, material often appears which can immediately be related to the clients' unfinished situations with caregivers from the past. The teacher should now have developed a better relational competence than the original caregivers in order to meet the student and intervene in an appropriate way.

In cybernetic psychology, one talks about process levels.[3] What can actually happen relatively quickly with mindfulness training is that it opens up to other process levels than those one is usually in contact with, so-called higher process levels. It can feel like a great energy intake, like clarity, like light, like visions or like religious experiences. After some time – from a few moments to hours or days – you are back in your normal self with your normal energy level. If the experiences are now interpreted from this 'lower' level, meaning with the ordinary everyday consciousness, then we have a problem. The ego mirrors itself in the experience with a high risk of inflation and grandiose behaviour. Vedfelt writes that, in therapy, he has often met people who practised meditation without adequate and continuous guidance. They are awakened to a high level too quickly, so to speak, and, since the self is not trained to accommodate this energy, it is projected into all sorts of internal or external conflicts (Vedfelt 1996, p. 121).

I myself, a few years ago, had a client who was a trained mindfulness instructor. He was required to attend an annual retreat to maintain his teaching licence. Coincidentally, it was during a time when he was in crisis owing to marital relationships. Many daily meditations and silence were the primary content of the retreat. When you fail to dissipate the energy, it will automatically accumulate in the system. The pressure gradually became so intense for the client in question that he complained of his distress to the instructors. But here was no 'dear mother'. He was told that he 'just' had to be 'mindful', meaning, of course, neutrally observant and, as the days went by, he got closer and closer to an actual mental collapse. When he came into therapy a few days after the course, I was close to proposing an admission to a psychiatric emergency room. With therapy, rest and good friends, however, balance was restored.

Mindfulness practices will always, at least at times, imply some inner pressure, but it is not appropriate to push oneself and others unnecessarily. To pressure others, as in the above case, is directly unethical. And the attitude of 'just being mindful, no matter what comes out' can be traumatic. Had it not been for that person's basic resources, it could have gone completely wrong. In the original traditions, where mindfulness has its roots, training was tightly structured and given under expert guidance, and so such conditions could be avoided to a greater extent.

The initial assumption that meditative experience is not necessarily proportional to personal maturation was sadly confirmed when the American international meditation teacher and spiritual teacher Andrew Cohen had to apologise publicly on his website. He admitted that, no matter how realised, transcended and enlightened a person is, yes, no matter how much meditation one has practised, one has an ego. In Cohen's case (even according to himself), this apparently unprocessed ego has made life difficult for others. The charges against him were many and very serious, everything from exploitation and manipulation to physical and psychological violence.

This topic has also been addressed by the American meditation teacher Jack Kornfield. He lived for some years as a monk in the East, practising intensive meditation. But, when he returned to the United States, he could see that it had not changed much in his way of relating to other people. He "was still emotionally immature, making acting-out of the same painful patterns of shame and fear, acceptance and rejection" (Kornfield in Vedfelt 2007b, p. 689).

So

With cybernetic psychotherapy's method of supramodal perception, it is possible to train both the function of consciousness itself, the conscious presence, and the neutral observation of mindfulness. And it is furthermore possible to do it in a way that allows the contents of consciousness to be welcomed. The *observing I* can be trained, while relating to what is observed. In this way, one avoids mindfulness becoming a cool, distance-creating, barren, repressing discipline. Content can be observed without the consciousness being lost in it, and emerging emotional material can subsequently be processed and integrated. It can be discovered how the inherent self-regulation and unconscious intelligence are constantly kindly knocking on the door, offering assistance to personal development alongside the mindfulness training.

According to Vedfelt, personal development takes place in sequences, from primitive to more differentiated, from lower to higher complexity. Humans are part of evolution (Vedfelt 1996, p. 113). Here, he is in line with the American philosopher Ken Wilber, who argues that evolution is moving towards an increasing degree of differentiation and complexity, and that there is an ongoing integration of this complexity. Does this evolution happen by itself, or do we have influence over it? Maybe we have. And perhaps awareness-raising activities such as creative expression, psychotherapy and mindfulness meditation actually might affect our common whole – for the better.

Notes

1 Walsh & Shapiro (2006).
2 Bertelsen points out, that it is possible to advance the meditation from the ordinary I-consciousness towards I-transcendent states of consciousness. In this process, neutral observation is but one step along the way. This process of reaching I-transcendent states is, according to Bertelsen, of a long duration and requires an extraordinary persistent effort.
3 The psychic processes organise themselves complexly and hierarchically – hence the concept of process levels.

References

Bertelsen, Jes (1999) *Bevidsthedens inderste*. Rosinante, Copenhagen.
Engler, Jack (2006) Promises and Perils of the Spiritual Path, in Mark Unno (Ed.), *Buddhism and Psychotherapy across Cultures, Essays on Theories and Practices*, pp. 17–30. Wisdoms Publications, Leicester.
Germer, C. (2005) *Mindfulness and Psychotherapy*. Guilford, London.
Gilbert, Poul (2010) *Compassion and Mindfulness*. Klim, Copenhagen.
Hass, Henrik & Hansen, Torben (2022) *Det ubevidstes potentiale*. Frydenlund, Copenhagen.
Hecksher, Morten Sveistrup, Nielsen, Louise Kronstrand & Piet, Jacob (2010) *Mindfulness manual til træning i bevidst nærvær*. Hans Reitzels Forlag, Copenhagen.
Højsgaard, Morten (2013) Kapløb mellem Jesus og Buddha. *Kristeligt Dagblad*, 12 April, Copenhagen.
Kabat-Zinn, Jon (1990) *Full Catastrophe Living*. Delta, London.
Kabat-Zinn, Jon (2005) *Coming to Our Senses*. Hyperion, New York.
Kjems, Jesper & Rasmussen, Marianne (2011) *Mindfulness og empati i skolen*. Interview with Jes Bertelsen. Filmkompagniet, Aarhus, Denmark.
Laing, R.D. (1985) *Wisdom, Madness and Folly: The Making of a Psychiatrist 1927–1957*. Macmillan, London.
Masters, Robert Augustus (2010) *Spiritual Bypassing*. North Atlantic Books, Berkeley, CA.
Risom, Jens-Erik (2013) *Mindfulness og meditation i liv og arbejde*. Hans Reitzels Forlag, Copenhagen.
Vedfelt, Ole (1996) *Bevidsthed*. Gyldendal, Copenhagen.
Vedfelt, Ole (2002) *Unconscious Intelligence – You Know More Than You Think*. Gyldendal, Copenhagen.
Vedfelt, Ole (2007a) *The Dimensions of Dreams*. Gyldendal, Copenhagen.
Vedfelt, Ole (2007b) Religious Peak Experiences in Transpersonal, Psychodynamic, and Cybernetic Perspective. *Psyche & Logos*, (28), pp. 675–705. Dansk Psykologisk Forlag, Copenhagen.
Walsh, Roger & Shapiro, S.L. (2006) The Meeting of Meditative Disciplines and Western Psychology. *American Psychology*, 61(3), pp. 227–239.
Washburn, M. (1990) Two Patterns of Transcendence. *Journal of Humanistic Psychology*, 30(3).
Wilber, Ken (2010) Integral Naked. www.integralnaked.org

7

Creativity, Life and Art in Cybernetic Psychology and Integrated Psychotherapy

Anne Hjort

The Russian writer Anton Chekhov once said that, to work with your art, you must work with your life. With a personal starting point, the chapter focuses on creativity in life and art. It poses the questions: How can one understand creativity? And how is it possible to create conditions that reduce inhibitions and blockages and promote creativity – both in life and art? Life is broadly understood as human evolution, and art is broadly understood as creativity that manifests itself in the world. With its theory of human consciousness, cybernetic psychology offers a framework for understanding creativity that, incidentally, is in line with existing modern research on creativity. In this chapter, I examine how cybernetic psychotherapy operates on the premises of creativity in its methodology, and how therapy supports creative processes – in people's lives as well as their work.

Making Room for Creativity

Turning 30, I had just finished a long period in education with a PhD in Comparative Literature and Media. In front of me lay a brilliant career as a researcher in media, either at the University of Copenhagen or in the Media Research Department at DR – the Danish Broadcasting Corporation – where I had been offered a job. I tried working in both places, for a short while, but had a nagging feeling that I would die if I stayed. The critical and analytical academic approach was no longer stimulating for me. In spite of a highly praised final thesis, my self-esteem was very low, and I felt restricted in many ways.

I sat in my small, dark office in the Media Research Department at DR, looking over at the tall building where all the creative people were working, making television. I knew I wanted to create something myself instead of continually criticising and analysing what others created. When I chose to leave the world of research, I spent years striving to become part of the creative class, years of anxiety and insecurity, inner and outer conflicts, economic sacrifice, hard work and many attempts in different directions. At the same time, I began seeing a psychotherapist, both in groups and on an individual basis, and this was to continue for many years. I am quite certain that, without this work, I would never have succeeded. The therapy gave me emotional support, insight about myself and greater self-esteem. It gave me courage and strength to do the work needed to accommodate more space for my

DOI: 10.4324/9781003360247-8

creativity as well as improving my economic situation owing to the documentary films and TV programmes I was directing.

In my personal life, I fell in love with talented, intelligent, sensitive and creative men with unfulfilled dreams of being artists. I even filmed such a man for more than a year. These were men who could easily become 'the eternal youth', who only reluctantly took adult responsibility for their life – or for me, for that matter – men in whom I invested a lot of hope and expectations. Committing to my own creativity became a focal point in therapy. Although I was making a living through my own creativity, it was still a big challenge to express it freely. Until a few years ago, I stubbornly insisted: "I am not creative". The therapeutic process has therefore focused on the question: What does creativity mean to me, and how does it manifest itself in my life and work? How do I establish the inner and outer conditions that make it easier and more enjoyable to display my creativity? It is, on the one hand, about having obtained a sense of professional security and, on the other hand, about handling the anxiety that is an inseparable part of the creative process. For many years now, I have made a living from directing TV documentaries, and my work plays a fundamental part in creating a joyful and meaningful life. Artistic men with large, unrealised potentials have, in this context, lost their appeal as potential partners.

In the following chapter, I shall investigate creativity. How to understand it. What inhibits and what facilitates creativity. How do we establish conditions that enhance creativity, in a balanced way, both in life and in art? By life, I mean human development and, by art, I mean creativity manifesting itself through work in the outside world, whether it be through craft skills, a TV programme, science, inventions, humour or a work of art.

In this chapter, the theory of cybernetic psychology is the framework for understanding creative consciousness. Furthermore, cybernetic integrated psychotherapy offers a method that is in accordance with creative consciousness and therefore suited to enhance the creative process in both life and art.

Understanding Creativity

Creativity is a special trait of the human psyche and consciousness. Spontaneous outbursts of creativity in life are a natural, innate skill, the reason why human beings are capable of creating something new. Modern creativity research suggests that creativity is the production of something new that is useful. Some talk of creativity with a lower case c as our everyday creativity and creativity with an upper case C when something is created that is new to all of us (Mikkelsen 2009, p. 24).

In his early writings, the father of psychoanalysis, Sigmund Freud, saw the creative state as a regression to more primitive psychic stages, to primary processes in the unconscious, a place for repression of both sexual desire and death wish. In opposition to this, the psychiatrist and psychoanalyst Carl Gustav Jung saw the unconscious as having a positive creative potential (Vestergaard 2012, p. 246; Vedfelt 1996, p. 79 f.).

More recent existential and humanistic psychologists (such as May and Csikszentmihalyi) see the creative state as more elevated in relation to the normal state, an understanding which is found in the concept of *flow* in positive psychology (Mikkelsen 2009, pp. 203, 205).

In early creativity research from the 1950s, the American psychologist J.P. Guilford, among others, focused on fantasy and ingenuity and the offbeat (divergent) thinking of the individual. Focus here was also on the testing of creativity – the so-called psychometric approach (Hammershøj 2012, p. 43; Bendixen & Nickelsen 2012, p. 39). A highly valuable contribution to research in creativity stems from the writer and journalist Arthur Koestler, *The Art of Creation*, from 1964. Koestler introduced the concept of *bisociation*, describing how a new idea combines what used to exist separately. It is not an association or a connecting of thoughts and ideas, but a creative leap that combines two frames of reference which formerly had not been connected, thereby creating an integration of understanding and experience into a new whole – a model that describes an essential aspect of creative processes in nature and human beings. Koestler's other contribution to the theory of creativity is the assumption that there are *three main domains* in which bisociation predominantly takes place – art, science and humour.

The Austrian psychoanalyst Anton Ehrenzweig describes the creative process as a deconstruction of fixed categories, giving way to a more complex and nuanced understanding of the topic of creative work. He calls it a *dedifferentiation of categories* and sees it as an opposite process to what happens in the educational system, where we learn to relate to the world in an analytical way. In an analytical understanding of the world, we differentiate between elements, we identify similarities and differences and we categorise them. Dedifferentiation is an opening up of the categories, and this is what happens in the creative state of mind. Many people experience having their best ideas when they relax, go for a walk or take a shower after having been focused at work. Recently, I had the experience of getting the right idea for a TV programme, which I had been thinking about for some time, when I skived off work and went to a museum instead. In these situations, when we are not being analytical or trying to find solutions, the experience of reality is more fluid and coupled to inner perceptions. A mental openness takes place, where thoughts, images and sensed feelings, flowing through our consciousness, mutually pollinate (Mikkelsen 2012, p. 199; Vedfelt 1996 pp. 133–134).

The Four Phases of the Creative Process

The pioneering French mathematician Henri Poincaré was one of the first to reflect on the different phases of the process, which had led to significant new discoveries. In 1927, these observations inspired the British social psychologist Graham Wallace to identify four phases in the creative process (Hammershøj 2012, p. 36 ff.):

1   The preparatory phase (*preparation*) – working consciously and focused on the problem to be solved.
2   The incubation phase (*incubation*) – no conscious work is executed, the person is in a relaxed state, active and unconscious labour with the problem is taking place, a 'mystic state' in the creative process.

3 The idea phase (*illumination*) – the moment a new idea emerges; accompanied by certainty and ecstasy/enthusiasm.
4 The editing phase (*verification*) – the idea is written down, compiled, adjusted and tested.

In relation to the last two phases, recent research points out that it is important not only to hold on to the first idea, but to allow more to emerge. It is furthermore evident that what characterises extraordinarily creative people is their ability to evaluate their ideas and act on the most interesting ones (Mikkelsen 2009, p. 54 ff.).

> The new inter-connections of knowledge happening in creative processes are usually unconscious. The American creativity researcher and cognitive psychologist, Mark Runco, says it is not possible to explain what precisely happens prior to the new, good idea arising. And there is general consensus that large parts of the creative process are unconscious – "beyond our awareness".
>
> (Mikkelsen 2012, p. 200)

In spite of almost one hundred years of research in creativity, there is still no definite answer to what happens during the creative process. There seems to be no centre for creativity in the brain. Recent brain research draws attention to the fact that what characterises the creative brain is a greater skill in using brain resources by interconnecting various centres of the brain (Vedfelt 2017, p. 20 f.; Mikkelsen 2020, p. 24 f.).

The general understanding among creativity researchers that a large part of the creative process is unconscious shows the necessity for having a theory of conscious and unconscious intelligence in order to comprehend what happens in the creative process. This theory is to be found in the psychoanalysis presented by Freud and his followers, in the work of Jung, as well as in cybernetic psychology, as presented by the Danish psychoanalyst, therapist and writer Ole Vedfelt in his theories of consciousness. It is surprising that these theories are still so marginalised, for this is where we find ways towards a better understanding of the creative process, in my opinion.

A Psychoanalytic Theory of Creativity

The Danish psychologist Thea Mikkelsen outlines an integrative model for the psychology of creativity, which she calls the psychic landscape of creativity. Here, she draws on Freudian psychoanalytic understanding of the self, which consists of the *ego*, the *superego* and the *id*. In terms of creativity, it is the part of the *superego* she has described as the *ego-ideal* that is relevant. This is the individual's goal and ideal perception of the self and the surrounding world that may result in a creative effort to make the world a better place. The *id* is responsible for imprinting the knowledge and experiences worked with, in a sensually meaningful direction. This is where the unconscious comes into play. In the unconscious, however, there are also complexes and conflicts. The role of the ego, in creative work, is to find useful and rational answers to how the innovations of the id and the goals of the ego-ideal find their concrete expression in a specific professional and organisational context (Mikkelsen 2012, p. 207).

Based on psychoanalysis, Thea Mikkelsen distinguishes between two ways of processing stimuli: Primary processes, which are visual, nonverbal and chaotic, and secondary processes, which are logical and linguistic. Creativity takes place in the universe of primary processes, where you feel omnipotent and have the sensation that what you are doing is remarkable and good. In fact, it is necessary to have that feeling when working creatively. In the early experience of omnipotence, which, at the age of two – with the development of language and social consciousness – is shifted to the unconscious, lies an important source of creativity. But, if the toddler is criticised at this stage, shame and feelings of being wrong also arise. When you open up to the feeling of omnipotence in creative work and get into flow, you there-fore also open up to all sorts of old insecurities, feelings of shame, defeat and forbid-den desires, emotions that can drain away self-confidence (Mikkelsen 2009, p. 185).

Thea Mikkelsen introduces the concept of *reverie* from the English doctor and psychoanalyst Wilfred Bion. Reverie is the dreamlike state that promotes idea gen-eration. It is "our thoughts, daydreams, fantasies, body sensations, fluid percep-tions, inner images, rhythms and melodies, sentences that run through our minds" (Mikkelsen 2012, p. 198). In reverie mode, the boundaries between different areas of knowledge are dissolved in a way that allows knowledge and experiences from different areas to inspire each other. Bion developed the concept to describe the state a mother is in when she imagines the child's needs and desires and thus thinks for the child and creates a space in which the child can learn to think. You, likewise, use yourself as an instrument when eyeing opportunities in the field in which you want to create something new. It is a theory for this state of reverie that cybernetic psychology offers, as well as a method to work with and within in.

Creativity in Cybernetic Psychology

In his innovative book *Consciousness* from 1996, Ole Vedfelt formulates cyber-netic psychology as a theory of consciousness, as a self-regulating and self-healing system that strives for integration and development throughout life. He states that a fundamental theme of cybernetic psychology is to recognise the constant and spontaneous creativity of the psyche. In therapy, this is experienced as a pressure from within towards personality development, which manifests itself in therapeutic material such as body expressions, fantasies, meditative experiences, symbols and dreams that can anticipate developments years ahead.

> Personality development is a form of subjective creativity, a creation of the per-sonality that works according to the same principles and phases as, for example, artistic and scientific creativity – objective creativity.
>
> (Vedfelt 1996, p. 133)

Inner, subjective creativity is active throughout life, pointing towards new life pos-sibilities which, if ignored, limit the personality. The ordered organisation of these creative processes, both subjective personality development and objective artistic creation, in Vedfelt's view, take place not as a stepwise sequential accumulation of details,

> but rather as a crystallisation of a whole [...] This whole is not a centralised process, but more like a germ, a potential, a structuring structure that permeates the whole psychic process or work of art in all its many details.
>
> (Vedfelt 1996, p. 133 f.)

When development of the psyche moves from one level to another, in its most crucial phases, it is, outwardly, a leap that leads to total reorganisation of the overall system. In the unconscious, as well as altered states of consciousness, this reorganisation can be developed through inner test actions and model simulations that take place at vastly different levels. Development of the psyche takes place in an open system which requires interaction with the environment. This applies to the young child, in therapy as well as in the creation of a work of art. Vedfelt does not believe there is a sharp distinction between subjective and objective creativity. In the ordinary human being, a process of personal change will also create external changes, and a lack of personal development will, in the creative human being, limit the ability to innovate. In total contrast to the popular myths that a miserable life is conducive to artistic creativity and that therapy will bring the creative, artistic process to a halt, it is Vedfelt's experience that therapy, such as cybernetic therapy, which in itself is creative, will stimulate creativity in a human being (Vedfelt 1996, p. 270).

The Danish musician Peter Bastian writes in his memoirs, *Master Class. A Life Story* (2011), how he, until late in life, had the idea that good, beautiful and true art would also create good, beautiful and true people. Eventually he had to admit to himself this was not the case, and that he himself had an increasingly schizophrenic experience of development as a musician, yet not as a human being.

Emergence

Freud believed that the most important driving force of the human psyche is the need for tension release, and he saw the death drive as an important control mechanism. Cybernetic psychology, on the other hand, regards life as continuous stages of development and personality transformations and sees the pursuit of integration as a driving force. It complies with the systems theory hypothesis of *emergence* – which is the spontaneous creation of new forms and higher levels – which makes it suitable for describing creativity. In systems theory, living systems are perceived as self-regulating, self-renewing, self-organising and having the capacity for creative development, also known as emergence (Vedfelt 1996, p. 108). These are processes that take place over time and can only be accelerated to a limited extent. This applies to the infant, therapy (both individual sessions as well as the whole process) and the creation of a work of art.

On the concept of emergence, the Danish professor of psychology Boje Katzenelson states: "Everything living is in the process of being created. In the process of unfolding itself based on the potentials lying within. Life wills itself" (Mikkelsen & Møller 2010, p. 78 f.).

The Danish theologian K.E. Løgstrup adds: "Man's foundation is goodness. Evil is not allowing goodness to prevail" – a psychological-philosophical understanding that life itself unfolding is good. "It is when we block the unfolding of life that problems arise" (Mikkelsen & Møller 2010). In addition to this, the Danish architect Bjarke Ingels has described his and his colleagues' work as making the yet invisible visible – in other words, with their buildings, the architects support and express an emerging process in culture and society.

Constraints and Contingencies

The term 'constraints' is used in psychology about the constraints that any system must impose on itself in order to function. The fewer restrictions a system has, the greater the freedom of choice – that is, the contingency. If a system has too much choice, it can become paralysed. Restrictions are therefore necessary to be able to act and know how to act in the most appropriate way in a given situation. American studies, for example, show that children who have too many toys stop playing, simply because there is too much choice. A famous example of the use of constraints to promote artistic process concerns the Danish Dogma films, where four film directors formulated ten rules to limit themselves, which released a creative energy and made several of the Danish films and their directors internationally famous.

> Development from the simple to the more complex means moving towards greater freedom of choice – increasing contingency, where a transfer of emotional energy to a higher level of control also takes place.
>
> (Vedfelt 1996, pp. 118, 137)

In other words, the development of a system means that it becomes more complex and thus functions with fewer restrictions and greater freedom of choice.

Breakthrough Experiences

According to Ole Vedfelt, high-intensity, information-dense states of consciousness can be seen as an insight into higher self-regulating control systems. They have strong creative potential because of their ability to set highly organising processes in motion with very long-term effect. It might be a subjective innovation in the process of personal change towards a new model for the overall personality. But breakthrough experiences can also be expressed in objective, creative actions. There are many examples of artistic innovation and scientific discoveries occurring as a form of revelation. Great creative personalities such as Poincaré, Mozart, Rodin and da Vinci all mention such intuitive, creative flashes of insight. A more recent example is the author J.K. Rowling, who, on a train journey, in a glimpse, saw the whole story of the wizard's son, Harry Potter. The creator of mindfulness-based stress reduction (MBSR), the physician and researcher Jon Kabat-Zinn, describes a similar experience. At a meditation retreat in 1979, he had a vision lasting ten seconds which included not only the model for MBSR but the entire implementation of the programme. At the same time, he envisioned the new scientific and clinical discoveries it would entail, along with its spreading to hospitals and clinics, both in the United States and worldwide (Kabat-Zinn 2011, p. 287).

Vedfelt describes these creative breakthroughs as an expansion of consciousness, where the mental processes are greatly increased. The experience is global – you see the work, in its entirety, at a glance. There may have been many frustrations associated with failed attempts, but, in the breakthrough, consciousness is fluid, and the feeling is ecstatic, euphoric, happy and boundless. Words such as revelation, illumination or enlightenment are often used to describe the decisive breakthrough (Vedfelt 1996, pp. 262, 264).

The Pulse of Consciousness

Psychoanalysis has perceived man as a being that is fundamentally in conflict with its inner instincts, and these are therefore fought with defence mechanisms. With a more modern perception, cybernetic psychology sees the personality as an open system that can connect to the greater network of its surroundings. The personality consists of complex inner states interplaying with many different programmes, constantly working to optimise themselves.

> In order to regulate the many processes that constantly take place in the personality, the mind switches between states processing information in different ways and performing different tasks. There is a pulse where consciousness swings between inward-facing and outward-facing states. The introverted states are vegetative, relaxed and self-reflective moments with relatively few external influences. Time for free imagination and creative ideas. Here we do not have to take care of the many tasks in the outside world that normally fill our everyday lives, and a surplus of information capacity arises, available for other purposes.
> (Vedfelt 2012, p. 53)

Jung describes two archetypes of essential significance for creativity. *Puer aeternus* or *puella aeterna* is the man or woman, respectively, who throughout his or her life retains youthful and/or puberty-like features. Puer is the bubbly and charming, creative and talented, mother-bound man with high spiritual aspirations and difficulty in bonding. Puella is close to the father and spiritually active but has difficulty dealing with the ordinary and close relationship attachments. The counterpart to these two is Senex, the old, wise man who ideally creates the necessary constraints for Puer's creativity to flourish. However, if Senex is too powerful, it can lead to rigidity and inhibition. This can be illustrated with a dream I had when I was studying at university – not a very happy time for me. I dreamed that Stalin cut my hair. It is almost superfluous to add that there was little room for either femininity or creativity at that time in my life. On the other hand, if Senex is too weak, Puer becomes the eternal youth who never takes responsibility in life but indulges in unrealistic identity dreams as an artist.

A few years ago, when I was studying to become a psychotherapist, I read an article by the Danish Jungian analyst Misser Berg: "A Myth about Addiction: Echo and Narcissus" (2001). It struck me how I had been fascinated by exactly that type of man. Then, I had a dream where I looked at an exclusive, glossy magazine, and in it, my ex-boyfriend B (who should have been an artist) posed in a variety of beautiful pictures. Suddenly, the picture crumbled before my eyes. I had had a passionate relationship with B, and it nearly killed me when he suddenly left me. Now, that unrealistic ideal finally crumbled.

In summary, cybernetic psychology focuses on systems at different levels in the unconscious, which hierarchically regulate each other (more complex regulates less complex). It also focuses on how something new spontaneously emerges in the interaction between constraints and contingency, during a creative process, as a sort of crystallisation of meaning and coherence from otherwise seemingly chaotic and disorganised material. This interaction has its archetypal parallel in Senex and Puer and in the Freudian understanding of secondary and primary processes – in other words, the fact that a creative process alternates between open, chaotic states and orderly, categorising states.

Dreams as Works of Creativity

It has been a widespread notion in Western philosophy and thinking that consciousness presupposes verbal thought activity. Ole Vedfelt (1996) argues that other modes of experience – also called modalities – such as emotions, inner images, body sensations and impulses of movement, have not had the same status despite the fact that every personal experience is stored in the memory of all experience modalities. In addition, we have an innate ability to transfer an experience from one modality to another. One can also argue that it is an innate ability of consciousness. In other words, we have, from birth, an inner *supramodal space* that encompasses the entirety of an experience. The supramodal ability is constantly present in our everyday life, though not on a conscious level. In dreams – as well as in creative states – the supramodal ability unfolds its full potential. All modes of experience are combined in one whole.

In his book *A Guide to the World of Dreams* (2017), Vedfelt describes ten core qualities of dreams. The ability of dreams to 'be online to unconscious intelligence' is one of them. He describes how we generally regard rational, everyday consciousness as consciousness itself. Rational consciousness is, of course, absolutely crucial for the personality and for our ability to cope in the world, but many overlook the fact that most of the time we are in other states of consciousness. Unconscious intelligence is constantly active, but it is only in free states that consciousness can connect to it and register a portion of the activity taking place. This happens especially in the dream state.

In dreams, the psyche rises above the troubles of everyday life, sorts out the many pieces of information received, and compares them to the greater patterns that govern our lives. Dreams thus operate on a higher organisational level in the psyche than normal awake, everyday consciousness.

(Vedfelt 2012, p. 53)

Vedfelt has, for many years, worked theoretically and practically with dreams, and he considers dreams to be on a par with creative enterprise, science and art. He thus opens up to a more flexible understanding of the unconscious. He rejects, inter alia, the widespread notion that the unconscious is incapable of thinking rationally. He argues that the unconscious is outstanding at handling cause and effect, time and space, imagination and reality. When a dream breaks away from principles of reality, it happens with the same means and expressive purpose as used by a playwright, for example. It does so to add something new, to add an extra meaning or in order to make a creative leap (Vedfelt 2002, pp. 147–159, 2007, pp. 465–483).

Dreams have an extraordinary ability to relate to a myriad of changing situations in reality, while at the same time being governed by specific, personal, inner experiences and behavioural patterns. The associative connections of dreams are neither random nor camouflage. They reflect an inner reality which is encoded on several levels and which is activated in an interaction with the surroundings. Dreams are considered by many to be meaningless and strange or seen as psychic garbage, but they are, according to Ole Vedfelt,

> meaningful expressions of a higher level of psychic organisation that handles more complexity than normal awake consciousness, and which has a larger content of knowledge. They are creative syntheses and possess an ingenuity and richness of image far superior to everyday consciousness.
>
> extract_source>(Vedfelt 2002, p. 151)

With reference to Koestler's concept of bisociation, Vedfelt demonstrates how dreams make a creative juxtaposition of levels otherwise kept separate by the more habitual thinking of awake consciousness. In this context, he queries the prejudice of seeing the unconscious as containing a deficit of mental capacity, when we otherwise look very positively at creative syntheses produced in the awake state. The unconscious masters tell stories and create a structured dramatic course within the dream, which is an expression of cognitive capacity far surpassing awake consciousness. "It is a narrative capacity that is fascinating in the way it manages, in symbolic form, to represent important inner psychic processes at a high level" (Vedfelt 2002, p. 157), and does so in a dream fable that makes psychological sense in relation to the life of the dreamer. In addition, dreams master an emotional and aesthetic quality the awake person would not be able to produce while awake.

Dreams of Creative Blockages

Among the important functions of dreams is a form of psychic long-term planning, as they reflect inner creation processes and the obstacles standing in their way. Dreams can therefore anticipate a person's development before the change of personality manifests itself in the external world. Artists and creative people remember more dreams than others (Vedfelt 2007, p. 466), and, for them, dreams can in many ways contribute to the creative process. Many creative discoveries have been made in dreams, but, in general, dreams first and foremost say something about the attitude to the creative process and do not present ready-made solutions. This can also, however, be a great help and support in creative work. Vedfelt tells, for instance, how he has been able to help clients whose dreams about ambition and anxiety about the opinion of others were obstacles in their creative work.

Creative blockages are often symbolically depicted in dreams of faeces, which, not infrequently, deal with complications surrounding creativity such as its being limited or controlled. In Danish, going to the toilet is also known as 'to make' and thus it can also have a positive meaning – for example, for young children who are praised for a self-made product. Rippling springs symbolise the source of life and creativity. Winter, cold and ice can often symbolise cooling of both emotions and creativity (Vedfelt 2012, pp. 297, 313, 323). I personally have often had dreams of ice and snow in connection with stressful periods in my life. In a stressed state, consciousness is in alarm, ready for fight or flight, and is far from the relaxed state that is conducive to creativity.

A journalist I know, at one point exposed herself to unreasonably harsh pressure. She then dreamed of a little horse that was whipped onwards by a riding instructor and, every time it had cleared an obstacle, it had to clear a new, even taller one. The dream made her realise she had to stop constantly pushing herself towards a new task, because it would never satisfy or be good enough, and instead allow herself to relax and praise herself for the effort she made. In that way, her creative work gradually became less strenuous and more fun.

One of my clients, a 60-year-old woman, had suffered from anxiety throughout most of her life. In connection with retirement and therapy, she resumed a lifelong dream of expressing herself artistically. After several archetypal dreams – among others, a house on fire – men began to appear in her dreams. At one point, she had a dream about a pale man, turned away from her. In a series of paintings, she entered into dialogue with the man, who gradually turned more and more towards her and became increasingly strong. In the end, he gave her a gift. This happened as she engaged more with her own way of expression, dared to stand by it and act upon it.

What Inhibits Creativity?

In *The Psychology of Creativity* (2009), Thea Mikkelsen gives a description of different types of creative blockages. Feelings of insecurity and anxiety are inevitable when being creative. You search for what you do not yet know, and it requires being ready to let go of what is safe and familiar. Sometimes, the incubation phase lasts a very long time, and it can be difficult to maintain confidence in the process. If anxiety becomes too dominating, a blockage can occur. The greater the anxiety, the more difficult it becomes, as anxiety causes stress and will inevitably force you to seek security and stick rigidly to what you know. And then it is almost impossible to have new and original ideas.

Mikkelsen defines a block as a feeling that one has lost connection with the creative impulse. To the outside world, such a block can be completely invisible – it can seem as if the person has finally come to her or his senses and has faced reality, instead of throwing her- or himself into risky and seemingly profitless projects. According to the English psychoanalyst Donald W. Winnicott, such people do not live their own lives; they conform to the norms of society and could just as well be dead. Their non-creativity is not necessarily the issue, but rather that they are not fulfilling their own creative impulse and cultivating the new opportunities this could provide for them and their surroundings. This was exactly the feeling I had when I, with my newly acquired master's degree, was offered a research scholarship at the university – that I would die if I accepted. I chose to decline despite all the uncertainty it brought. As I had rather blurry notions of what I wanted instead, an inevitable consequence was, among other things, periodic unemployment, fluctuating income and lack of a pension scheme.

The Destructive Aspect of Creativity

The new requires destruction of the old, which can be provocative. According to the English psychoanalyst Juliet Miller, women especially withhold their creativity for fear of the destructiveness it causes (Miller 2008), all that must be rejected to make room for the new. What will it entail to show that destructiveness, and how will it affect the woman's ability to be a mother, a wife or a lover? Men too may end up with such extreme responsibility that they forget what really turns them on. Creativity can seriously test one's self-image, and one can feel selfish, unreliable and awkward – which may involve feelings of both shame and guilt. Social expectations and the desire to be there for people they care about also mean that many put their creativity aside. Miller believes it is crucial for creative women to be able to recognise and use their aggression. She mentions Louise Bourgeois as an example of how a female artist has used aggression as a positive force to find her own identity and her own language as an artist and, thus, freed herself from the particular constraints female creativity is subjected to.

For most people, it is not until they feel the meaningfulness and the rewards of creativity that they convince themselves it is valuable enough in itself and thereby break with conventions and risk the social exclusion they feared as a result of the creative 'norm breach'. In 1993, the American psychologist Howard Gardner examined some of the great creative personalities in history, such as Freud, Einstein, Picasso and Gandhi. He concluded that, early in their lives, they had all recognised that conformity was not an option for them – they chose to develop their very own theories and practices (Mikkelsen 2009, p. 162).

Creativity generally seems to be a greater challenge for women than for men. Today, it is not so much finances and having one's own room that is the issue, as the English writer Virginia Woolf described. Now, it is more about being able to have your own inner space intact, which Donald Winnicott calls "an undisputed resting place". Many women want to be there for those who need them and therefore arrange their lives to always be prepared to put their own things aside for others. This cannot be reconciled with an artistic life, where, in the American film director David Lynch's words, there must be freedom and time for the good things to happen.

It is not uncommon for women to realise their creative potential late in life (Vedfelt 2003, p. 324). One example is the Danish writer Karen Blixen (Isak Dinesen), who did not realise herself as a writer until after her love affair with the big game hunter Denys Finch Hatton, as well as the possibility of having children, had finally passed. Despite her world fame, on her deathbed, she is said to have told her sister-in-law, who lived a full life with husband and children, that it was she who had made the happy choice.

Psychic Openings

In the creative process, there is interaction between unconscious assessment and conscious assembling. The psychoanalytic point of view, represented by Thea Mikkelsen, describes this as an interaction between primary processes governed by desire and anxiety and secondary processes that distinguish between reality and fantasy, right and wrong, the possible and the impossible. Creative people are generally more open to impressions than others. Some even find it difficult to distinguish between fantasy and reality. Experiences of opening to the unconscious can even lead to blockages.

One could say that creativity balances between an inner fantasy world and its principle of pleasure on the one hand, and an experience of real life with a principle of reality on the other. If you hold on too tightly to the principle of reality, with its conventions and professionalism, it can block the emergence of new ideas. If the inner fantasies take over, they can block the perception of reality and even lead to a form of psychosis (Mikkelsen 2009, p. 164). Such experiences may lead to great anxiety about creativity, and the approach must therefore be slow; this is also the case in a therapeutic context, where it is crucial not to open up to greater amounts of unconscious material than there are resources to integrate. Likewise, the therapeutic framework and the security it creates are of the utmost importance to proceed into the creative processes of therapy.

Loss of Control and Performance Anxiety

Doing something new is risky and will always cause anxiety about losing control – from butterflies in the stomach to actual fear. Creativity depends on daring to move into the unknown and letting go of control. In order to work creatively, it is necessary to be able to endure anxiety. The amount of anxiety and loss of control we humans tolerate varies. In psychoanalytic terms, anxiety is linked to two fundamental challenges. The first is about the fear of losing one's ability to cope in the world. The second is concerned with the fear of losing oneself. The first is linked to the feeling of being small and dependent and to the risk of being abandoned or attacked and unable to survive. The second is linked to the experience of the ego being a fragile structure which might crumble.

Performance anxiety often deals with the fear of being exposed. It deals with destroying the illusion of omnipotence, which one must be in contact with in order to work creatively. It is a fear of being neither brilliant nor on the verge of becoming world famous, of not being as professionally skilled as you would like to be, of not being good at anything, just incompetent. Performance anxiety is thus linked to the fear of losing one's ability to cope in the world. It is the only form of anxiety worth doing a reality check on by examining whether you actually have the necessary skills to do what it is you want to do (Mikkelsen 2020, pp. 120–121).

Although the anxiety that may be experienced in connection with creative processes is based on inner psychic conflicts, it is often experienced as a real danger. It can lead to avoidance behaviour, where one avoids taking on a new task or postpones things until the last minute. What can appear as laziness and procrastination may, in fact, be due to anxiety. One may also overreact and automatically reject new proposals without necessarily having any good reason for doing so. Or one may think of solutions, in order to maintain control, which creatively are bad solutions (Mikkelsen 2009, p. 166). Ultimately one wants to shut down the conflict-filled emotions as well as the anxiety. The problem is that, as a result, you also shut down creativity. Creatively speaking, it is far better to feel grief, pain, anxiety, anger, shame and guilt and engage in the conflicts you encounter than shut them down.

In relation to the therapeutic process, this is exactly what happens in therapy when you teach the client to be aware of their thoughts, feelings, body sensations and inner images; to feel them, meet them with acceptance and a neutral presence, thereby not turning off the creative flow. It is this presence, this contact with unpleasant emotions, that enables a transformation and something new to develop.

Facilitating Creative Processes in Cybernetic Psychotherapy

The American psychoanalyst Otto F. Kernberg published the article "Thirty Ways to Destroy the Creativity of Psychoanalytic Candidates" in 1996. He states that "our problem is not so much to foster creativity, but to try not to inhibit the creativity naturally stimulated by the nature of the work" (Kernberg 1996, p. 85). In the article, he criticises the training of psychoanalysts for being normative, authoritarian, patriarchal, anxiety-producing and power-oriented in both theory and practice – and almost dead. He hereby points at the importance of keeping a tradition alive, open and constantly evolving in order not to become rigid in a normative and closed practice. He simultaneously underlines that working with people in a therapeutic relationship requires set boundaries, high ethics and awareness of the potential relationship of power between client and therapist. If not, it may inhibit and destroy both the creative as well as the personal development process which the therapy is meant to support.

Cybernetic psychotherapy is, per definition, an open, integrative method and is thus able to incorporate new developments, new knowledge, new interests – in accordance with the overall cybernetic theory of consciousness. It integrates several different psychotherapeutic traditions into one therapeutic practice. With various therapeutic tools such as conversation, mirroring, drawing, dreamwork, bodywork, touch and meditation, inter alia, access is secured to the different levels of consciousness through different processing channels.

In *Consciousness* (Vedfelt 1996), Vedfelt describes cybernetic and integrated psychotherapy as a fundamentally creative form of therapy. He draws parallels between the creative and the therapeutic processes. When observing a creative person at work, it may, at times, seem as if nothing is happening, whereupon these periods are replaced by fierce activity. In therapy, you do not steam ahead either; first, you create a relaxed atmosphere and, then, you delve into the deeper experiences. In both therapy and creativity, there are phases in the process that are beyond the control of volition, and it is a dynamic process that cannot be divided up (Vedfelt 1996, p. 137). In order to facilitate the process, it is important to adopt an observant openness that allows it to proceed freely within certain given frameworks. If it is met with assessments and judgements instead of an exploratory attitude, it most often comes to a halt. As a therapist, you therefore train, among other things through meditation, to be able to work from a state of expanded and intensified attention.

Introspection

In cybernetic psychotherapy, work is focused on strengthening individual, creative processes of the unconscious. Introspection occurs when consciousness, in an altered state, is attentively reflective and observes thoughts, feelings, body sensations and inner images. When the client is guided in this, it is called guided introspection. When the therapist is attentive to her or his own sensations and, in this way, tries to understand the client's feelings, it is called vicarious introspection. In other words, with the open, exploratory attitude of introspection, dialogue becomes a creative process and a way of removing obstacles in order to facilitate spontaneous creative forces being expressed between human beings (Vedfelt 2002, pp. 111, 134).

Creative Methods in Cybernetic Psychotherapy

Vedfelt talks of a "Picasso Principle" in therapy, referring to the painter Picasso's description of how an artist must destroy his beautiful discoveries in the painting, time and time again, in order to give it more substance, to hone and transform the piece of art. Transferred to the dialogue in a therapy session, it is seen as a creative process, where therapists should hold back on fine ideas and good suggestions and instead turn their attention to the creative processes that seek to express themselves from within the client. Hereby they experience a honing, more substance and a better empathy with the universe of the other person (Vedfelt 2002, p. 134). Cybernetic psychotherapy is "literally a creative process in which new structures emerge in a manner that probably follows certain laws, but which, in their actual expression, are unpredictable" (Vedfelt 1996, p. 296). He compares therapy to jazz improvisation, "where you have melodic freedom within certain harmonious frameworks, where you have a large repertoire of rehearsed standard figures, which can be used freely wherever it serves the interplay but where the overall course is a unique phenomenon" (Vedfelt 1996, p. 298).

The therapy's repertoire of rehearsed standard figures includes various techniques for disconnecting normal, focused consciousness. This is in order to access sufficient mental resources to tune in to associative connections in the unconscious which are meaningful on another level. This is done in therapy with, among other things, the help of the free association technique, developed by Freud, Jung's active imagination technique, fantasy journeys, drawing, chair work (role play with different people or subpersonalities), body sensing (possibly with touching), psychodrama and meditation. All techniques are useful to relax normal consciousness and open it up. These techniques simultaneously stimulate creativity.

In other words, cybernetic psychotherapy aims at being 'online to unconscious intelligence' in the same way as parts of the creative process, as described earlier, with the concept of the reverie state. Leaps of consciousness link between the various modalities of experience and processing channels, an approach, on the premises of the creative mind, and a state where new connections can be created on higher and more complex levels. In dreamwork, a synthesis of cybernetic theory and practice takes place. Dreams may point at blockages – both in the person's life and in the therapy itself – and, cybernetically, one works multidimensionally to unfold the relevant meanings of the dreams' creative synthesis. This happens in a creative process including several modalities of experience (Vedfelt 2012, pp. 79 f., 96). Thus, cybernetic psychotherapy also becomes a way to practise facilitating creative processes, as it is simulation in a safe space. Once the framework is set and necessary confidence established, you can initiate an investigation borne by acceptance, interest and creativity, where something new is allowed to emerge from consciousness.

> In successful therapy … reflection and process evolve simultaneously. Reflection is used to dispel prejudices that block both the ability to observe and the flow of life. Since we constantly evaluate parts of our personality negatively and displace them, they live a crumpled existence, and we are unable to see their potentials of growth. The opposite to this blockage is acceptance. It is the core of all wisdom. One could also describe it as love, which the system directs towards itself.
>
> (Vedfelt 1996, pp. 140–141)

It is through this loving attention that negative emotions, such as anxiety, can be transformed and the natural creative process may unfold unhindered – in life and in art.

Creativity – Life and Art

Creativity is a natural capacity in the human consciousness and psyche – creativity understood as the ability to create something new. Cybernetic psychology presents a theory of consciousness that includes creativity – both subjective as well as objective creativity, in both life and art. The cybernetic integrated psychotherapeutic method works, in practice, on the premises of the unconscious and thus facilitates creative processes, both in the personal development process and in manifest – objective – creativity.

Cybernetic psychology also makes a special contribution to the understanding of dreams, which in themselves are seen as being creative. Cybernetic psychology has developed a method of working creatively and openly to unfold the multidimensional meaning of dreams. Cybernetic psychology exemplifies that a special quality of dreams is to be 'online to unconscious intelligence', in similarity with parts of the creative process. Cybernetic psychotherapy offers methods to evoke the fluid states of consciousness that promote creativity. It does so within a framework ensuring security and thus the opportunity for change and development to take place in a balanced way, without forcing the natural process. Both therapy and creativity require frameworks (constraints) to unfold. The more blockages are lessened, the more the self-regulatory powers of consciousness are brought to practice – and the greater the freedom becomes (contingency).

In relation to my own story, the dictators are no longer present in my dreams, and, in both my inner and outer life, there is more freedom than ever before and, therefore, also much more room for both subjective and objective creativity in my life. Some years ago, when I had come to a complete standstill in the development of a project, a very creative friend said to me: "You must be brave enough to investigate, what you don't know". I recalled the phrase writing this chapter and, the following night, dreamed that a red-haired woman in a sex shop said to me, "Nothing is fruitful until you examine it". With this statement, my unconscious got the final say, a humorous juxtaposition of creativity and sexuality – sexuality that can lead to the ultimate creation – new life.

References

Bastian, Peter (2011) *Mesterlære. En livsfortælling*. Gyldendal, Copenhagen.

Bendixen, Mads & Nickelsen, Niels Christian Mossfeldt (Eds.) (2012) *Innovationspsykologi*. Dansk Psykologisk Forlag, Copenhagen.

Berg, Misser (2001) En myte om afhængighed: Ekko og Narcissus, in Pia Skogemann (Ed.), *Symbol, analyse, virkelighed. Jungiansk teori og praksis i Danmark*. Lindhardt & Ringhof, Copenhagen.

Hammershøj, Lars (2012) *Kreativitet – et spørgsmål om dannelse*. Hans Reitzel, Copenhagen.

Kabat-Zinn, Jon (2011) Some Reflections on the Origins of MBSR, Skillful Means, and the Trouble with Maps. *Contemporary Buddhism*, 12(1).

Kernberg, Otto F. (1996) Thirty Ways to Destroy the Creativity of Psychoanalytic Candidates. *International Journal of Psychoanalysis*, 77, pp. 1031–1040.

Mikkelsen, Thea (2009) *Kreativitetens psykologi*. Nyt Nordisk Forlag Arnold Busck, Copenhagen.

Mikkelsen, Thea (2012) Det usynlige arbejde bag innovation, in M. Bendixen & N.C.M. Nickelsen (Eds.), *Innovationspsykologi*. Dansk Psykologisk Forlag, Copenhagen.

Mikkelsen, Thea (2020) *Coaching the Creative Impulse. Psychological dynamics and professional creativity*. Routledge, London.

Mikkelsen, Thea & Møller, Mette (2010) *Den kreative kraft i innovationsledelse. Teori U's psykologi i praksis*. Dansk Psykologisk Forlag, Copenhagen.

Miller, Juliet (2008) *The Creative Feminine and her Discontents*. Karnac, London.

Vedfelt, Ole (1996) *Bevidsthed. Bevidsthedens niveauer*. Gyldendal, Copenhagen.

Vedfelt, Ole (2002) *Ubevidst intelligens* (2nd ed.). Gyldendal, Copenhagen.

Vedfelt, Ole (2003) *Manden og hans indre kvinder*. Gyldendal, Copenhagen.

Vedfelt, Ole (2007) *Drømmenes dimensioner*. Gyldendal, Copenhagen.

Vedfelt, Ole (2012) *Din guide til drømmenes verden*. Gyldendal, Copenhagen.

Vedfelt, Ole (2017) *A Guide to the World of Dreams*. Routledge, London.

Vestergaard, Arne (2012) Individuation og innovation, in M. Bendixen & N.C.M. Nickelsen (Eds.), *Innovationspsykologi*. Dansk Psykologisk Forlag, Copenhagen.

8

The Cybernetics of Anxiety

Britta Karlshøj

This chapter is written for people who experience or have experienced anxiety, live with anxiety. It is written for anybody who is curious about anxiety as a phenomenon. It is also written for you who, by virtue of your profession, meet people in your work who have experienced or are experiencing anxiety. For you who would like to meet the person who experiences anxiety in a welcoming way and perhaps be a support on this person's way forward. The chapter shows how cybernetic psychology sees the concept of anxiety, mainly as a possibility for transformation of personality. Recognising the fact that anxiety is an emotion, the chapter emphasises the cybernetic perception of anxiety as a condition which the cybernetic self 'initiates' in an attempt to get the personal self to create a necessary life change that may seem unwelcome, disturbing and confusing, but that benefits the whole of the personality. I intend to point out that we are dealing here with a perspective that will meet anxiety in such a way that it becomes possible to master life with anxiety as a companion, and I want to show that the transformation of anxiety can become an opening to personal growth.

Meeting Anxiety

We are many who remember 11th September 2001 very well. We remember where we were and who we were with. We remember what happened before and what happened after. That, too, is how it is for me. I was a physiotherapy student and was an intern in a hospital in Canada. In retrospect, I also see that I was on the run from myself. When the towers toppled in New York, I toppled too. I encountered anxiety for the first time with such violence that I was sure I was going to die. And, at the same time, at this point, I was not at all aware that it was anxiety I had encountered.

The Danish National Board of Health states that there are 52,000 men and 84,000 women in Denmark who have been diagnosed with anxiety (Flachs et al. 2015 p. 195). I imagine that, in addition, there are many, many more who experience anxiety to varying degrees without being diagnosed. Of course, it has social and economic consequences for a country and, particularly, it can have crippling consequences for the individual. That was the case for me. With anxiety, one's life

DOI: 10.4324/9781003360247-9

is not lived. Everything comes to a standstill. Anxiety about anxiety is a concept that occurs over and over again in the literature. I think it is because anxiety about anxiety is what can slow down the unfolding of life in every way.

Treating or Transforming

I think everyone who has experienced anxiety or has met people who have experienced anxiety has thought, "if only the anxiety would disappear, then ..."; the idea that everything would be easier if only anxiety did not exist is completely understandable. I have thought so myself many times. And people who come to my psychotherapeutic clinic because of anxiety have thought the same, over and over. What I learned when I realised I needed help to deal with my anxiety was that it turned out to be a widespread idea that treating anxiety was about getting the anxiety to go away, to disappear. My path became different. It became a path of transformation, a path of transformation in which skilled cybernetic psychotherapists insisted on looking for resources in the personality revealed by the anxiety, resources that could be used to solve what might seem insoluble. In the following, I shall present some basic ideas and thoughts from existential psychology, as I shall later show how this perspective can be integrated into the resource-oriented cybernetic psychotherapeutic work that is the main theme of this chapter.

Existential Psychotherapy

Existential psychotherapy has philosophical roots. There are many contributors. In this context, I have chosen to focus on American professor of psychiatry and existential psychotherapist Irvin D. Yalom's contributions to existential psychotherapy and on the German philosopher Martin Heidegger and the Danish theologian and philosopher Søren Kierkegaard for the philosophical foundations. In an attempt to place existential psychotherapy on the map of psychology, I have particularly noticed that Yalom calls existential psychotherapy "something of a homeless wanderer" (Yalom 1998), and he also shows that existential psychotherapy is related to humanistic psychology. Existential psychotherapy is a form of 'dynamic psychotherapy' in which the word 'dynamic' is to be understood as a professional term associated with the concept of 'force'. Man's 'forces', says Yalom, exist at different levels of consciousness, and some of them are unconscious. A person's psychodynamics thus encompasses the various conscious and unconscious forces, motives and notions of fear that act in him or her. The dynamic psychotherapies are based on this basic model of the psychic functions (ibid.). The existential standpoint emphasises a particular type of basic conflict in man which is particularly relevant in this context. It is a conflict that stems from human confrontation with what the existentialists call the basic conditions of existence. Yalom has designated, from Heidegger, four basic existential conditions: Death, freedom, isolation and meaninglessness (ibid.). In the next section, let us look at 'death' as one of the basic conditions of life, as it is here that we can approach an existential understanding of the concept of anxiety.

Death

Existentialists say that there is one thing we can be absolutely sure of, and that is that we must all die one day and that we must do it 'alone'. We cannot let others die for us, or, in Yalom's words, "Without life – no death. Without death – no life" (Yalom 1998).

Now, as I am writing this, it may somehow seem completely commonplace. And at the same time, if we dare take note of it, it can also be felt to be very provoking. There is a deep truth in this knowledge – it is felt as quite a landmark. We could call it achieving some form of death consciousness, just as banal as it may seem, just as anxiety-provoking as it can be. Yalom postulates that death is a primordial source of anxiety and believes that fear of death underlies any mental problem (ibid.). Death reminds us that life cannot be postponed, and that there is still a time to live. Kierkegaard says that the lucky ones are those who face their own death and recognise life as "the opportunity of opportunity" (Staubrand 2014). Heidegger says that "death can save man", and it is precisely these central thoughts that, according to Yalom, have contributed to the development of existential psychotherapy (Yalom 1998).

According to Heidegger, there are two basic ways of being in the world: A state of forgetfulness of being and a state of consciousness of being. In short, living in the state of forgetfulness of being is a state where man has forgotten that he is – in other words, that he exists. Man stays in him- or herself and is engulfed by everyday distractions of life. One is preoccupied with 'unimportant talk', lost in oneself, indulges in trivial daily life and focuses on 'how' things are. One knows that one must die, but one is no one, and man has not made him- or herself aware that 'I myself' must also die. Heidegger calls it an "inauthentic mode of being".

If, on the other hand, one lives in a state of being contemplative, one does not wonder 'how things are' but 'that they are'. To exist in a state of being contemplative is to be conscious of one's being. One is aware of life and one's own self-creation, where one discovers the ability to change oneself. Heidegger calls it "the true/real mode of being" (Heidegger 2007). Heidegger uses these two basic ways of being in the world to explain how "death can save man". He says that the awareness of our own death acts as a spur that causes us to move from one mode of being to a higher one (Yalom 1998). The theory here may seem contradictory, and one might feel like asking oneself, "why fear death?" The answer is hard to give, but Yalom shows, through empirical studies, that fear of death is prevalent everywhere and with such strength that he believes we spend a great deal of our life energy on denying death (Yalom 1998). Yalom uses the term "anxiety of death" – not "fear of death", which has its roots in Kierkegaard. Kierkegaard clearly distinguished between "fear" and "anxiety", which was completely new in his time.

> The concept of anxiety is hardly ever seen treated in psychology, I must therefore point out that it is completely different from fear and similar concepts that refer to something specific, while anxiety is the reality of freedom as the possibility of possibility.
>
> (Kierkegaard in Staubrand 2014 p. 69)

Thus, fear is directed at something specific – for example, being afraid of spiders – while anxiety is not directed at something specific but is characterised by having fear of nothing. Thus, Kierkegaard says: "what effect has nothing. It gives birth to anxiety" (Kierkegaard in Staubrand 2014 p. 68). Anxiety is always forward-looking – that is, directed at something that can happen but that we do not know will happen. If it concerns something that has happened, we can regret that it did happen, but, if we are anxious, it is because we imagine that it may happen again in the future (Staubrand 2014). According to Yalom, the primary fear of death will always be transformed into something less destructive for the individual through the psychic defence system, and so, for the therapist, it is manifested by the client fearing various events – for example, going shopping – but Yalom argues that treatment of these shifts requires treatment of the primary problem, which Yalom considers to be anxiety of death (Yalom 1998).

Existential Therapy

Attempting to describe an existential method is not easy. I shall here try to give an insight into why this is the case. Once, Yalom was in a cooking class where an Armenian woman and her helper, neither of whom spoke English, would teach by visual instruction. All the students made an effort to do exactly what the Armenian woman did, but it never turned out quite as well – it was as though something was missing. One day, Yalom discovered that, when the helper carried the Armenian woman's dish to the oven in the kitchen, the helper, in passing, added a handful of exotic spice.

In several of his books, Yalom wonders about what "ingredients" are needed to make the therapy successful. Yalom believes that textbooks, journal articles and lectures often portray therapy as something exact and systematic, with carefully defined stages, strategic technical interventions, methodological development and resolution of transference, analysis of object relations, and a well-considered, rational programme of insightful interpretations. He has come to the conclusion that, when no one is watching, the therapist adds "the real thing". This little narrative perhaps illustrates why it can be difficult to find a structural method in Yalom's books. Yalom himself says: "Everything I have done with my patients is accessible to anyone: All techniques can be modified and used" (Yalom 2008 p. 37).

Basically, Yalom's attitude is that diagnosis should be avoided, as it will 'make' the client sick. Yalom does not allow his psychotherapeutic method to be 'controlled' by diagnosis. Yalom recommends that therapy should be based on the "here-and-now", as he calls it. He encourages researching the client's "here-and-now" with the client and thereby trying to spot the client's themes. Furthermore, Yalom emphasises that he sees the therapeutic relationship as a healing force, and that we should not be afraid to touch clients. At the same time, he shows that he uses dreams to expand his understanding of what is at stake for the client (Yalom 2009). Yalom tells about a 60-year-old woman who experienced the 'intellectual' part of the therapy as 'nice enough', but the real benefit turned out to be in the relational interaction. The client attached special importance to the sense of togetherness that arose with the therapist (Yalom 2008). He asks his client about experiences around death, because – as already mentioned – he believes that a lot of anxiety is due to fear of death. He asks directly about notions of death and experiences of the death of others. He has learned that, if he asks, "what exactly is it about death that you fear?" it accelerates the pace of the therapy, and he may also recommend his client to meditate – for instance, at the parents' grave. At the same time, he shows that he uses dreams to expand the understanding of what is at stake for the client. And, in the dreamwork, it is seen that he uses free association and that he himself is cautious with his own hypotheses (Yalom 2008). He advises therapists to pay special attention to the first dream or dreams in which the therapist appears (Yalom 2009). In summary, Yalom's existential method is based on long-term therapy, basically built on the client's 'here-and-now' and not on diagnoses. In the therapeutic relationship, he uses free association, meditation, touching, reading of facial expressions and dreamwork. He works on the basis of the attitude to life that we all experience confrontation with the basic conditions of life, which, among others, is shown when he enquires directly into these basic conditions and how these are experienced by the client. In the next section, it will become clear that a lot of the methods from the existential perspective can readily be integrated into cybernetic psychology and psychotherapy. In the following, we shall look at how cybernetic psychology offers what I perceive to be a strong theoretical perspective that can be the foundation of professionally based choices of methods in psychotherapeutic work.

Concept of Consciousness

Cybernetic psychology is an integrative theory based on cybernetic network theory. The theory serves as a model for the way in which information and energy are regulated in the complex neural network of the human psyche. Overall, cybernetic psychology introduces a special understanding of consciousness. Consciousness is described in theory as having many levels that work in different states of mind. These states can be expressed via different experience channels – for example, through body perceptions, emotions, imagery and thoughts. These channels of experience are equated in cybernetic psychology. They are thus equally valid channels for information and are all perceived as different processing channels for consciousness (Vedfelt 2012 pp. 45–50).

- *States of consciousness*: We are all familiar with our normal wakefulness, the awareness we have when we are awake and living our daily lives. Another state of consciousness that most of us are also familiar with is the night's dream sleep – that is, the state of consciousness that produces our dreams, which many of us can remember more or less of when we wake up from our sleep. In addition, our consciousness can be relaxed states, contemplative states and spontaneous breakthrough experiences of expanded consciousness with a special feeling of clarity in the mind. The fact that, as humans, we have access to different states of consciousness is considered in cybernetic psychology to be a valuable and natural part of the human psyche (Vedfelt 2002 pp. 91–108).

- *Levels of consciousness*: When we think of levels of consciousness, we in the Western part of the world are especially familiar with the rational, awake level of consciousness. The rational, awake consciousness has a limited capacity for information. There are other levels of control in our consciousness that communicate much faster than the rational, awake level of consciousness. It is why, therefore, we cannot 'just' rationally make anxiety go away. The other levels of control that communicate faster appear to be directly related to overall levels of the total personality. It is possible to reflect on these levels of governance, and they are constantly present. We detect them best when we are in relaxed states (ibid.).
- *Processing channels*: This concept is an information-theoretical expression of the various experience channels. In our normal waking state of consciousness, we can transport information through one processing channel at a time. We feel a trickle down our backs. Next, we bring to mind a dark, eerie street where we once walked and were scared. Next, we feel the emotion fear and so on – that is, either we feel a body sensation, or we think, or feel an emotion, or ... – but mainly one thing at a time. In addition, there are supramodal states of consciousness where it is possible to rise above our usually one-dimensional experience system (ibid.). The interesting thing is that it is possible to train our consciousness on an equal footing with the training of muscles, for example. This is what you look for in, for instance, mindfulness practice and meditation.

Unconscious Intelligence

Unconscious intelligence is a central concept in cybernetic psychology. It is basically about not just accepting the 'unconscious' as a phenomenon but understanding the unconscious part of our total intelligence as a valuable resource that can be translated into life in general and into psychotherapeutic practice in particular. The way I explain it to my clients is that unconscious intelligence is a real resource, and getting accustomed to it is like learning a language, a language that many of us have forgotten. No one really knows why – maybe in adaptation to the culture we are a part of, maybe for other reasons. What strikes me time and again is that people who listen to this intuitively understand what it is all about. Our unconscious intelligence is expressed, among other things, through our nocturnal dreams, our body language, our facial expressions, our associations, emotions and fantasies via our processing channels (Vedfelt 2002). Part of our intelligence is conscious, and a large part of our intelligence is unconscious. Many people have a conscious relationship with their thoughts and feel comfortable and at home communicating rationally. Many are adept at articulating their thoughts both to themselves and others. Fewer people may be aware of the information they receive through other processing channels – for example, in the form of body perceptions, emotions and imagery. It is thought-provoking how much information from our intelligence system is often lost that way. And again, there is the opportunity of practice. It is possible to practise verbalising perceptions from the body, verbalising emotions, inner images and other inner experiences. From a cybernetic perspective, it is important to clarify that all processing channels contribute equally valuable information. Nothing is worth more or worth less. A body perception thus contributes information that is as important as a rational thought.

If we want to be able to become better at receiving information from more than one processing channel at a time as a human being – and as a professional – it is crucial to practise our ability to orient ourselves in the supramodal space, where it is possible to receive information from several processing channels at a time. It requires in-depth mindfulness training and practice to be in more contemplative states, where the normal awake, one-dimensional consciousness steps a little into the background for a while. It is a method that is enriching for everyone to practise, especially when working professionally with other people. It is a practice that is different from our cultural background, a practice that requires elaboration, teaching and training – in this perspective, Ole Vedfelt calls it *apprenticeship*.

The Person Model

In cybernetic psychology, the normal consciousness is called the personal self. The personal self is the subjective experience or self-perception. In the cybernetic psychological perspective, it is assumed that the personal self only makes up an infinitely small part of our total consciousness. The total consciousness is called the cybernetic self (Hansen 2015 pp. 248–250). The cybernetic self is considered the highest level of human consciousness. Everything is included (Vedfelt 2002 p. 264). The personality is believed to have self-regulating qualities, and the higher levels are believed to be able to regulate the lower levels of the personality. Thus, Ole Vedfelt writes, "I have described the personality as a self-regulating and multi-layered cybernetic system, where the more complex levels have the highest information capacity and can regulate less complex levels" (Vedfelt 2002 p. 312). The image I formed in my mind when I was introduced to these concepts was of the cybernetic self as a kind of umbrella. An umbrella – the cybernetic self – that embraced the whole personality. From the umbrella, I imagined, were hanging a lot of threads that also interfered with each other crosswise. One of these threads is the personal self and thus forms part of the personality. If we tip the umbrella a little to one side, all the threads will move and be affected by the new position of the umbrella. In other words, our entire personality network will be affected by what is going on at the highest level – here described pictorially. According to Ole Vedfelt, the personality is self-regulating, which means that it works to create balance in the overall system. The personality has many layers. The more complex levels of the personality have the highest information capacity and are able to regulate less-complex levels. What is important here is to understand that, in this perspective, it is perceived as problematic if, in therapy, you try at a 'low level' of the personality to change a 'higher level's' attempt at self-regulation (Vedfelt 1996 pp. 138–139). This is what happens if, with the help of the rational part of our consciousness – which, we remember, constitutes a smaller part of the total consciousness – we try to make a wilful change to what is perceived as a problem for the personal self.

Let us imagine that the person experiencing anxiety has heard that it is irrational to experience anxiety. The person with anxiety may have heard that one 'just' has to learn to think differently about anxiety. Then, the person thinks that, somehow, there must be something wrong with the way he or she thinks about his or her anxiety. That person uses his or her will to think differently about anxiety. Tells him- or herself that it is irrational. That it will go away when he or she thinks differently about anxiety. Or neglects the anxiety. We can try to think differently about anxiety. We can try to tell ourselves that anxiety is harmless, and that it disappears by itself. But it does not remove the source of anxiety. It does not remove the cause of the anxiety.

In the cybernetic personality model, it is essential to understand that our personal self – our rational subjective experience of being a whole human being – is understood as a practical, way-finding level of the personality. Thus, the personal self constitutes a lower level than the cybernetic self. The personal self is perceived as the most important subpersonality but still just a part; not the whole (ibid. pp. 259–264). The phenomenon of subpersonality must be perceived as a naturally occurring phenomenon in a normally functioning psyche. Subpersonalities are inner representations, and their activity relieves our consciousness. While we think abstractly and purposefully and solve rational problems, the subpersonalities, for example, automatically take care of our emotional and bodily aspects of communication (ibid. pp. 264–276). The development of subpersonalities will, in many cases, start in the relationship with the mother and lead to a 'mother-subpersonality'. Do not many of us know what our 'inner mother' will think about the things we do, even if our real mother, in our adult life, does not – physically – play a direct role as when we were children? As our development continues, we will build new inner subpersonalities from our relationship with our father and/or caregivers, siblings, peers, teachers and other significant people in our lives.

The Role of Anxiety

Anxiety is assigned different meanings in different theoretical perspectives. The theoretical perspective is going to determine how we think about anxiety and what role we assign to anxiety. The theoretical perspective determines how we perceive anxiety, talk about anxiety, encounter or do not encounter anxiety and how we relate to and deal with anxiety.

The most common perception I have encountered is that anxiety is a symptom that points to a disorder of the personality; a fault, so to speak. It is a cognitive perception of anxiety that anxiety is a disorder of the personality (Mørch & Rosenberg 2005 p. 84). Another perception of anxiety comes from Danish philosopher Søren Kierkegaard, who describes anxiety as an existential part of life, an existential part of being human; something we all encounter – to varying degrees and in different ways, but inevitably. The American existential psychotherapist Irvin D. Yalom is strongly inspired by Kierkegaard and calls anxiety one of the basic conditions of life (Yalom 1998). In cybernetic psychology, anxiety is understood as a condition or an emotion; a state that must be seen as created by the cybernetic self in an attempt at self-regulation; an emotion that has the effect of 'shutting off' and may have an inhibiting and limiting effect on our way of life. Among other things, we see many people who have experienced or are experiencing anxiety developing a form of evasive or avoidant behaviour in an attempt not to activate the anxiety in their system. Let us examine here what consequences it will have when we bring the cybernetic perspective into play. What significance does it have for our perception of anxiety? And how does this particular perspective affect the way we relate to and deal with anxiety in therapy? And in life in general?

Psychotherapeutic Method: The Supramodal Space

In cybernetic integrated psychotherapy, the overall method is that we strive to orient ourselves in the supramodal space – that is, the space which, on the one hand, is difficult to define, as language has limited capacity, and which, on the other hand, seems clear once the supramodal space becomes a personal experience. When we orient ourselves in the supramodal space, we are not limited to receiving information from one processing channel. We are not limited by our one-dimensional way of experiencing. Our path to the supramodal space consists of training, teaching, sparring and more training, over and over again.

Our path into supramodal space is through the body, through our breathing, through the space of consciousness, through the heart and through accepting that everything seems to be changeable. On our way to supramodal space, we practise as neutral a behaviour as possible, as free from prejudice as possible. We imagine that it is possible to become like a mirror. A mirror that does not prefer any content over anything else; a mirror that does not mind what might occur and also does not want anything special to occur; a mirror from which we strive to look at the world as it is. In the supramodal space, we experience being in a state of consciousness where we know that we are in contact with ourselves at the same time as we are in contact with the other who, in the therapeutic space, is represented by the client, and we are open to whatever may arise and manifest itself in the client and in our own system. When I meet a client who experiences anxiety, I focus on creating security and trust in the relationship and also examine where there is an experience of 'safe places' in the body. If there are no safe places, I start working with the client to establish a sense of safe places in the body. It is one of the techniques to create a concrete bodily and mental contact with the client's resources, so that it is always possible to return to safe places. Another way of working which is integrated into the cybernetic perspective is to work with the dreams of the night. We do this because dreams always deal with what is important to us (Vedfelt 2012 pp. 51–56). In case of anxiety in the client, it is not uncommon to have nightmare-like dreams as well. The dreams are often experienced as 'bad' dreams by the client, but gradually the client will discover that, even if a dream is experienced as unpleasant, there are no 'bad' dreams as such. The client builds an experience through the therapeutic work that it is always possible to find a resource in any dream. There are many good reasons to take dreams seriously in therapeutic work. In this context, my focus is on how dreams can help to build contact with the dreamer's personal resources. In therapy, we spend time building the necessary internal resources to slowly approach what is difficult – in this context, anxiety. It is important to tread carefully and, in a gentle way, approach the anxiety and constantly orient ourselves in the supramodal space to observe and be alert to what signals the client will send. My experience is that, when a client comes to me because of anxiety, the goal for the client is to 'get rid of the anxiety' and preferably as soon as possible. My focus as a therapist is to build up the relationship so that he or she feels safe, to build up the client's personality so that it becomes safe, flexible and spacious enough to take in more of the essence of anxiety and meet it as a natural part of being human. Here, I experience that the concept of 'anxiety for anxiety' is slowly fading away, which is a necessary step to meet the anxiety and start up a dialogue with it. Now, curiosity can arise as to what the anxiety *wants*, what its purpose is, and this approach replaces the desire for the anxiety just to go away as soon as possible. I find this to be a longer-term solution – to face the anxiety and learn from it, rather than pushing it away and working to make it go away, as it seems the anxiety will always return, which can lead to an experience of discouragement if no stable and balanced contact has been built up with the personal resources that must be used to move forward in the process of meeting anxiety as a condition of life.

One way to enter into dialogue with inner psychological content is through externalisation. One possible technique is to externalise psychological content by working with drawing therapy as a method (Løvdal 2015 pp. 73–77). In cybernetically integrated psychotherapy, many years of experience have been accumulated by letting the client draw elements from dreams or draw a bodily experience. It is working on a different level of consciousness, in a different state, through a different way of experiencing. The client has crayons and can let the hand speak instead of the mouth. It is easier for the client to be allowed to express an inner experience, state or feeling in the drawing therapy. I often hear that it is "easier to share an inner experience when I am allowed to draw it" or that it is "easier for me to relate to my bodily experience when I have drawn it and can look at it". In relation to working with anxiety, I find that drawing therapy is very beneficial. It can provide an opportunity to be allowed to express, for example, emotions, body experiences and dreams on paper and perhaps discover that, along the way, something is changing.

In summary, I have now mentioned the overall method of cybernetic integrated psychotherapy, which is to orient oneself in the supramodal space in many ways and at many levels. In addition, four techniques are mentioned, all of which can be integrated into cybernetic psychotherapeutic work – namely, the conscious building of the therapeutic relationship, establishing or creating contact with safe places in the body, dreamwork and drawing therapy.

I understand working psychotherapeutically as a form of play or dance, where the client's creativity is an active participant in influencing which techniques are involved. In this perspective, being in an interaction between different states of consciousness is beneficial for the therapy. The above techniques do not necessarily have to be included in the order in which they are presented here, nor is this an exhaustive list of techniques used in cybernetic integrated psychotherapy. The essential thing in this context is to exercise the supramodal ability.

Meeting the Anxious Person

When, as a newly qualified teacher, I faced a student for the first time who was so full of anxiety inside that she could not master even the smallest everyday tasks, I felt a degree of paralysis of action. Sometimes, she was the bubbliest and most talented student in the class and, other days, she did not even dare to go to the toilet alone. Something in me was scared. I did not know what to do. I consulted more experienced colleagues: No help. I went to my leader: No help. I decided that she should not be alone and made myself available to her. She told me what she experienced. She told me her stories. Her trauma. She shook. She cried. She laughed. As time went on, it became clearer and clearer to me that I was lacking knowledge. I lacked sparring. I made my ears available. I made my empathy available. I let my light shine without putting a bushel over it. And it burned. I burned. And I burned out.

My path became a theoretical superstructure in educational psychology, which was fruitful and instructive and laid the foundation for my professional understanding of educational and psychological topics. But I did not really become more competent in the practical meeting with the student, the citizen, the client or what we call people we meet in our working life. I was hungry for more, which is why I trained as a psychotherapist at the Vedfelt Institute and learned to work methodically and practically from a cybernetic psychological perspective. You could say that I went into apprenticeship as a human being and as a professional. I experienced getting better at my work with other people. I found that I became better able to take care of my own personal resources. It dawned on me that it is not actually possible, or beneficial for that matter, to try to help a human being if we are 'in deficit' ourselves. For me, it is imperative to build up a 'personal surplus' if we are to do something good for other people. Internal sustainability is essential to take externally sustainable action in order to help other people. It is important and it is underestimated.

Many people who experience anxiety are not aware that it is anxiety they have encountered. It may be a little enigmatic, but I think it is true. Anyone who experiences anxiety may go to their own doctor. They may tell of chest tightness, lack of energy, fatigue, dry mouth, sweaty hands, inexplicable experiences of sudden cold or heat arising in the body. Or they may give up in resignation. And they may come to life in the meeting with the doctor in the hope of receiving help. The doctor examines everything that could be suspected as physical illness, which of course is important. But, for those who experience anxiety, it can unfortunately increase the experience of anxiety and may even cause frustration and discouragement. I have had clients with anxiety problems who, for a long time, were 'banging their heads against a wall'. The frustrations of the client may be unconscious and may cause a form of stress in the body. Here, dreamwork can be a resource. Thus, a client who experienced disabling anxiety during the investigation phase had this dream:

> I see myself walking in some long hallways. I think I'm at a hospital. It is very white. I pass nurses dressed in white. White-dressed doctors. I'm trying to get in touch with some of them. I seek eye contact, but do not succeed. I'm trying to say something. My lips move, but no sound comes out of my mouth. I wake up with palpitations and am completely sweaty.

The therapist meeting this client on the basis of the experiences of the dream-self is absolutely crucial for the client's increased self-understanding and self-insight. Let us keep in mind that anxiety comes in varying degrees. A touch of anxiety is completely natural and beneficial if an aggressive barking dog comes running straight towards you and you have to take to your heels. Where anxiety reaches another level of severity, with life-threatening consequences, is when anxiety occurs for no apparent reason. Or, as Kierkegaard wrote: "Anxiety is the fear of nothing". It is the severe anxiety. In cybernetic psychology, it is 'anxiety as an emotion or a condition' that inhibits the unfolding of life which requires some form of treatment. It requires a supportive environment. It requires backing-up. It requires someone to believe in you, believe that what you experience is what you experience; someone who shows you that it is possible to get better. It is a journey, and it can be a long journey that can bear fruit and lead to healing.

The Potential of Anxiety

It is not unusual for anxiety to occur in different life transitions. There are several different suggestions on how life transitions can lead to different types of crises in humans. I shall here confine myself to mentioning four common life transitions, which relate to adulthood, and which Ole Vedfelt has pointed out in his books: From apprentice to journeyman, parenthood as entry into a master role, the professional master crisis and the midway turn (Vedfelt 2002 pp. 337–357). When anxiety takes hold of a human being, it can be experienced as if it 'comes out of thin air'. A completely normal, manageable task, such as peeling carrots, laying the table or drinking coffee with colleagues can trigger anxiety. That, I think, is important. As I see it, it shows the inexplicable when we talk about anxiety. It can be difficult to understand why anxiety arises in just that context and not in other contexts. It is important to understand that those who experience anxiety will not be able to answer that very question. And maybe it is not that important either. The important thing is probably that the person who wants to meet the person who experiences anxiety is able to 'be with' him or her. Without explaining. Not trying to assess. No judgement. Just being. Without turning away. Anxiety can be overwhelming and disabling. It is not my purpose to disprove that fact. Still, I would like to try to gently point out that anxiety can also have a function for personal development. Recognising the fact that anxiety is an emotion, I would like to emphasise here the cybernetic perception of anxiety as a condition which the cybernetic self 'initiates' in an attempt to get the personal self to create a necessary life change that may seem unwelcome, disturbing and confusing but benefits the whole of the personality. Experience from cybernetic integrated psychotherapy is that anxiety can arise to make the personal self aware that 'there is something important you have overlooked'. And this 'something' is essential for you and for the life you live. When we are overwhelmed by anxiety in a life transition, it makes sense in the cybernetic perspective to examine what the anxiety wants. Anxiety often creates so much restlessness that the person who experiences anxiety may feel compelled to seek help to deal with the anxiety, to deal with life, the life situation.

My hope is that the person who experiences anxiety will meet a professional therapist who will not turn away. One who does not become afraid of anxiety. One who does not just want the anxiety to go away. One who dares – with cautious curiosity and careful openness – to ask, "What will the anxiety show you?" I hope that the anxious person will meet a resource-oriented professional adult who believes that anxiety holds transformational possibilities, one who dares to walk the line with the one who suffers, as long as it may be necessary and beneficial.

The Therapeutic Journey

The therapeutic journey is to tell one's story, one's biography, again and again, in several ways – new ways, old ways, different ways. Recognise and gain greater insight into the life that became yours. And, over time, discover that seemingly insoluble issues can change character. I experience that transformation is one of the gifts it is possible to become aware of by choosing to work deeply psychologically with one's problems and/or life crises with the help of a qualified psychotherapist. On the journey of life, we need to create meaning. Meaning in what has happened to us. Meaning in the 'now' that is ours. Meaning that can somehow help to create direction in our lives. I think most people – for some, perhaps, just in very brief glimpses – have experienced or are experiencing an inner longing for 'something'. Something meaningful. Something higher. Something deeper. Something else. *Something*. Generally, we project our longing out into the world, on to other people. Maybe we think, "he's charismatic" or "she has a special insight", "How lucky he is", "She is so incredibly enriching to be together with". We might also think, "I do not like her". We are attracted. We are repulsed. We project our own unconscious psychic content on to others. The other. We are somehow looking for some kind of meaning in 'something', in the other, in things, in knowledge, in what we do. And, somehow, it is probably the necessary step on the road – on the journey of life. It is necessary to meet our shadow, our antipathies, our sympathies. For many people, therapy is extremely beneficial for just this. It is necessary to meet all our emotions – including those we prefer to avoid meeting, such as anxiety. It is necessary to discover that we contain sides we are proud of and sides we are less proud of. Telling our story seems necessary to achieve increased self-awareness, and here we meet one of life's great paradoxes. All stories must be told, to acknowledge oneself. But where is the real meaning? Where do we get our longing for 'something else' – 'something more' fulfilled? It seems to me that, in some peculiar way, the real meaning lies behind one's language – behind the possibility of the narrative. Beyond the speech. And, at the same time, it does not seem possible to get there without the words.

A Possible Further Journey

After a long psychotherapeutic course, in which I had told my stories from every conceivable angle and through many possible processing channels, I experienced that, where I was now in my life, the stories seemed to ebb away.

The words ran out. Anxiety felt recognised. It relaxed. Patterns changed. Life became different.

I travelled that wave for a while. Over time, I could see that what I knew from myself, I began to meet and recognise in other people. Perhaps it is a universal human process to be forced to stop from time to time and listen. In cybernetic psychotherapeutic work, the individual's ability for introspection is trained. To feel the body. Feel the breath. The heart. The emotions. Feel what the individual wants. And what it does not want. This training of our ability for introspection can lead us in many directions. I found that new questions arose. What is the meaning of life? The real meaning of my life? Of human life as such? It was as if I was experiencing another pressure from inside for 'something more'. Not an unpleasant pressure as I knew it from the anxiety. But a pressure, a longing, an urge for individuation.

My path became a path into meditation and creativity. I think that, even on such a journey, we need a supervisor – a teacher – just as much as we need a psychotherapist on the therapeutic journey. For me, meditation and mindfulness form a navigable journey to gain better contact with the unconscious part of ourselves and integrate larger parts of our cybernetic self. I imagine it is a journey that never ends. And that the journey is a goal in itself.

References

Flachs, E.M., Eriksen, L., Koch, M.B., Ryd, J.T., Dibba, E., Skov-Ettrup, L., Juel, K., Statens Institut for Folkesundhed, Syddansk Universitet. (2015) *Sygdomsbyrden i Danmark – sygdomme*. Sundhedsstyrelsen, Copenhagen.
Hansen, Torben (Ed.) (2015) *Det ubevidstes potentiale – kybernetisk psykologi i anvendelse*. Frydenlund, Copenhagen.
Heidegger, Martin (2007) *Væren og tid*. Forlaget Klim. Copenhagen.
Løvdal, Henriette (2015) Integration – om at integrere forskellige metoder i den psykoterapeutiske praksis, in Hansen. T., *Det ubevidstes potentiale*. Frydenlund, Copenhagen.

Mørch, Merete M. & Rosenberg, Nicole K. (2005) *Kognitiv terapi*. Hans Reitzels Forlag, Copenhagen.

Staubrand, Jens (2014) *Søren Kierkegaard Angst*. SK Books, Søren Kierkegaard Kulturproduktion, Copenhagen.

Vedfelt, Ole (1996) *Bevidsthed. Bevidsthedens niveauer*. Gyldendal, Copenhagen.

Vedfelt, Ole (2002) *Ubevidst intelligens. Du ved mere end du tror*. Gyldendal, Copenhagen.

Vedfelt, Ole (2012) *Din guide til drømmenes verden*. Gyldendal. Copenhagen.

Yalom, Irvin D. (1998) *Eksistentiel psykoterapi*. Hans Reitzels Forlag. Copenhagen.

Yalom, Irvin D. (2008) *Som at se på solen – at leve med døden*. Hans Reitzels Forlag, Copenhagen.

Yalom, Irvin D. (2009) *Terapiens essens. Åbent brev til en ny generation af terapeuter og patienter*. Hans Reitzels Forlag. Copenhagen.

9

Integration

On Integrating Methods in Psychotherapeutic Practice

Henriette Løvdal

In this chapter, I focus on cybernetic psychotherapy in practice. I will examine, in particular, the integration of methods from many different therapeutic movements into one coherent form of therapy. Studies show that, while few therapeutic schools openly recognise other schools' discoveries, most therapists integrate different methods in their practice. But what does it mean to integrate therapeutic methods in practice? How, in an integrated therapy, do we form a coherent theoretical basis for the methodological choices to be made in practice? And how do we establish the clear concepts and terminology necessary to reflect upon the practice. The chapter will present a view of cybernetic therapy and method integration as they unfold during sessions – as well as a theoretical understanding of why and how different therapeutic approaches may be integrated in cybernetic therapy.

The Need for an Integrated Psychotherapy

Putting therapeutic practice into words is no easy task. The therapeutic situation is a complex one, and all our senses and means of perception are involved in the process – bodily expressions and experiences, cognitive functions, memories, inner images, prejudices and dreams. It is a personal process, but, for the client, it takes place in relation to another person, someone to whom the client does not usually have any personal connection. Small changes in intonation and body language contribute to the process, in which both the conscious and unconscious parts of our minds are hard at work. Among other things, this complexity is what makes therapeutic practice so endlessly fascinating – moments that might seem simple but cannot be planned, or when a difficult task is suddenly transformed into an easy one.

Working therapeutically from a single method is in itself a complex thing. So why add even more complexity by beginning to bring together many different approaches – and the theories behind them?

In the last few years, a number of studies have been carried out trying to prove the effect of various forms of therapy. Comparing their results, we find that therapy works – but also that there is, in fact, no appreciable difference between the effects of the different forms of therapy (Bateman & Holmes 2002, 14, 28; O'Leary &

DOI: 10.4324/9781003360247-10

Murphy 2006, 3). Even so, in literature on the subject we find quite heavy lines drawn between various therapeutic schools of thought – lines often deepened by scientific studies documenting the effect of this *particular* therapeutic approach. In the aftermath of Freud and Jung, it has become almost a tradition to uphold a rivalry between the various approaches. As the American psychologist Jerold Gold has also noted, one often gets the impression that the opposing schools of thought would rather look for inspiration in completely different fields of study – such as quantum physics, neuroscience or literary studies – than deign to find it in each other (Stricker & Gold 1993, 6).

In practice, however, the various schools of thought are less distinctly divided. Many psychologists and therapists have pursued several different courses of education and employ several forms of therapy in their daily work. An American study has shown that the majority of therapists and psychologists define their methods as 'eclectic' – that is, combining various therapeutic methods and understandings (Norcross & Prochaska 2007, 2–3). However, even though the integration of different methods takes place daily in a relatively uncomplicated manner, it is – when seen from a scientific point of view – rather difficult to get a grasp on it. How do we know that an integrative therapy will not simply be a jumble of the therapist's personal preferences and chance experience? How can we – working with ourselves or as therapists – take a reflective approach to the integration of different therapeutic methods? And how do we deal with the fact that many of those ways of meeting clients which seem to work best are founded on theories that are vastly dissimilar – sometimes even polar opposites?

These ought to be important questions to consider for everyone who practises any sort of combination of several therapeutic approaches. After all, what good is a clear and coherent theory if practice is always random and disorganised? Cybernetic psychology offers an example of how to reflect on and work with this type of integration.

On Integrating

The word 'integration' comes from the Latin *integratio*, making whole, either in the sense of 'recreating' or 'renewing'. In the context of this chapter, the word is used to mean 'creating a new whole'. As a reflection of different ways of perceiving this 'whole', integration research distinguishes between three ways of integrating (e.g. O'Leary & Murphy 2006, p. 4):

1 Technical eclecticism.
2 Theoretical integration.
3 The common factor approach.

Technical eclecticism denotes a therapy with a primarily pragmatic approach in which the new whole consists of the therapy situation with its various choices. This concept was introduced by the South African psychologist Arnold A. Lazarus, and it describes a practice in which therapists employ techniques from various schools of thought without taking the theoretical implications into consideration – and without necessarily agreeing with the theoretical bases. It is, then, a sort of combination of methods. Focus will often be on finding the best method of treatment for the client's specific symptoms.

Theoretical integration attempts to incorporate various therapeutic approaches on a theoretical level in order to create a coherent theoretical whole to support practice. In other words, it is the attempt to synthesise theories in order to create a new frame of reference, or to create a completely new theory that can use new words to encompass other theories, the methods of which can then be understood in a new context. Such an operation can be very difficult, not least because many of the therapeutic schools of thought are often in opposition to each other on a philosophical level. Because of this, critics often claim that the result is more of a 'theory porridge' than an actual theory (London 1988). On the other hand, American psychologist John C. Norcross and psychiatrist James O. Prochaska consider that the act of theoretical integration expresses a positive attempt to override the fragmented, confusing and contradictory jungle of methods and theories and create a 'trans-theoretical therapy' (Norcross & Prochaska 2007, xv, 1). In Denmark, Ole Vedfelt has established cybernetic psychology based on a wish to create a sort of 'umbrella theory' able to hold within it the advantages of various psychological approaches (Vedfelt 2001, 294).

The *common factor approach* is built upon the observation that certain factors are common to nearly all therapeutic schools of thought, and on the idea that it might be these common elements, rather than the individual therapies' particular characteristics or theoretical foundations, that make up the effective ingredients. It is generally agreed upon that essential common factors exist. However, what these are and which are the most important have been the subject of ongoing discussion since the American psychologist Saul Rosenzweig began to take an interest in the matter, as early as the mid-1930s. The common factors most often mentioned may tentatively be categorised thus:[1]

- The therapeutic relationship (the creation of an alliance between therapist and client).
- The characteristics of the client (e.g. her or his ability to have positive expectations).
- The characteristics of the therapist (e.g. his or her powers of empathy or ability to inspire the client with hope).
- The treatment structure (that the therapy progresses in a safe and transparent manner, or that the sessions contain reassuring and familiar rituals).
- Clear processes of change (e.g. practising new ways of reacting in specific situations, or giving the client a regular outlet for strong emotions).
- Rational basis (that there is a comprehensible conceptual frame within which to think and speak, be it scientific or spiritual. In this respect, it is more important for the theory to be clear and accessible than for it to be true).

The Complexity of Practice

I have sketched out an academic way of categorising therapeutic integration approaches. In practice, most integrative therapies contain a little from each, in various degrees and combinations. This is, in my opinion, a good thing. If, for example, one were to imagine an entirely technical eclecticism, one would quickly meet with some difficulty: New studies show that there is no one specific method most suitable for one particular symptom (Stricker & Gold 1993, 32). What, then, are the selection criteria used in this technical eclecticism? Are choices based on the therapist's intuition or on the chance courses or seminars he or she has attended? Or does coherence in the course of therapy in fact come from the therapist's personal characteristics and intuitive focus on creating, for example, a good alliance, as described in the common factor approach?

In a further attempt to put the complex practice into words and theory, the American psychologist Stanley B. Messer suggests a fourth method of integration called *assimilative integration* (Messer, in Norcross & Goldfried 1992, 151). Here, the therapist (or person working with her or his personal development) maintains a solid foundation in a specific theoretical framework but is willing to, and interested in, assimilating techniques and understandings from other schools of thought. This ensures a clarity of theory, because the theoretical implications of the integration are not taken into account. A clear theoretical background provides a feeling of safety. I would presume that this is, in practice, a very common way of integrating.

Cybernetic theory expresses a wish for theoretical integration but, thanks to its basis in the systematic approach and information theory, it is sufficiently open and flexible to support a very high degree of integration of new knowledge. This is very useful in a reality in which new theories and methods constantly appear, and in which technological progress makes so much new research into psychological and neurological matters possible. The necessity of considering a great deal of complexity and different approaches and perspectives is part of the theory. This may be seen as an attempt to embrace the practical complexity rather than simplifying it.

In an attempt to describe how the integration of different methods takes place, the British theorists Anthony Bateman and Jeremy Holmes have described another important element in connection with this: They speak of a "practical flexibility in the mature therapist" (Bateman & Holmes 2002, 3). In Aristotelian concepts, one would say that *phronesis* (practical virtue) illustrates that knowledge of therapy cannot, in practice, be reduced to a *techne* (craft; Falkum 2008).

Apprenticeship

So, how can we incorporate the idea of *phronesis*, or "practical flexibility in the mature therapist", in a theoretical frame? Studies have shown that, when it comes to the ability to establish an effective relationship with another person, experienced therapists from different schools of thought are more similar to each other than are inexperienced and experienced therapists from the same school (Bateman &

Holmes 2002, 14, 28; O'Leary & Murphy 2006, 3). This seems to suggest that something occurs in practice in the therapeutic relationship and situation that is not described in the textbooks.

An important element of the training to become a cybernetic psychotherapist is apprenticeship. Lectures alone are not enough; it is necessary to work continuously through the roles of client, therapist, assistant or observer in many variations of the therapeutic situation. When we learn something through practical experience, we employ a learning process quite fundamental to human beings, parallel to the way in which young children learn (Vedfelt 2002, 78). Situations in which human beings communicate are full of nuances of body language, emotions, thoughts, words and intonation. In fact, new research shows that the greater part of the information picked up by our minds is perceived subconsciously (Vedfelt 2002, 21–25). This means that practical experience is extremely important in the therapeutic relationship. By strongly emphasising the principle of apprenticeship, cybernetics tries to bring practice into theory, thereby lessening the distance between textbook and therapy room. Cybernetic psychology implies that there *must* be a certain degree of intuition or phronesis/practical flexibility in the therapy. There probably is in all therapy situations, but here it is being explicitly stated and actively worked with. Therapy is an extremely complex situation and cannot be reduced to a rational analysis of cognitive processes, even though reason and analysis are definitely necessary.

In the following, I will present part of a course of therapy. This sort of case description is, of course, only an impression of a past colourful phenomenon.[2] But the purpose is to give an *impression* of how cybernetic integration of different forms of therapy can look in practice. The first case description spans a period of eight months, with sessions every week for the first two months and every second week after that. I mean to sketch out one of the thematic threads of the client Christian's progress. The description of the interaction that took place must, of course, also be seen as a sort of sketch.

Christian in the Tree House

Christian is in his late 40s. When I speak to him on the phone for the first time, he tells me that he would like to meet in order to do something about the discomfort he feels when speaking in front of a crowd. When he arrives for his first therapy session, however, I gather that he has not come of his own accord. As Christian expresses it, "my wife sent me" because she thinks he ought to make a speech at his eldest daughter's graduation party. He has never liked speaking in public or getting too much attention in general. But he has never viewed this as any great problem either. At least, not until a couple of years ago, when he met his current wife, Betina, who asks a number of things of him that he is not used to being asked.

We talk about that a bit, and I ask Christian what he thinks about going to therapy because another person felt he should. Christian determines with himself that he simply wants some help to figure out how he would like to celebrate his daughter.

He gets the idea that he will write her a letter, which he will present to her and which she can then read later, by herself. For the remainder of the session, we work on how he can explain this decision to Betina in a good way – and explain that it is his decision to make. After that, I do not actually expect to see Christian again.

A couple of weeks later, however, he calls me up. He says: "Right, there was something else, as well. There are those shaking fits. Maybe we could also do something about them". He tells me that, in the last five years, since the divorce from his first wife, in fact, he has suffered from inexplicable shaking fits at regular intervals. He has been examined, but the doctors have not been able to locate any physical problem and have put the issue down to mental strain. Christian himself has an unpleasant fantasy that he might be going mad.

The next couple of sessions we spend talking about what it is he feels when the fits arrive. We also talk about how serious they are in various situations and what has happened, and what he has felt in the time immediately before their arrival. Christian says that it is very difficult to explain. He does not feel that there are any particular bodily sensations before the fits or any particular events leading up to them. His body simply starts shaking, and he becomes very afraid. It makes it worse that he has no idea when the problem will arise. I explain to him a little about the nervous system and about what happens physically when the amygdala is activated and anxiety sets in. Christian says that is nice to be given a logical explanation. Understanding that there are natural functions at work and that he is not going crazy gives him some peace of mind. We talk about good, realistic responses he can give himself when the thought "I am going mad" appears.

In the first session, my point of departure was an enquiring, phenomenological approach, because I agree with cybernetic psychotherapy (and with most forms of therapy, really) that it is important not to let my opinion or interpretation of the situation disturb the client's own judgement. I was particularly conscious of this in connection with the question of whether to begin a therapy course when, in fact, Christian has felt that his wife sent him to me. It was important that he did not feel as if he had to adjust to the opinions he sensed from his (female) therapist, but rather had the opportunity to examine his own feelings and thoughts. In this way, I tried the best I could to create a trustful relationship in which there was room for curiosity and open-minded investigation of Christian's feelings.

After this, we approached Christian's anxiety symptoms through technical eclecticism. He was afraid of the symptoms, and empirical analyses show that psychoeducation – that is, the explanation of what happens in the brain, nervous system and body in general – is helpful in many such cases. Experience from cognitive therapy was integrated with mindfulness and a systemic psychodynamic approach. In Christian's case, we supported his ability to refrain from being carried away by the physical expressions and to observe in an accepting manner when the overwhelming bodily conditions appeared. The purpose of this was to enable him to take a step back from his emotions. Behavioural training, for which cognitive therapy is known, provided a practical method for handling the negative thoughts ("I am going mad"). Making Christian aware, through analysis, of the underlying thoughts which contributed to controlling the pattern involving the fits provided a background for practising other, less destructive thought responses (such as "experiencing this anxiety is unpleasant, but it will pass").

A couple of times, I tried asking Christian about his bodily sensations in the moment, but he clearly did not like this, and he answered that he felt nothing in particular and that no particular thoughts appeared, either. At some point, however, he told me that he felt uncomfortable before the fits began.

H: Alright, so you feel uncomfortable. Can you describe how?

C: Just uncomfortable. [He crosses his arms.]

H: Okay, there is some experience that it can be a good idea to look into the bodily sensations, too. It can be worked into a sort of tool for handling the uncomfortable feelings. So try to describe to me where and how you feel the discomfort in your body?

C: Well, it feels uncomfortable, of course …

H: So which body sensations do you experience right now?

C: Nothing. I actually don't feel anything at all. [His right leg, which is crossed over his left, twitches lightly, like a small, almost invisible kick.]

I (finally) focus on something else and ask him:

H: So how does it feel to sit here and talk about it?

C: Well, it's not very pleasant, of course. But if it can help me get better, then … [he pauses for a moment and looks thoughtful] … you know, I just remembered that I actually had a fit like that when I was a kid, too. It happened in connection with a nightmare. Because I often had the same nightmare again and again. And I normally never dream of anything, I don't think. But it was always something about me sitting in our tree house, which dad had built, and some kind of dragon, or whatever it was, tried to get to me and pull me out to kill me. But it was only able to just reach my clothes. The clothes were completely shredded.

I realise that, by pressuring Christian to examine and describe his symptoms, I have repeated the behaviour he experiences from his new wife, and that the dragon from the dream he has remembered is a pretty common archetypal dream symbol in connection with negative experiences with mothers or women in general. I ask some more questions about the dream and, at one point, I also ask, smiling a little:

H: And I'm a bit like that dragon, trying to pull you out of your tree house with all my questions?

C: [Lights up and smiles.] No … or, well, yeah, in a way. It's as if I always need to do all these things I can't live up to. It's like I can't ever be left in peace.

H: Okay, try to describe the dragon to me, then.

C: It's sort of brown. And it's kind of hysterical … women are so damned hysterical, too. [He laughs a little.]

H: How old do you think you were when you had that dream?

C: Maybe eight or nine years old. Probably eight.

H: So what happened when you were eight years old?

C: Well, I guess my parents were getting divorced about that time. But it can't be about that. I've always been happy that they got a divorce. My dad was an alcoholic. With the hysteria, it's more my ex-wife I'm thinking about. She's hysterical in this kind of controlled manner. It was scary when she first started planning our divorce, I couldn't say anything, just had to do as I was told if I wanted to see the kids.

H: How does it feel to sit here and talk about these things?

C: It's actually really nice to talk about it. It's like I feel calmer now.

In the process, Christian makes a drawing of the dragon. It is a relief to him to see the dragon on paper, the feeling being externalised. It now looks more sad than angry.

We then talk about the feeling of being left in peace and having a safe 'tree house' of one's own. Christian associates it with spending time in the woods with his grandmother's dog, which he did a lot as a kid. I ask him to describe his bodily sensations when reimagining these situations. He describes a fluffy, light blue "cloud" in his chest. A very pleasant sensation, that grows stronger as he makes a drawing of the cloud. We look at the drawing for a long time. Some sessions later, he tells me that, for the first time in a long while, he has gone for several weeks straight without being afraid of the fits.

When I first asked Christian to examine his bodily sensations, his feelings were clearly expressed in his answer ("I don't feel anything"), in his body language (arms crossed, leg twitching) and in my system as a therapist (a tension in my diaphragm and a light, prickly sensation in my hands). In traditional psychoanalysis, this would have been termed *resistance*. In cybernetic psychotherapy, we see this as a sign that the client is not being met on the right level of organisation. This means that the client is not met in the most appropriate manner, and that the therapist needs to move the process on to a higher level. In this case, I moved our focus away from the symptom to how it felt to talk about the symptom.

The idea of levels of organisation is part of the cybernetic theory of consciousness.[3] Another way to approach the situation might have been asking Christian to repeat and enlarge his leg twitch, asking him to make it an actual kick and examine how that felt, thus changing the *process channel* to focus on bodily sensations – giving room for feelings such as anger and resentment.

In accordance with cybernetic theory, it was important to strengthen Christian's own resources during our process. His positive bodily sensations were given as much weight as the 'problems'. Every time we worked with the uncomfortable sensations, I made sure that we also touched upon safer and more pleasant sensations. Within cybernetic apprenticeship, we often use the image of 'circling' the difficult subjects to look at them from various angles and in various ways. Integrated psychotherapy can be used to ensure that one does not always approach a problem from the same perspective. Within cybernetic psychology, we talk of process channels – different functions of perception and cognition – for example, bodily sensations, thoughts, visual expressions, sounds, touches and body language. These various functions are a natural part of our experiences, memories and learning processes and, as such, they are also part of the more difficult feelings which these may influence. With this in mind, cybernetic psychotherapy is very apparently an attempt at theoretical integration. It is a kind of new systemic approach in which the relationships of various elements with each other are expressed in a conceptuality that is cybernetic, because it has to do with levels of information processing and mind organisation.

In the latter years of their marriage, Christian's relationship with his first wife had been characterised by routines and an atmosphere that was polite but not very warm. She had been in charge of planning and the house. When she left him, it had been difficult because he missed the children, but he did not miss her. He had thought that there was a pattern to him being attracted to controlling women, and so he had at one time decided to put a stop to that. He feels that Betina is a different sort of person. He describes her as lively, funny and erotic. She had, in his words, "swept him off his feet". But he wouldn't mind being allowed back on his feet now. He feels that she is asking too much of him and is beginning to be increasingly dissatisfied with him. She wants new energy in their sex life and more affirmation and recognition, and she feels that he is closing up so that she has no idea what he is thinking. She has noticed that Christian has lately become happier but, as he has decided not to share with her what he is working on during the therapy sessions, she feels rejected and is more worried than happy with his development.

I ask Christian about his relationship with his mother. He explains that theirs was a very good and close relationship, but that, sadly, she died when he was in his late 20s. Christian becomes very emotional when speaking of her. She had a difficult life, he tells me. When married to Christian's father, she had, for many years, tried to keep his drinking secret from family and friends. After the divorce, she sometimes had to work a lot, night shifts too, in order to provide for them. She always tried to hide it when she was sad.

Christian has no great fondness for his father. He has only seen him twice since the divorce, and on both occasions the father complained that Christian's mother had kept Christian and his siblings away from him. The father had not been able to see his own part in the business. Christian's youngest brother is still in occasional contact with their father and he tells Christian that the father has, he believes, stopped drinking. Christian thinks his brother was too young at the time of the divorce to realise how much of an idiot their father was. Christian remembers how the father once spent a whole day, Christian's birthday, sleeping off his drink, and how on another occasion he fell asleep in a flowerbed in the front garden. And he remembers their mother being very unhappy.

Christian and I spend a good deal of time talking about his mother. He feels he never properly got to say his goodbyes to her because her illness developed so quickly; she lost consciousness a relatively short while after she was diagnosed. At one point, we set up a small role-playing exercise: We invite her in, and Christian has the opportunity to put into words some of those things he would have liked to tell her. Afterwards, he is very moved and relieved. But he also laughs a little at the whole thing, saying he had never in his life imagined that he would one day be talking quite so intimately to a pillow on a chair.

Throughout the process, working with Christian's relationship with his mother and the other women in his life, I mirror what he is telling me, inspired by the Imago technique.[4] I thus repeat what he says, both to make sure I have understood correctly and to approach more closely to feeling what he felt. Furthermore, it gives him the opportunity to correct his statements or add to them. In our role-playing exercise, I employ techniques from gestalt therapy (the so-called empty chair technique, which encourages dialogue between different sides of the personality or between the client and a person who is not physically present). I also include elements taken from narrative therapy (the 'saying hello' idea used in grief work, with its emphasis on including the person who has been lost rather than working towards letting go).

One day, Christian tells me that he has had a dream, and that it reminds him of his childhood nightmare:

C: I am driving through a large tunnel in Switzerland when I suddenly realise that it's sealed off, because they're drilling a new tunnel directly above it. I try to brake, but the brakes aren't working, and at that moment, huge drills begin to crash through the ceiling right in front of me, accelerating in speed. I rush on and think that I can't possibly keep on avoiding them. Then I wake up.

I ask Christian to tell me his associations to the elements of the dream. He associates Switzerland with a place he was very fascinated by as a child, because of the skill of the Swiss in making watches and knives and because of the lovely mountains. His father had a Swiss knife that contained, among other things, a magnifying glass. The drills he associates with the dragon, which has simply become mechanical. He imagines that the car he drives in the dream is rented in Switzerland and is quite a cool model. But then again, he admits, it might not be that cool, really, as the brakes are not working.

At this point, Christian has been through eight therapy sessions since he started the second time. There is no doubt that he still does not find it pleasant to examine his physical sensations, but by now we have established such good contact that I decide to take a risk and I ask him to close his eyes. I then guide him through a brief relaxation exercise. I ask him to think about Switzerland and the wonderful mountains and notice what comes into his mind. Suddenly, he opens his eyes and tells me that he had a very pleasant sensation – at first. Then, on an unpleasant impulse, he had come to think of a situation he had otherwise forgotten – sitting on the sofa in the living room with his father and looking through a picture book. They sit talking and are having a really nice time together. But then his mother comes home and sits down, apparently very angry with the father. The father then gets up, puts on his coat and leaves, and Christian feels very sad.

Then comes a long period of therapeutic work focusing on Christian's relationship with his father and mother, in which we return several times to the language of symbols used in the two dreams. After his parents' divorce, Christian felt a huge responsibility, especially to his younger siblings. Their mother did her best, but he had clearly been able to feel her bitterness towards his father, and Christian had wholly sided with her. It is a relief to him to feel that there might after all have been something good in his father and in their relationship.

Christian now thinks that he has so far been 'renting' an identity (a Swiss car) that he was unable to stop. According to this identity, he is a thoroughly stable man (in our common catalogue of symbols, Switzerland has by now come to symbolise male rationality, skill and stability – the positive father figure Christian might have needed). But he has not been completely himself. We understand the inability to brake as a symbol of the feeling he gets when anxiety sets in. The faulty car is a parallel to the shredded clothes from the first dream – an identity that breaks down in the face of a battle with dragons. To Christian, the parallel tunnelling becomes a symbol of his mother's image of the father as a big idiot, and of the way in which Christian has felt somehow prohibited from driving along the old route, where his father was also a good father.

Towards the end of the therapy course, we commit a session to looking into how Christian can better communicate with Betina. We analyse a situation that led to a conflict between them, and Christian becomes aware that his inner thoughts in connection with such conflicts are "If I express my wants and needs, people will abandon me; others' feelings are more important". Christian expresses a feeling that, following his parents' divorce, he was often afraid that his mother would disappear, as well. The session ends with Christian concluding that what Betina really wants is for him to tell her what he wants and needs. He also concludes that this is the main problem with their current sex life, that he is not fully present. Far too many distressing parallel thoughts are going through his head: "What's she thinking now?" "Is she bored now?" "Why can't I be a bit more spontaneous?" and so on.

Christian brings a new dream to our next session:

C: I'm on a camping trip with Betina. I don't know where, maybe Sweden. I'm sitting inside our tent, and suddenly I see a hand touch the canvas from outside, and I'm stricken by panic, like in a horror movie. But then I think that hey, I can just open the tent and go outside, and I do that. It feels nice to open the zipper with a swishing move, and outside Betina is sitting, warming some food on a camping stove. She tells me she just had to hang a towel to dry on the tent, and that that was why she'd touched it before.

Christian demonstrates the move with the zipper in the air, and we repeat it together several times. He says that making this movement gives him a feeling of calm. A feeling of being in control of the situation and taking action. I ask him to associate freely over this symbol, and Christian comes into contact with a feeling of controlling the zipper in his jeans himself; this gives him hope that he will come to "feel like a man" in his relationship with Betina. Christian feels that he would like to get down from his tree house, but he needs to decide the timing and pacing himself. At the same time, he comes to understand Betina's feelings, realising that all his inner worries had made him less empathetic towards her.

We explored the content of Christian's dreams. To begin with, my approach was a phenomenological one, just allowing the dreams to come forward and then asking elaborating questions. But, as Christian interpreted the symbols for himself, we gradually developed a process for working with symbols inspired by Jung's symbols teaching and by gestalt therapy. Cybernetic psychology includes a broad understanding of dreams, and as such this became the overriding perspective on our work (e.g. Vedfelt 2017). The use of movement is also found in body and trauma therapy.

Integration and Conscious Relationship Work

Christian's therapy did not introduce a conceptual frame belonging to cybernetic psychology, but one of which he himself was the co-creator. This is a characteristic of the cybernetic therapeutic practice. With time, we both came to immediately understand what was meant when one of us used, for example, "motherly tunnel vision" about his mother's view of his father, or when we used "tree house state" to describe Christian's feelings when he was introverted. These were Christian's own concepts. They helped render complex emotions tangible and make it possible to explore them – as well as to make some methods more obviously useful than others. In this way, integration always takes place *in* the relationship rather than *before* it.

One example of how integration can be used in the relationship relates to the question of touch. When is it a good idea to use touch in the therapy situation? It calls for methodological and theoretical knowledge, but it is not necessarily a good idea to use touch simply because the therapist has a background within the relevant methods and theories. In each particular case, it also depends on the trust and relationship that exists between client and therapist. Another example is Christian's dreams. We could have approached them in a number of ways. We could have made drawings or role-playing exercises, reflected on the underlying patterns and so on – or we could have chosen not to focus on them at all. In both examples, the essential thing is that the relationship between therapist and client – their body language, word choice, inner sensations and so on – are in a constant process of balancing and harmonisation that involves all process channels.

Central to cybernetic psychology is the conscious and active reflection on the relationship and on the process of emotional balancing. This is trained as a method (focusing on form, content, intensity and frequency) and based on a psychological theory of integration. The basis of the relationship is a curious, open approach that is always aware of the client's resources. Simultaneously, the therapist is continuously considering *transference* – that is, the feelings the client might have in relation to the therapist and which traits or intentions the client might ascribe to the therapist based on her or his own process/background and the strong parts of her or his own personality. At the same time, the therapist has to consider *countertransference* – that is, those often-unconscious feelings awoken by working with the client.

In cybernetic therapy, transference and countertransference are seen as instances of communication on a higher level of organisation and viewed as valuable tools rather than unwanted side effects. They are dynamic processes that partly determine which methods are useful in the therapy. For example (and this is a very simple illustration), one may consider whether a client has a motherly or a fatherly transference to the therapist, and what this means for the client's needs in the therapeutic situation.

The idea is not to impose methods and theories on the therapy in cybernetic practice, but rather to put them at the disposal of the client's self-regulating processes.[5] However, people who are in a trying situation often have difficulty feeling their own needs. During therapy, the therapist's own experiences from therapy situations and his or her knowledge of various approaches – both practical and theoretical – are put at the disposal of the client's wish to examine and change some of the ways in which she or he thinks, feels or acts. In this way, cybernetic therapy is also very much an example of technical eclecticism and a therapeutic common factor approach.

Christian's work with his dreams lifted the themes of his 'problems' on to a higher level of organisation than the level on which those problems were visible – that is, in his daily life with Betina. On this higher level, the structures behind his experience of the world became clearer. The feeling of being 'in control of the zipper' and able to go in and out of the tent was generated by his unconscious, self-regulating processes, and it gave him a sense of freedom. The realisations he came to in his work were no longer designated for just one area of his life. They were relevant for his relationship with Betina and also his relationships with his ex-wife, his parents and (as later became evident) his colleagues, himself, politics and authorities in general.

Integration in the Relationship

In the described session with Christian, where I first put a little pressure on him to make him describe his physical sensations, my questions had a negative effect on his transference on me, and I became a negative mother-aspect – became 'dragon-like'. It called for a change in approach. Working consciously with transference was a central part of Freud's teachings, and the approach was developed further by neo-Freudians such as Kernberg and Kohut, among others. The integration of various therapy methods happened in interaction with the relationship work. It was characterised by his transference on to me as a motherly figure and helped him get in contact with a more nuanced view of his complex emotions in relation to women.

As a tool to react to these self-regulating changes in the relationship, the therapist can look into her or his own emotions and physical sensations along the way. The concept is called vicarious introspection and it requires mental and physical awareness training. A conscious observation of inner sensations and countertrans-ference is required to make the necessary methodological adjustments.

The integration of methods in Christian's therapy was a combination of the three types of integration described above. Reading about cybernetic psychotherapy without considering it in a practical context, one might think that it mainly employs theoretical integration, simply because the approach involves integrative theory. In practice, however, just as large a part is played by technical eclecticism – conscious thinking about how to approach the situation based on the therapist's knowledge of effect and of focus on common factors. The method is also suitable for assimilative integration, as cybernetic theory can easily be a point of departure for the integra-tion of new knowledge from newer forms of therapy, without the therapist having to turn a blind eye to conflicts of theory.

In cybernetic therapy, the therapeutic expression – the concrete of how the inte-gration takes place – is inseparable from the particular situation. That is also why it is so difficult to set it down in writing in any precise manner. The full experience requires an experience of practice. This is why cybernetic psychology puts such an emphasis on achieving phronesis or 'practical flexibility in the mature therapist', here learned through *apprenticeship*.

The Therapeutic Netherworld, the Therapy beneath the Surface

I have tried to give an impression of cybernetic integrative therapy as it looks in practice. But, as James O. Prochaska also stated, it is a matter of course that integrative psychotherapy cannot be described through a single individual case (Norcross & Goldfried 1992, 317). Examining and attempting to describe an in-tegrative psychotherapy is to invite the complex and relative into the theoretical. There is a striving for simplicity within integrative therapy, a wish to create clar-ity after a period of a cacophony of conflicting 'brand name theories'. We are unlikely ever to find an absolute truth within psychotherapy, but theory can help us move closer to some form of truth (Norcross & Prochaska 2007, 1–4). The strength of integrative theory is that it does not focus on dictating new methods, but rather tries to say something about what happens in the therapy room when therapy succeeds. In other words, the idea behind this theory is to get closer to the knowledge of what works in practice and strengthen the flexibility inherent in practical therapy.

Many processes take place in therapy rooms and in clients' and therapists' self-work that are not mentioned in the textbooks. We know that therapy works. And we know that most therapists integrate. But to describe precisely how the processes take place to such a degree that they are entirely predictable is not yet possible. The division of integration methods into three categories is a useful tool for discussing integration, but very few integrative therapies can be contained within a single category. For example, we might say that cognitive theory, which emphasises in-ner cognitive processes, has limited the importance of the relationship, otherwise an important element in the common factor approach. But even so, most cognitive therapists probably do build up a therapeutic alliance that functions as an element in their therapy. As mentioned before, it is my opinion that it is beneficial for integration that the three integration types are not distinctly divided in practice. For example, the common factor approach may be criticised for overlooking specific techniques that might be useful, as it emphasises common factors rather than individual traits of the various schools of thought – at least, that is, if we keep strictly to the definition of this one type of integration. In practice, however, this is no great problem, as most therapists probably integrate using an element of technical eclecticism as well, making them attentive to whether particular methods could be suitable for clients with certain problems.

In cybernetics, it is important to put equal emphasis on all three types of integration: One should strive for an 'umbrella theory' from which to think about the newest knowledge about what works in various cases and to understand the active ingredients in effective therapy.

Perhaps it is true, as Klein and Dittman have stated, that there is a "therapeutic netherworld" that never gets out into the textbooks and, in many cases, does not inform training and education either (Stricker & Gold 1993, 45). This is the part of therapy that is not addressed in most theories. And perhaps it is especially the part of therapy that has to do with the practical flexibility of the mature therapist, with phronesis and integration. It is the driving force behind the common factor approach, but it has not yet been put into words as a part of it, and it dissolves the differences and the strengths of the various therapeutic approaches. This therapeutic netherworld is concerned with navigating the extremely complex situation made up by therapy. And it might still be where the real wisdom of how therapy works is to be found. Until we reach a better understanding of this, I believe our best option is to become increasingly aware of therapeutic relationship and integration. Cybernetic psychotherapy is one way to reach this awareness.

Notes

1 This categorisation is inspired (with variations) by the one presented by Stricker and Gold (1993).

2 Furthermore, and for obvious reasons, the description only presents a small part of what took place during the therapy sessions. And, of course, it is only the conscious processes which can be interpreted here. In my opinion, a case description can only give an impression of, but by no means document, a course of therapy.

3 The notions of 'higher' and 'lower' levels of consciousness tie in with cybernetic psychology's roots in the systems theory (Vedfelt 1996, 108). The documented fact that our 'normal consciousness' is only able to handle a small part of the total information capacity of our mind makes it relevant to speak figuratively of higher and lower in relation to the degree of control – i.e., whether it is a primary or a secondary system. It is not, then, to be understood as a hierarchy of values. The higher levels of consciousness provide an image of a larger (and completely or partly unconscious) system of information processing, working as a level of control. Our normal consciousness does not have unobstructed access to these levels, but it can reflect on them and, through relaxed states such as dreaming, it can gain knowledge of these levels.

4 Imago is a relation therapy developed in the USA in the 1980s by the couple Harville Hendrix and Helen Hunt. They took as their point of departure experiences from couples' therapy, and the central element of the method is a controlled dialogue stimulating meaningful narration, recognition and empathy.

5 When we speak of self-regulating within cybernetic psychology, it is because of our confidence in the fact that unconscious processes possess self-regulating properties for the mind in general.

References

Bateman, Anthony & Holmes, Jeremy (Eds.) (2002) *Integration in Psychotherapy: Models and Methods*. Oxford: Oxford University Press.

Falkum, Erik (2008) Phronesis and Techne: The Debate on Evidence-Based Medicine in Psychiatry and Psychotherapy. *Philosophy, Psychiatry & Psychology*, vol. 15, no. 2, pp. 141 ff.

London, Perry (1988) Metamorphosis in Psychotherapy: Slouching toward Integration. *Journal of Integrative and Eclectic Psychotherapy*, vol. 7, no. 1, pp. 3–12.

Norcross, John C. & Goldfried, Marvin R. (Eds.) (1992) *Handbook of Psychotherapy Integration*. London/New York: Basic Books/Harper Collins.

Norcross, John C. & Prochaska, James O. (2007) *Systems of Psychotherapy: A Transtheoretical Analysis*. Salt Lake City: Brooks/Cole Cengage Learning.

O'Leary, Eleanor & Murphy, Mike (Eds.) (2006) *ew Approaches to Integration in Psychotherapy*. London: Routledge.

Stricker, George & Gold, Jerold R. (Eds.) (1993) *Comprehensive Handbook of Psychotherapy Integration*. New York: Plenum Press.

Vedfelt, Ole (1996) *Bevidsthed*. Copenhagen: Gyldendal.

Vedfelt, Ole (2001) Fra Jung til kybernetisk psykolog, in Pia Skogemann (Ed.), *Symbol, analyse, virkelighed. Jungiansk teori og praksis i Danmark*. Copenhagen: Lindhardt og Ringhof, pp. 288–316.

Vedfelt, Ole (2002) *Ubevidst intelligens – du ved mere end du tror*. Copenhagen: Gyldendal.

Vedfelt, O. (2017). *A Guide to the World of Dreams. An Integrative Approach to Dreamwork*. London: Routledge.

10

The Cybernetic Psychology View of Nature

Dorte Mikuta

The chapter examines human nature viewed through cybernetic psychology. Looking at key concepts in the tension between two scientific
paradigms, it is interesting that cybernetic psychology builds bridges between cognitive and constructivist views of human nature. Cybernetic
psychology integrates the biological, social and cultural aspects of man in
its method. By examining the scientific and therapeutic positions, considerations about the view of human nature become relevant in a contemporary culture. In this light, the chapter defines central qualities the
therapist must possess when working with psychological symptoms in the
therapeutic space.

View on Human Nature

Various kinds of news media, both academic and social, deal with human beings,
their behaviour, emotions and thoughts. A growing number of sciences produce
knowledge about humans, which generates new questions. New angles and more
advanced techniques thus expand the total amount of information about the subject. All this information affects the direction in which our society develops and
influences the different discourses and discussions that take place in the public
domain. This influences the way in which we assess ourselves and the demands
we make on ourselves and each other. The weight of this focus on human beings is
centred on the normative question of how we live a good life. For this reason, I find
it both current and pressing to raise awareness of what lies behind our assumptions
about humans and our development. When, at the same time, it is clear that many
are challenged by psychological imbalances, including anxiety, stress and depression, it may seem paradoxical that we, on the one hand, have the normative desire
for human well-being and happiness, while, on the other hand, the focus is on the
individual having to meet the demand for adaptability and a high utilisation of potential. These seemingly contradictory expectations are operating in many places.
And this is, of course, also the motivation for my study. For example, it is interesting to look at how, in some contexts, we assume that the development of potentials
and talents is better supported separately from society's institutions and external

DOI: 10.4324/9781003360247-11

requirements in general – for example, in the communication that takes place via meditative yoga practices – while, in educational and labour-market contexts, for example, the focus is on the targeted education of citizens, with a requirement to develop and adapt. It is the question of *the solitary* versus *the social*, and it is of crucial importance in the debate about how we build society in its interest to support and develop good and harmonious lives. An early and persistent requirement for humans from the surrounding relationships could seem both disturbing *and* motivating. That is why I am investigating whether we think of people as *essentially preprogrammed* in the way in which we, via genetic dispositions, have specific ways of being in an individual core that forms the basis for our development of our emotions, ways of thinking and actions, or whether, as some people claim, we are exclusively shaped by the socially constructed, where the formation and development are conditioned by the surrounding environment and where motivation arises through the social matrix.

It is my wish to place Ole Vedfelt's cybernetic psychology in a scientific and historical perspective. At the same time, I would like to emphasise how important it is to be aware of the view of human nature that we presume in a therapeutic practice. For this reason, I will present key aspects of Vedfelt's cybernetic psychology and analyse the area of tension between *cognitivism* and *constructivism*, which are two paradigms that are often in opposition in academic considerations and discussions about human development. Second, the cybernetic psychology of Vedfelt will be used as a foundation in a presentation of three Western European thinkers, Jean-Jacques Rousseau, Carl Gustav Jung and Michel Foucault. Among others, they have expressed their interest in the development of human beings in sociological, anthropological, philosophical and psychological terms, and their ideas are important background voices in the discourses of society when we discuss upbringing, education and human psychological well-being.

Clarification of Views of Human Nature – Cognitive versus Constructivist

The two scientific-theoretical positions, *cognitive and constructivist*, influence modern paradigms within the human sciences, and their mindset is influenced by divergent views of humans. In *cognitivist* understanding, there is an assumption that humans are primarily biological beings whose understanding of the world is fundamentally governed by evolutionarily developed neurocognitive functions. Historically, this position can be traced back to psychology and natural science, where studies of human culture, language and social activity are linked to studies of human consciousness, cognition and the brain. Cognitive science has seen many different variations, but there can be said to be a joint attempt to relate human cognitive and psychological structures to behavioural forms and ways of perceiving and categorising the world. In this way, human nature in cognitivism is based on the cognitive structures of consciousness, and humans' self-understanding and understanding of the world are located in the brain's function.

In the *constructivist* understanding of humans, on the other hand, human nature is formed in the interaction with the outside world, and not only the human being but also what we refer to as reality is first and foremost a social and historical construction. On the basis of this perspective, brain research is seen as a non-concrete science without objective foundation, because it is believed that the concepts and the basic world-view that the brain research serves are socially constructed. Constructivism can be traced back to sociology and social science, and it is preoccupied with critical studies of the social and historical conditions for knowledge. Because it sees the human being as a product of linguistic discourses and social practices, it is preoccupied with critical studies of the social and historical conditions for the ability to acquire knowledge. Constructivism positions itself by demonstrating that something that is normally perceived as natural, universal or even necessary is in reality contingent and historically variable, constructed by the community that defines power (Jensen 2011).

The View of Human Nature in Cybernetic Psychology

In this way, when I seek to clarify the view of human nature in the scientific context between the *cognitive* and *constructivist* positions, it is a crucial point that Vedfelt has developed cybernetic psychology based on the feelings, inner images, body experiences and thoughts that he has experienced in his clients. In his cybernetic therapeutic practice, there is a correlation between his practical experience and the cybernetic teaching about the regulation of information in complex systems. Against this background, the human personality can be defined as a hyper-complex, layered information network where many levels of consciousness are active at the same time, and where the *intelligent unconsciousness* functions as a self-regulating and self-organising potential (Vedfelt 2002, p. 34).

In a comparison of the view of human nature between Vedfelt and the two scientific-theoretical positions, the concept of the *ecological niche* and the concept of *self-regulation* are particularly useful.

> The identification of universal (human) ability to decode body language, the existence of common human emotions, experience modes and forms of behavior, all point to a common unconscious foundation for being human. So do the infant's formidable innate abilities and the ecological niche's just as impressive and complex responses.
>
> (Vedfelt 2002, p. 356)

Regardless of cultural background, Vedfelt finds that humans have the same innate abilities to live in the particular human environment. Humankind has genetic abilities that have been developed during human evolution, which are thus adapted to their particular environment just as other organisms, from birth, are adapted to their unique environment. The high complexity of the exchange of information in relation to other living organisms is unique to the interaction that takes place between humans. However, in order to develop this innate potential for the high level of complexity, humans are dependent on a caring environment that teaches us advanced communication via feedback. As communicative and interaction-oriented individuals, humans' intentions are in their expressions, which means that they can already influence their interaction with the outside world from the outset. This is necessary in order to develop in the ecological niche. By virtue of their inherent structure, they can draw the attention of the caretaker – for example, by showing discomfort, joy, anger, disappointment or pain – in a way that resonates with the surroundings. In the same way, a child is able to receive and understand the caregiver – for example, in the nuanced moods and body signals that emanate from the mother. The social function is developed in a reciprocal adjustment and to be able to read moods, emotions and other signals, and, based on this, we align ourselves with each other in an interaction that becomes the foundation for how we function with ourselves and with each other (Vedfelt 2002, p. 90).

In the key question of whether humans have essential preprogrammed dispositions, Vedfelt is thus in line with cognitive theory, which documents that human cognition and consciousness interact with the outside world via feedback. However, the concept of humans' fundamental dependence on interaction and reconciliation via their surroundings is in line with the constructivist concept. Human development depends on mirroring and interaction with the outside world, so that both values and ways of life are formed in a social context, and, as social constructivism points out, the current power structures in society are automatically taken over in the adaptation to the ecological niche. But an important prerequisite for human psychological growth is that human beings are simultaneously supported by the importance of self-regulation. Self-regulation is an important concept in Vedfelt's theory. Through self-regulation, a balance is practised in such a way that it is not just an adjustment to the external 'power structures', because, in harmonious psychological development, there is a balanced adjustment between the internal and external adaptation. Therefore, the quality of the mirroring and regulation that take place in the early years is crucial. Here, the ability to self-regulate is stimulated when the closest caregivers react with a well-developed ability to understand and respond to fundamental needs. This interaction shows the child's recognition of the spontaneous emotions and a way through emotions, which will enable it to handle inner emotional states while gradually adapting to the surroundings. But, conversely, if the natural impulses are only understood and mirrored to a lesser extent or not at all, the impulse is suppressed, and the child is forced to seek out other strategies in order to adapt to the outside world. In this situation, the ability to balance self-regulation between the outer and the inner is weakened. This means we will lack the flexibility needed to cope with the growing complexity that is required by the natural developmental phases of human life (Vedfelt 2002, p. 82). According to Vedfelt, the self-regulation mechanism is congenital and it is impressionable all through life. This is documented by cognitive theory, which considers a brain-based foundation for the feedback received via interaction with the outside world to effect change to the plastic brain (Jensen 2011, p. 242).

The Therapist's Role as a Reparative Body

When we increasingly see people suffering from depression, anxiety and stress, cybernetic psychology will see it as an expression of a lack of balance between internal and external adaptation, because the information exchanges between the individual and the outside world have been exposed to stressful conditions for the client (Vedfelt 2002, p. 313). The therapeutic work is therefore to seek a balance between the internal and external adjustment in the client.

What is special about cybernetic therapy is that the therapist understands the client's problems as the overall psyche's attempt at self-regulation. With developed ability to read body language, movements, facial expressions and use of voice, the therapist can support the client's self-regulating ability through empathetic feeling. Where the client's emotions and impulses have been hampered as a result of excessive adjustment, it may, for example, make it difficult for the client to handle stressful situations. The therapist becomes the client's new ecological niche (Vedfelt 1996, p. 112).

In order to further explore the supportive function that the therapist carries out in collaboration with the innate ability to self-regulate, we need to consult Vedfelt's theory about the overall processes in the human psyche. When describing man as an intelligent information system, a central concept is the *unconscious intelligence*. This concept has a correlation with the neuropsychological perception that human behaviour can be read in the brain, and that humans are actively structuring and seeking meaning in their way of recognition, so that there is a correlation between the brain and psychological processes. However, as Vedfelt expresses:

> The way in which man's spiritual networks process information makes it clear, that we in our everyday lives function on a practical intelligence, built up since the beginning of time, which is a prerequisite for our mutual understanding of each other.
>
> (Vedfelt 2002, p. 356)

According to Vedfelt, the surroundings' feedback is processed by a *practical intelligence* that ensures that we are able to record, store, organise and use information in a way that allows us to act flexibly in the complex social interaction. However, the information processing takes place in such a way that the majority of the information that we perceive and store takes place unknowingly via what is known by Vedfelt to be a subliminal information intake. The rational waking consciousness does not have the capacity to store all the information that is gathered continuously via the human senses. It focuses on targeted tasks – for example, organising everyday life, meeting at certain times, being able to complete a planned activity. The rational consciousness performs tasks based on logical principles (Vedfelt 2002, p. 51, 1996, p. 127).

This means we have a control of the rational consciousness that we are not immediately able to see but that shows through the reactions and behaviour of personality, which is a more general governance. According to Vedfelt, this control is intelligent but unconscious. He explains that, when analysing unconscious processes, we find that human beings, in their reaction and action, trigger huge amounts of information that is stored outside the rational consciousness. However, since these actions turn out to be reflective, constructive, problem-solving, long-term-relating and with an abstraction capacity and the ability to distinguish between significant and unimportant, this is described as a *practical intelligence*.

Just as Vedfelt describes that humans contain an inexhaustible collection of practical knowledge about the world and the human being, cognitive research proves that the brain is a medium for knowledge in which huge amounts of knowledge can be activated simultaneously without us being aware of it. Unconscious knowledge is organised in what Vedfelt describes as different networks in the psyche, with overlapping memory systems and with varying degrees of consciousness (Vedfelt 1996, pp. 112–113). This theory has a significant influence on the therapeutic method and places expectations on the therapist's own personal development, as the aim of cybernetic therapy is to contact these general management systems, which are not accessible to rational consciousness.

The Cybernetic Psychology's Practice

As previously mentioned, the client's issues are seen as intelligent attempts to optimise the inner balance in relation to their surroundings. This can be seen as a communication from the higher consciousness structures, so that problems reveal vulnerable places in the psyche where we have not been stimulated to develop or are hampered by traumatic events that are persecuting and disturbing us later in life. However, healing in therapy consists of searching beyond the rational consciousness, because, if we can reach the unconscious and underlying psychological levels, then we can achieve what controls humans at a higher level of control. According to Vedfelt, this is possible when we can establish contact with what he calls *changed states of consciousness* (Vedfelt 1996, pp. 130–131).

Changes to states of consciousness are, for example, creative, imaginative, sensitive and meditative, as well as dream and trance states. In cybernetic therapy, when you seek contact with these higher control systems in the client, it is because you get deeper contact with the unconscious impulses, where the normal consciousness is disconnected. It is the therapist's supramodal ability that facilitates contact via the changed states of consciousness, if the therapist is trained and able to navigate in multiple simultaneous states of consciousness, with the client and in themselves. This means an awareness, for example, of emotions, intellect, outward sensations such as body expressions and inner bodily sensations. Then, the therapist can rise above the individual experience modes and be led by the client's subconscious intelligence. In this way, it is possible to be led to the areas in the psyche that are responsible for rigid and difficult regulation of internal emotions in the client. Images, body language, fantasy material and dreams are reflections of the client's psychological systems' communications. And, in therapy, the therapist's empathetic mirroring can involve new coding in the changed states of consciousness, where there is contact with the many levels of the person's control systems. When there is new coding in the client's psyche, this is described as a creative and problem-solving development. Situations that were previously stressful can then be handled with greater flexibility, using the ability to self-regulate (Vedfelt 1996, pp. 112–113).

Human Well-being and Development

In the previous text, Vedfelt's theory of humans' psychological formation and the causes that can form the basis for a lack of well-being and the consequent psychological problems have been clarified. But, on the overall question of how human beings are considered to live well, I return to one of the initial questions of whether individual dispositions to develop exist – a distinctive individuality that differentiates the way in which one develops.

In the question of human development, Vedfelt refers to the human unconscious intelligence as a preprogrammed structure in the human psyche:

> I envision the unconscious intelligence with all its facets, as a natural information pool continuously unfolding. Long before humans were created, information about development existed.
>
> (Vedfelt 2002, p. 356)

We instinctively collect information about the ecological niche's living conditions, norms and possibilities via feedback from our surroundings and target the organisation of information towards experiencing the development phases that are specifically human. New phases of life demand that the person is able to handle greater complexity. This succeeds when systems and subsystems communicate with each other and constantly ensure self-regulation and a greater understanding and balance in the personality. It is a natural development when, for example, the child goes from seeking one to several close caregivers from a certain age and, later, goes further into the social network, moving from childhood to puberty, parenthood to the mid-life phase and, eventually, old age. In this process, for example, you become aware of your own individuality, free of family bonds. You try your hand at new sides of your personality, prepare for parenthood, seek out development that challenges both physical and mental abilities. According to Vedfelt, throughout the entire process, unconscious intelligence will seek to optimise the personality by seeking positive growth-generating relationships while moving from a primitive to a highly advanced and complex information level. At each new development stage, a higher-level steering system will be activated, and the targeted search for information to use in the new developmental stage means that the psyche usually finds itself in a new overall personality structure without major problems, as the higher level's control systems integrate the lower level. However, on the question of whether human beings have individual dispositions to develop that differentiate the way in which they develop, Vedfelt writes that it is basically a matter of self-realisation *within* a more comprehensive whole and, later, as a crystallisation *based on* a whole. I imagine that, as a whole, it is the *cybernetic self* that human beings cannot experience in its entirety, which is the total personality and the overall operating system. It seems like a movement "inside and out" and, in that case, as an individual core, which humans have an impulse to express and which is seen as a more comprehensive process of creation from the inside. Vedfelt claims that, in any case, something more was added to the personality than what we learn via the interaction with the outside world. It is a creation of individual properties, which can happen in a creative revelation.

But I understand that the surrounding environment is still an important partner in realising this potential, as the work consists of creating the conditions for expressing one's particular talents in an optimal way, achieving this in a balanced manner in relation to one's ambitions and the opportunities that society controls. In other words, it is also very much an acceptance of reality that the process takes place in interaction with the outside world. However, Vedfelt writes that, in the same way as it is for other developmental processes, it is necessary to give in to the changed states of consciousness and let the unconscious processes of transition control the psyche to a higher process level. At the same time, he believes that inspiration from others who have lived through the same process is necessary. In the self-realisation process, you will be able to tune into areas where a new, creative individual development is resolved (Vedfelt 1996, pp. 133–135).

If we compare Vedfelt's statements about human development with the two scientific-theoretical positions, then cognitive theory documents that the brain is shaped by experiences and thereby changes throughout life. Based on the biology that identifies humans' cognition and forms of behaviour, it is argued that there is development in the sense that human self-experience and the world's understanding are changed. Constructivists claim that the knowledge that humans gain about themselves in the therapeutic space results in a change of identity and world-view, but that it is just another construction that is shaped by the new context in the therapeutic space. The question is whether there is even talk of development if, in reality, we are talking about a variability in an adjustment process in which there is no individual growth. With Vedfelt's concept of development as a sense of purpose, I sense that he identifies more with the idea of a purpose-specific process in which there is a movement towards higher complexity and development in the psyche's control system.

Summary of Cybernetic Psychology between Cognitivism and Constructivism

In the previous text, it has been shown that cybernetic psychology is moving towards social constructivism in the concept of the ecological niche, whereas the idea of the preprogrammed human being is moving towards cognitivism. Cybernetic psychology is constructivist in the fact that we take into consideration the power structures that characterise our surroundings through the current norms for how we live and interact. But Vedfelt has a foot in both camps, since he is also considering the innate structures that work in the psyche of man and that determine the way in which we develop. It is a cognitive approach in therapy, where we try to get in contact with the higher control systems via the changed states of consciousness. The flow of information is given in a special order, a system of information, but, as we relate to the client as a hyper-complex information system, the client's operating system provides us with guidance on where it should be reprogrammed. The new, changed position of the client's psyche is created on a high control-system level, in a creative process in the communication field between client and therapist, which is a constructivist process.

Overview of Three Historical Thinkers

After drawing up key concepts that qualify cybernetic psychology in relation to the theories and ideas that are topical in current scientific discourses, it is relevant to consider how the cybernetic psychologist's view of human nature and therapeutic methods relates to other theories. The overall question still remains about how we envisage humans evolving to be able to live well, and how, because of the underlying view of human nature, we believe that humans can be supported to counteract serious distress. By putting into perspective three different, but each very significant, thinkers – Jean-Jacques Rousseau (1712–1778), Carl Gustav Jung (1875–1961) and Michel Foucault (1926–1984) – one can get the impression that an awareness of the underlying view of human nature is a crucial starting point in a therapeutic practice, as well as in the considerations that precede pedagogical principles in the culture of education.

   With their sociological, anthropological, philosophical and psychological observations about humans, the following three thinkers influenced the discourses from which we now speak when we discuss upbringing, education and human development today. But it will be shown that they have deeply diverging views of humans and our path to living well and harmoniously.

Jean-Jacques Rousseau

The French philosopher Rousseau was one of the key thinkers of the Enlightenment. It is said that he created romanticism with his encouragement to let the feeling reign. At a time when it was believed that common sense and knowledge were able to free man from tradition and the close ties of force of habit, his view was groundbreaking as he spoke against rational materialism and the mechanical world-view that reigned during the Enlightenment. Instead, he emphasised feelings and the value of nature. In 1762, in his novel on upbringing, Émile, he focuses on how best to form a human being and he is convinced that human beings are formed on the basis of the influences to which they are exposed. But, because he believes that humans are best in their natural state, it is important to search for a state in which they best unfold their natural aptitudes and tendencies. Rousseau thus wishes to give the child strength via upbringing, which must take place through a stay in nature, because nature teaches people about the conditions of life while at the same time encouraging patience. When the child in nature learns from his or her own experience, a certain attitude is practised that best ensures a harmonious state throughout life. To be formed via society means that the opportunities for development are limited, and there is a risk of being seduced by the values exchanged in society, so that humans become alienated from themselves. The child must therefore be protected from too many assaults from the surrounding society, as humans cannot be adapted to both themselves and fancies from the surrounding culture (Rousseau, 1962).

In other words, Rousseau's view on human nature is a clear manifestation of the fact that human development consists of unlocking an inner potential, for which it requires freedom to find the truth in a solitary and introverted journey. This radical distancing from social structures is also an important voice in our time, as Rousseau's thoughts are still used as an inspiration in much children's literature and in the formulation of pedagogical principles in the Western world. The conviction that human beings are formed based on the influences to which they are exposed leads to the distinction we also see in terms of internal and external adaptation. But, where natural and harmonious development is found in a predominantly inward-directed attention with Rousseau, the balance with Vedfelt is found in the alternation between the outer and the inner.

Carl Gustav Jung

Carl Gustav Jung was the founder of analytical psychology, which is a depth-psychology theory that emerged from psychoanalysis. He considered *the unconscious* as a spiritual depth from which inspiration could be obtained. He found that the strongest and most unavoidable driving force in human beings was the desire for self-realisation. Like Rousseau, Jung also thought that we inevitably suppress certain aspects of our being when we are affected by our surroundings during our upbringing. If this happens to such an extent that repressed thoughts, feelings and tendencies prevent our personal development, it creates disturbances such as anxiety, depression and psychosomatic disorders. For Jung, these disorders are symptoms of the fact that humans are not in a healthy relationship with themselves. But Jung approaches it differently from Rousseau in recommending an attempt to gain freedom from the surrounding society. Jung developed a method for engaging in dialogue with these original parts of the psyche, especially via the unconscious expression in dreams. It is a method to heal the division that follows when the external influence prevents the unfolding of the inner. Jung believed that there is potentially an innate development plan for the individual person, and the process in development is driven from the inside in an individuation process. In a psychological development process, the purpose is to help people to become *the* specific single creature that they are. Jungian analysis is an awareness-raising process in which one changes the perceptions and behaviour patterns that stand in the way of psychological development through contact with unconscious impulses, as well as archetypal structures. One's attitude is transformed when one integrates the repressed psychological impulses. In an encounter with the personal unconscious, and partly with the collective unconscious and instinctive part, one can come into contact with the original parts of one's own psyche. However, Jung emphasises the individual as a collective being, and therefore the purpose is to become one both with oneself and also with mankind. In a successful development process, as Jung calls the *individuation process*, one becomes self-conscious in one's uniqueness but accepts both the personal limitations and those limitations which belong to human life. Jung believes that the fulfillment of individual and collective characteristics is interconnected. The individual can be absorbed by society if he or she is not centred in his- or herself, but, on the other hand, he does not believe a true society can exist if there is no freedom and independence for the individual (Grønkjær 2010).

Jung has been a great source of inspiration for creatives such as artists and researchers in many areas of the humanities and natural sciences. However, according to Vedfelt, Jung is particularly useful when you seek to obtain theoretical insight into the human psyche, and when you work with therapy and personality development (Vedfelt 2001, p. 294). In this regard, Jung also introduces the predisposed cognitive structures that he calls archetypes. However, Jung views the development process differently from Vedfelt, because Jung emphasises that it is about *getting in the right relationship with oneself*, whereas Vedfelt sees the psyche as an inter-psychological system that is constantly in relation to the psychological development process (Vedfelt 2001, p. 294). For Vedfelt, it is the lack of support from the surroundings that inhibits the ability to experience development phases in order to be able to process greater complexity. Jungians primarily claim that the external influence prevents the unfolding of the internal. In other words, Jung clearly has a solitarian aim for the development process. There is 'potentially' an innately embedded development plan in which only through an awareness process will you become the person you were once determined to be. When you understand it in depth, and only then, you can begin to consider the social situation.

Michel Foucault

Foucault was a historian of ideas, philosopher and psychologist. He was an international celebrity, and his books have been translated into multiple languages. Today, he is more popular than ever. Both in Denmark and internationally, social constructivist arguments are becoming increasingly popular in university environments. Foucault examines humans on the basis of their behaviour throughout history. According to Foucault, we cannot find the essence and nature of mankind by studying human beings because there are no eternal truths about the human mind. Humans do not have a goal and a determination. They just function. On the other hand, Foucault believes that we can find some unconscious structures that determine the framework we use when we talk about humans within. Foucault attempts to find the origins of the human consciousness outside the subject. In this way, he seeks to put a stop to the phenomena that we habitually perceive as nature, which are merely ideological constructions in his theory. He does not believe that there are predisposed structures in humans. In fact, he tends to assert that they are completely empty of given prerequisites. 'Modern power', which he defines as the discourses that have led to the world we are currently a part of, appears as natural and is therefore not a tangible power that has its starting point in, for example, the state. There is something that runs internally in us through discourses and practices that helps to determine our opinions and actions. For example, *our* diagnosis of people as mentally ill is an example of a modern power discourse. He was therefore also sceptical in his views on therapeutic practice because he thought it was just another construction. His thoughts have nevertheless given rise to a form of therapy, namely narrative therapy. This is a way of changing the client's self-understanding via new narratives. New narratives create new frameworks for understanding, and, when the special concepts and stories that exert power over the client are changed, the client's sense of identity will change (Jensen 2011, p. 79; Heede 2012).

Foucault is an interesting source in my study as he is an important marker for the thoughts in our time, and he has thereby an underlying discourse of his own, which we speak from when we discuss how human well-being and growth must be supported and interpreted gradually, without making us aware.

Foucault does not look to human biology when he examines what human beings are. Like Vedfelt, he looks to human behaviour. Where Vedfelt finds that humans are fixed on development, Foucault finds that humans have no determination but merely falsely believe that they operate on their nature. It is a myth that Foucault tries to expose, and instead he seeks to prove that we are shaped by the changing power structures of history. However, Vedfelt would probably respond to Foucault that our determination is to develop the ability to function in ever more developed and advanced complexity, in interaction with our surroundings, and, at some point, to make contact with our uniqueness, which is sought to be unfolded in interaction with the surroundings. Vedfelt states that it is a basic condition for human consciousness that it interprets reality and makes sense from it, so that it is a continual interplay between consciousness and the world (Vedfelt 2002, p. 80). In this way, cybernetic therapy differs from a therapy that has Foucault as the main inspiration, where human identity is nothing more than narratives that can be transformed and strengthened in new and powerful narratives by way of therapy.

Conclusion

The perspectives above show, for example, that Rousseau and Jung see it as crucial for human beings to be able to unfold their individual core, in seclusion from society, and this is incompatible with Foucault's and Vedfelt's theories, in which humans are created in a social context.

Many concepts have been formed throughout history, such as Rousseau's emphasis on feeling, Jung's theories about the unconscious and Foucault's thoughts on power structures. They have all made their mark. These are concepts that Vedfelt continues to build on in his own thoughts and theories. However, as mentioned above, these concepts are discourses on which we speak and discuss. They are therefore important for our assumptions about humans when we conduct pedagogical practice and discuss and conduct social politics, health promotion and social work, because their ideas still influence educational institutions and public and cultural discourse. These concepts become part of a common foundation of knowledge that we may not be aware of but that has an impact on how we interact with each other and our society.

The individual theories and assumptions are based on a theory embedded in a more comprehensive theory about the human psyche, and one perspective on humans can, on closer scrutiny, turn out to be incompatible with another. That is why it is crucial that we spread awareness of the view of human nature when we decide on initiatives in caretaking areas, in educational institutions and in interpersonal relationships such as therapeutic practice.

In relation to the two scientific-theoretical positions, we see that cybernetic psychology has a foot in both camps. Vedfelt is actually able to integrate the biological view of human nature, where there is a brain basis for every emotion and experience, with the knowledge we have about the plastic brain that is shaped by the experiences we have. What people have experienced in therapy will thus show up in the brain's structure. For this reason, I believe that cybernetic psychology shows the way for interdisciplinary integration between the two perceptions – humans as products of biology and humans as products of sociality and culture – as cybernetic psychology's understanding of consciousness has a theory that contains aspects of both positions.

This chapter illustrates that the different sources have divergent views of human nature, and this difference will manifest itself in the relationship between client and therapist in therapeutic practice. In the cybernetic psychology of Vedfelt, however, it is not the therapist who has knowledge of how the client should be developed. The psyche can only succeed in a creative field where there is regulation in the internal and as a part of an interaction with the outer ecological niche that the therapist represents in the therapy room. In cybernetic therapeutic practice, it is therefore important that the therapist goes through a psychotherapeutic process and is able to navigate in supramodal perception in order to consider the modalities with which the client is in contact, in changed states of consciousness, while at the same time being able to maintain open-mindedness. If the client tries to adapt to the therapy space, no redemption will take place.

This leads to the central question of the therapist's position in the relationship between client and therapist. When we invite the client inside in therapy, it is in a context where the client 'puts his or her life in our hands'. That is why it is of the utmost importance that the therapist is anchored in a view of human nature that he or she can vouch for. Therefore, it is important that he or she has taken a position on this, and a derived focal point becomes how we perceive power in the therapy room. In his cybernetic psychology, Vedfelt shows that it is contact with the process channels that work behind the client's rational consciousness that supports the creative development of the client's personality. However, I see the condition for therapy being successful depending on whether the therapist, through a trust-inspiring connection, has the ability to expertly and empathetically perceive and be led by the client's unconscious intelligence, so that, in the process, the client is healed in the emotional and repressed areas. The 'power' in the therapy room thus becomes the client's unconscious intelligence.

Finally, I would like to quote a statement from Ole Vedfelt in his book *Unconscious intelligence*, concerning the entire human being:

> Even though science is fragmented in its view of man, the human being is fundamentally not. It is connected and forms a general whole, which can be contacted through the unconscious intelligence.

(Vedfelt 2002 p. 308)

References

Grønkjær, Preben (2010) *Jungs analytiske psykologi, En introduktion*, Hans Reitzels Forlag, Copenhagen.

Heede, Dag (2012) *Det tomme menneske, Introduktion til Michel Foucault*. Museum Tusculanums Forlag, Copenhagen.

Jensen, Thomas Wiben (2011) *Kognition og konstruktion. To tendenser i humaniora og den offentlige debat*. Samfundslitteratur, Frederiksberg.

Rousseau, Jean-Jacques (1962) *Emile*, Books 1–3. Del, Borgens Forlag, Copenhagen.

Vedfelt, Ole (2002) *Ubevidst intelligens – Du ved mere end du tror* (New revised ed.). Gyldendal, Copenhagen.

Vedfelt, Ole (1996) *Bevidsthed – Bevidsthedens niveauer*. Gyldendal Copenhagen.

Vedfelt, Ole (2001) Fra Jung til kybernetisk psykologi. In Skogemann, P., *Symbol, Analyse, virkelighed – Jungiansk teori og praksis*. Saxo, Copenhagen.

11

Algorithms of the Heart
A Fugue about Consciousness

Lisa Carew Dahlager

In cybernetic psychology, consciousness is a network of complex systems. This chapter examines how we can understand the functioning and algorithms of consciousness, and how this understanding can be translated into a psychotherapeutic practice. The chapter is composed as a fugue with seven themes, each expressing an aspect – an algorithm – of consciousness. The first algorithm, wholeness, depicts consciousness as a phenomenon that includes both the so-called conscious and unconscious aspects of consciousness. The second algorithm, relations, describes the body, mind and matter as one entity, with consciousness as the 'relating' aspect of this entity. The third algorithm, integration, explores the ability of consciousness to integrate. Through integration, new systems emerge that incorporate the properties of prior systems. According to the fourth algorithm, organisation, consciousness is arranged in networks in which more complex levels have more information capacity and therefore the ability to regulate less complex levels. By communicating with these higher, more complex levels of organisation, using the language of consciousness, the power to learn and create can be activated. These are the fifth and sixth algorithms. The chapter concludes with the seventh algorithm, healing, which illustrates how cybernetic psychotherapy, by following the algorithms of the heart, can promote not only learning and creativity but also the healing powers of consciousness.

Algorithms

The heart has its reasons which the reason does not at all perceive.

Thus wrote the mathematician Blaise Pascal (quoted in Bateson, 1972, p. 321). Anthropologist Gregory Bateson, one of the fathers of cybernetics, reformulated Pascal's words as follows:

Consciousness has its own algorithms.

(Bateson, 1972, p. 138)

DOI: 10.4324/9781003360247-12

This chapter examines the algorithms of consciousness, which are denoted 'algorithms of the heart'. The heart is used here as a metaphor for consciousness. This metaphor is chosen to capture a paradox inherent in consciousness. On the one hand, consciousness is not very rational; rather, it is characterised by a kind of irrationality. For example, consciousness uses metaphors such as 'the heart' to communicate what we cannot express in more logical language. On the other hand, although consciousness may seem irrational, it has its own logic, a precise mode of action. It has its own algorithms.

An algorithm – for example, a food recipe – is a logical pattern or guide for how to undertake a particular process, step by step, regardless of the specific situation. However, the algorithms of consciousness – unlike a food recipe – do not prescribe a straightforward, rigorous procedure. If one wants to work with the algorithms of consciousness, one must be prepared to constantly search for new paths in an unknown landscape, to jump from level to level and listen to resonance.

This adaptability is central to cybernetic psychotherapy. In cybernetic theory, verbal language and reason play a secondary role in the overall ecology of consciousness. This stands in contrast to many psychological and philosophical traditions where verbal language is considered a necessary precondition for the categorisation of consciousness and for the formation of general meaning and the creation of knowledge. Instead, cybernetic theory proposes unconsciousness as the wellspring of knowledge.

This chapter therefore examines the following: What are the algorithms of the heart? Or, how can we interpret the algorithms of consciousness? Drawing primarily on the cybernetic thinking of Bateson and the Danish cybernetic theorist and psychotherapist Ole Vedfelt, the chapter attempts to understand how such an insight can be translated into cybernetic psychotherapy to create learning, creativity and healing.

The chapter is composed as a fugue. A fugue is a compositional technique in music in which a short melody or phrase is introduced by one voice, successively taken up or imitated by other voices and developed by interweaving the voices. Most fugues open with a short main theme, followed by a second voice repeating the theme at a different pitch and so on. This chapter is composed as a fugue consisting of seven voices, or seven 'algorithms', as no one voice by itself defines consciousness; rather, each is an imitation of the theme on a different level, which explores a different aspect of consciousness. The seventh algorithm focuses on how these voices of consciousness can be brought into play in psychotherapy.

Algorithm 1: Wholeness

In *The Sickness unto Death*, Danish philosopher Søren Kierkegaard compared the human spirit to a house with three floors – a basement, a ground floor and a first floor. Kierkegaard claimed that, although the first floor (which is closest to the spiritual realm) is at our disposal, we prefer to live in the basement, in the sensory world (Kierkegaard, 1989). In *The Interpretation of Dreams* (Freud and Brill,

1997), Sigmund Freud reused the house as a metaphor for consciousness. However, he suggested that the upper floor is inhabited by the super-ego (conscience and norms), the ground floor by the ego (the I we identify with) and the basement by the id (instinctive impulses and the unconscious). Accordingly, the ego is founded on the unconscious. Freud's theory of psychoanalysis thus introduced a basic idea of consciousness as divided into a conscious level and an unconscious level. Furthermore, it dethroned rationality – elevated during the Enlightenment – as the dominant aspect of human consciousness. Instead, man, according to Freud, is ruled by a force beyond his control: The unconscious.

In contrast to this idea, in cybernetic thinking, the deeper, more unconscious layers are described as *more* complex than the more conscious layers of consciousness. Further, rather than forming a static structure, like a house, consciousness is described as a complex, open system, constantly exchanging information with other complex systems and with its environment, which is imagined as an organising field. Just as trees use fungi and their large network of underground mycorrhizae (called by some the 'wood wide web'; McKinney, 2011), the rhizome for communication and energy distribution, consciousness, in cybernetic thinking, acts as "a multi-layered, self-optimising complex information system" (Vedfelt, 2020, p. 89) comprising far-ranging interconnected networks. In other words, the basement is inhabited by unconscious intelligence, connected to a worldwide web of consciousness.

In cybernetic thinking, consciousness also consists of a multitude of subsystems. These subsystems are differentiations and specialisations of consciousness, just as the different spaces in a house (the kitchen, the bathroom etc.) each have their own function and distinctive characteristics. For example, the personality may be organised into subpersonalities, which are differentiations of the self into relatively autonomous, specialised units with their own identities. In this way, the personality can process information on several different levels. Several schools of thought in dream analysis claim that the characters in our dreams reflect our inner subpersonalities (Vedfelt, 1996).

These subsystems can exist in different states. Whereas planning or reflection involves a high degree of cognitive consciousness, dreaming, for example, is a state of consciousness with a small degree of rational (cognitive) consciousness (Vedfelt, 2002);. Thus, consciousness "swings rhythmically between states more or less in contact with the outer world" (Vedfelt, 2020). Subsystems work together to ensure self-regulation and regulation in relation to the outer world. The different states of consciousness have different degrees of complexity, information density and information processing capacity, and many degrees of intensity, with the most complex, information-dense and intense states of consciousness being holistic experiences, such as near-death experiences, archetypal dreams and creative breakthroughs. In cybernetic psychology, such states of consciousness are seen as expressions of activity at higher levels of organisation.

Despite this differentiation into parts or subsystems, however, each part remains a whole in and of itself, as well as a part of a larger whole. Here, Arthur Koestler's notion of 'holons', as described in his book *The Ghost in the Machine*

(1982), is a useful way to understand the relationship of subsystems in cybernetic consciousness. A holon is a subsystem within a larger system. It is simultaneously an evolving, self-organising, dissipative structure and also part of a greater system composed of other holons. A hierarchy of holons is called a holarchy, which Koestler defines as a hierarchy of self-regulating holons that function (a) as autonomous wholes in supra-ordination to their parts; (b) as dependent parts in subordination to controls on higher levels; or (c) in coordination with their local environment (Wikipedia, n.d.).

This concept of 'wholeness' as constant dialogues between parts and whole and between the system and the outside world, through a network, is the core of the cybernetics understanding of consciousness. This understanding is repeated in the cybernetic view of the relationship between the body and consciousness. That is the next algorithm.

Algorithm 2: Relations

In Ancient Greek as well as in Christian culture, there is often an oppositional relationship between body and spirit, matter and mind. The body is to be controlled to serve the spirit ('mind over matter'), or the body is cultivated, and the notion of spirit is viewed as irrational ('matter over mind'). By contrast, in cybernetic psychology, as described by Vedfelt, body and psyche are connected:

> The connection between psyche and matter is present in the human personality and consciousness in a thousand observable ways. Every emotion, every inner image, every bodily sensation is the ticket to the psychophysical relationship and is subordinate to a psychophysical process, which encompasses the whole personality and its environment ... One can imagine the psyche and the body as complementary expressions of the same phenomenon, like wave and particle within quantum physics.
>
> (Vedfelt, 1996, pp. 225–226; author's translation)

Likewise, Bateson imagines matter and consciousness – or matter and mind – as inseparable. Thus, the cybernetic approach to consciousness set out by Bateson and Vedfelt posits mind and matter as one whole, a psychophysical relationship.

In this approach, consciousness is understood as a property of all complex systems, of all cybernetic systems. It is the ability of these systems to compare and react to differences or relations between things. Bateson suggests that, when matter is organised into orbits, something arises that we can call 'mind' or 'consciousness' (Bateson, 1972). Differences or relations are the 'substance' that can be recognised by consciousness. For example, if one touches a table with one's finger and experiences the table as hard, then one can only recognise it through the difference or relationship between the table and one's finger. Consciousness is thus the recognition of, and reaction to, differences and relations.

Consciousness can be characterised as a verb – the 'relating' aspect of the psychophysical whole – that is, the ability to create, experience and respond to relations and differences so that each part and the system as a whole can exchange information internally and with the outside world. But consciousness can also be seen as a noun – a structure that can integrate new relations between things and thus develop and evolve, as will be described in the next algorithm.

Algorithm 3: Integration

One of the basic laws of physics, that of entropy, holds that shapes, patterns and structures tend to disintegrate into disorder. According to cybernetics, however, cybernetic systems can maintain and increase their complexity and give form to new patterns and structures (Bateson, 1972). In fact, cybernetic consciousness constantly moves towards *increasing* complexity through integration. Thus, the cybernetic theory of consciousness defies the law of entropy.

Vedfelt's notion of integration in the cybernetic approach to consciousness flows from his understanding of how our brains process information:

> It is in the concept of biological development that the higher forms of development always include features of the lower forms … The brain is thus built up in many levels, where the mental processes correspond to different stages in human evolution, i.e., information processing takes place both at different physical levels (cells, tissues, organs) and in interaction with higher mental functions.
>
> (Vedfelt, 1996, pp. 99–100; author's translation)

In Vedfelt's model, humans – comprising biological, psychological, social, cultural and transpersonal systems – are far more complex than a cell, for example, but include and integrate the cell's abilities.

The development of consciousness is necessarily closely woven together with the 'ecological niche' – that is, the outside world or system of which it is a part. Vedfelt's cybernetic consciousness is thus a complex system that integrates properties from less complex systems that are part of its environment, causing new systems, new wholes, to emerge. These systems organise themselves into networks. This is the fourth algorithm.

Algorithm 4: Organisation

In cybernetic thinking, consciousness is understood as organised in networks, where small information units ('parts' or 'holons') are associated with each other in a coherent pattern (the 'whole' or 'holarchy'). The strength or weakness (the so-called 'energy charge') of the associations between the parts in a network determines which information patterns are activated by different influences. The relative strength of the associations varies in different states of consciousness.

Some parts are connected to many other parts within their own and other networks and thus have a large number of associations, enabling them to play a lead role in regulating the system. This aspect of cybernetic thinking is in accordance with recent network theory, where emphasis is placed on the relations ('links') between each part (called a 'node' or 'nodal') in the network and on the network's number of relationships to other networks. Cybernetic consciousness is similarly organised in holarchies of greater or lesser complexity and breadth. More complex (higher) levels of consciousness have more information capacity and can regulate less complex (lower) levels. The higher levels integrate and transcend the lower ones. In contrast to the Freudian psychoanalytic tradition, as discussed above, however, the more complex, more information-dense levels are the more *unconscious* levels. They are referred to in cybernetic psychology as 'unconscious intelligence'.

In cybernetic psychology, this high-level unconscious intelligence is the prerequisite for rational thinking. The self and rational consciousness are considered to be lower levels, constituting only a small part of consciousness (Vedfelt, 1996, 2000). These less complex levels of consciousness can either support or interfere with higher levels, but they cannot regulate them. Thus, cybernetic psychology distinguishes between the I or ego (the subjectively experienced, personal self with a unifying function) and the cybernetic self or self (the coordination and regulation of overall processes; Vedfelt, 2000).

Consciousness is thus organised as a network in which more complex levels regulate less complex ones, with the cybernetic self as the overall system, the highest organising level. The cybernetic self is the total personality, understood as a whole (Vedfelt, 1996, 2000). We can promote learning and creativity in this system by communicating with consciousness in its own language. This is the fifth algorithm.

Algorithm 5: Communication

As described in Algorithm 2, according to Bateson, consciousness can be viewed as the ability of complex systems to compare and respond to differences or relations between 'things'. However, consciousness is also the ability of systems to *communicate* these differences or relationships. Since cybernetic systems are part of an environment (their 'ecological niche'), they must be able to communicate with their environment or community to ensure wholeness.

According to Bateson, it is the emic (meaning 'what is uttered') aspect of events and phenomena that is communicated. That is, it is not the event or phenomenon itself, but rather the *message* that is relevant to the system that receives it. Thus, the recipient is part of the communication, as it decodes or brings meaning to the message.

Information – or messages – can be gathered in patterns. These patterns can be understood as a collection of a large amount of information brought together through a meaningful associative process. Metaphors – such as the 'heart' of consciousness – and symbols are examples of such collections of information.

Bateson distinguishes between iconic communication (e.g., metaphors and symbols), analogue communication and digital communication. In analogue, nonverbal communication – such as tone of voice, hand movements, posture and so on – there is a correspondence between the sign and the signified. For example, if a scream indicates pain, there will be a correspondence between the intensity of the scream and the intensity of the pain. In digital communication – that is, the spoken or written word – there is no correspondence between the term or 'sign' and what is signified – for example, the word 'cup' and the cup itself (Bateson, 1972).

Bateson argues that, in the overall complex system, communication is primarily analogue and iconic. Digital language can communicate information about objects but is not well suited to communicating information about relations. By contrast, analogue language operates almost exclusively in the realm of relations and can communicate precise information about such vital relations as dominance and submission, addiction and love. Iconic communication is more information-dense than digital communication and can communicate complex meaning. Thus, in cybernetic psychotherapy, emphasis is placed on describing and using analogue and iconic communication, such as emotions, bodily sensations, mental images and dreams.

Cybernetic psychotherapy posits further that all experiences are processed through communication channels or 'information modalities'. Our everyday experience stems from a so-called 'supramodal' ability not only to experience the world across these different modalities, which may include various kinds of analogue, iconic and digital communication, but also to experience a unity between these modalities. Consciousness is perceived as a supramodal space, an intelligent network, where all these various kinds of information are stored and processed (Vedfelt, 2002).

Consciousness thus communicates through a network of languages comprising many different information modalities. It is by using these languages, jumping from level to level, and switching from one modality to another that a dialogue is created with information-dense levels of consciousness ('unconscious intelligence') to which rational consciousness does not have access. Accessing these information-rich levels of consciousness promotes learning and creativity in the system. This is the next algorithm.

Algorithm 6: Learning and Creativity

Stability, according to Bateson, is a descriptive statement about a system that remains true. Cybernetic systems tend to maintain the truth of statements, to be stable. To remain so, the cybernetic consciousness places statements that remain true regardless of changes in the outside world into the deeper layers of consciousness, while those that need to be adapted to the outside world are placed on the surface where they are more accessible. The process of these truisms sinking to the deeper, more unconscious layers of consciousness can be described as the creation of 'habits'. These habits are animated as soon as a person enters a relationship with the outside world. They are fundamental patterns or algorithms which a person activates to act, think and perceive (Bateson, 1972). The I can be understood as a cybernetic system of habits that perpetuates its form and the algorithms it engages in order to act by processing information using habitual truisms.

Some habits, however, exist only in individual subsystems (so-called 'subpersonalities') and thus can cause an overall system to become unstable. Cybernetic systems typically contain some such subsystems that can run amok if not corrected but that are kept in check via constant feedback from the overall system to ensure that a stable state is maintained. In several theories of learning, feedback processes are described as necessary for learning to take place. In cybernetic theory, feedback is one of the mechanisms that causes learning in that system. Since cybernetic systems are open, they balance and evolve using the feedback they receive and process, adapting to changing circumstances and continuously recreating reality (Lindvang, 2010). The changes that emerge through this contact with, and processing of, external influences are disseminated throughout the system. This process creates learning.

Learning, in the cybernetic consciousness as described by Bateson, is distinguishable into different degrees. Zero-degree learning is action based on a certain expectation, where neither the action nor the expectation is subsequently corrected through feedback. First-degree learning occurs when actions are corrected based on feedback – that is, trial and error. Second-degree learning results when the number of alternative actions considered increases or when the context is defined in new ways. The notion of second-degree learning is based on the idea that the individual acts based on pattern recognition, recognising which context they are in and reacting relevantly to that particular context. Second-degree learning helps to simplify an individual's information processing, enabling the individual to handle many different situations within the same general context because they can recognise the common expectation scheme. Second-degree learning is therefore closely linked to habits (Bateson, 1972).

Learning, according to cybernetic psychology, primarily takes the form of what one might call 'apprenticeship'. The cybernetic consciousness slowly builds up an array of templates, synthesising information into patterns illustrating how the world is shaped in different situations and a corresponding set of algorithms for action in those situations. These templates function as a pattern-recognising information network, a form of second-degree learning. Pattern recognition is thus a form of intuitive expertise in which the 'apprentice' is trained in childhood and which they later submerge into more unconscious parts of consciousness (Vedfelt, 2000).

As the cybernetic system learns via second-degree learning, it moves towards a higher degree of complexity, where more and more components can be accommodated and put into play. However, Bateson posits a yet higher form of learning, third-degree learning, in which one becomes able to observe the way one has learned to divide one's surroundings into different contexts and the criteria one uses in the division. It is a form of meta-learning that is rare and requires a profound impact to activate – for example, as may occur in intensive psychotherapy. Third-degree learning requires greater flexibility than is acquired by second-degree learning alone, as one must be free of constraints imposed by habits (Bateson, 1972).

Third-degree learning is facilitated in cybernetic psychotherapy by activating the system's own self-organisation and creative resources via contact with highly complex levels of consciousness. The transition from a less developed to a more developed phase of consciousness involves the emergence of a higher level of organisation through a creative process. Energy that was previously bound at a lower system level is released and used to 'charge' the higher, more complex system level, making it possible for the higher level to integrate the lower level into a new overall structure. Differentiation of the personality can thus take place within the new structural framework.

In sum, consciousness constantly uses systemic feedback among different interior levels of consciousness, as well as with the outside world, to engage in learning levels that allow it to evolve creatively towards more complexity. This evolution results in what cybernetic psychologists refer to as 'emergence' – that is, "The spontaneous creation of new forms of consciousness and higher levels of consciousness" (Vedfelt, 1996, p. 135; author's translation). It is this capacity for learning and creativity that forms one of the cornerstones of cybernetic psychotherapy. In the concluding section, we shall see how emergence enables healing, and how insight into the algorithms of the heart is translated into cybernetic psychotherapy.

Algorithm 7: Healing

The word 'healing' is derived from the Old Nordic word *heill*, meaning 'undamaged' (Den Store Danske, n.d.). According to Bateson, consciousness has the ability to heal itself. If left undisturbed, it will tend to arrange itself as a tautology – a circular argument that is true under every possible interpretation. This tautology can be disrupted, however, like the surface of a pond when a stone is thrown into it (Bateson, 1972). Trauma, for example, can act as a force that tears consciousness apart.

Vedfelt uses the image of the psyche as a landscape with soft hills and pointed peaks. The pointed peaks can occur when the memory of a trauma is triggered, causing a certain part of the system of consciousness to take control over the entire network or large parts of it. Such a memory thus initiates a cascade effect in which the whole system switches to a state of consciousness where those parts of the system that could activate a self-healing process are rendered inoperative (Vedfelt, 1996).

Cybernetic psychotherapy seeks to remediate this effect of trauma by enhancing those states of consciousness that have access to higher consciousness levels with the capacity to reorganise the system. These states of consciousness are activated by switching between process channels in the supramodal space. The purpose of activating these states of consciousness is to prevent the more rational and habitual levels of consciousness from slowing down the self-healing processes and to increase the level of complexity engaged by the consciousness (Vedfelt, 1996). Under this approach, as an example, a client's attention is directed to a feeling. In exploring the feeling, the focus can move away from the rational levels of consciousness and towards an inner bodily sensation, a mental image, a memory or a transference experience, for example. By drawing attention to the supramodal flow of information, the client and therapist can engage in a creative process (Vedfelt, 2009).

In addition to working with states of consciousness and communication channels, cybernetic psychotherapy uses a number of other therapeutic approaches to promote self-healing that are characterised by the notion that self-healing can be enhanced by exchange with the community. We can picture the therapeutic space as a safe community in which a more comprehensive personality has the latitude to emerge. With these approaches, the therapist can, for example, actively step in and act as a substitute for the client's awareness and self-regulatory system by using vicarious introspection. Or the therapist can personify a possible missing element in a systemic relation by, for example, taking on the role of a mother or father (Vedfelt, 1996).

Bateson argues that therapy is an attempt to change a client's metacommunicative habits – that is, the rules or premises that govern how messages are interpreted (a form of third-degree learning, as opposed to second-degree learning). These 'habits' are unconscious before the therapy, but, throughout the therapy, communication takes place at a level that is meta in relation to these habits. Third-degree learning becomes possible as the client learns to perceive and act from a meta-perspective. At the second-degree learning level, the I is the unity of characteristics that one calls oneself and is governed by the habits one uses to perceive, shape and divide contexts. In third-degree learning, a redefinition of the self takes place, and the I no longer functions as the heart of the system, the locus for the division of experiences into different contexts (Bateson, 1972). Instead, the cybernetic self becomes the heart of the system, fully equipped with its own reasons.

Thus, we can say that the basis of cybernetic therapy is the idea that consciousness is always a unity of part and community, with the capacity for self-healing. The community – including the therapist – can promote the ability inherent in all cybernetic systems to self-heal by helping clients to engage in meta-learning through harnessing the power of cybernetic consciousness. Consciousness is undamaged in itself. We need only give it the right conditions, and it will return to its state of wholeness.

Conclusion: Following the Algorithms of the Heart

In this chapter, we have examined the algorithms of the heart, or how we can understand the workings of consciousness in the context of cybernetic psychology. The purpose is to understand how such an insight can be translated into cybernetic psychotherapy. The chapter has shown that cybernetics not only offers a language to describe consciousness, but also provides guidelines for a psychotherapeutic practice aimed at supporting clients' learning, creativity and self-healing powers.

Cybernetic psychotherapy is based on the premise that we, as individuals, evolve not on our own but by virtue of a community that we share with all complex systems, with all living entities. The power for healing and growth made available through this interconnectivity is part of consciousness's own mode of being – its algorithms.

Cybernetic psychotherapy follows the algorithms of the heart by allying itself with reasons which reason knows not of. It follows consciousness like Ariadne's thread through an unknown landscape, in the confidence that consciousness's own propensity for self-healing will show the way.

References

Bateson, G. (1972). *Steps to an Ecology of Mind*. Intertext Books.

Den Store Danske. (n.d.). Retrieved from www.denstoredanske.dk/Kunstogkultur/Musik/Klassisk_musik/Kompositionogarrangement/fuga.dk, 5 September 2021.

Freud, S., and Brill, A.A. (1997). *The Interpretation of Dreams*. Wordsworth Classics of World Literature.

Kierkegaard, S. (1989). *The Sickness unto Death: A Christian psychological exposition for Upbuilding and Awakening*. Penguin Classics.

Koestler, A. (1982). *The Ghost in the Machine*. Last Century Media.

Lindvang, C. (2010). A Field of Resonant Learning. Self-experiential Training and the Development of Music Therapeutic Competencies. Thesis. Department of Communication, Aalborg University. www.mt-phd.aau.dk/phd-theses/

McKinney, D. (Director). (2011). *Wood Wide Web* [Film]. Black Forrest Productions. http://woodwideweb.no/src/v2.mp4

Vedfelt, O. (1996). *Bevidsthed*. Gyldendal, Denmark.

Vedfelt, O. (2000). *Ubevidst intelligens – Du Ved Mere End Du Tror*. Gyldendal, Denmark.

Vedfelt, O. (2002). *The Dimensions of Dreams: The nature, function, and interpretation of dreams*. Jessica Kingsley.

Vedfelt, O. (2009). Cultivating Feelings through Working with Dreams. *Jung Journal: Culture & Psyche*, *3*(4), p. 88–102. https://doi.org/10.1525/jung.2009.3.4.88

Vedfelt, O. (2020). Integration versus Conflict between Schools of Dream Theory and Dreamwork: Integrating the psychological core qualities of dreams with the contemporary knowledge of the dreaming brain. *Journal of Analytical Psychology*, *65*(1)1, 88–115. https://doi.org/10.1111/1468-5922.12574

Wikipedia. (n.d.). Holons. Retrieved from https://en.wikipedia.org/wiki/Holon_(philosophy), 5 September 2021.

12

Calls from the Unconscious

Maria F. Sejersen

An increasing number of people are experiencing a growing restlessness, meaninglessness and emptiness in life. The World Health Organization (WHO) has drawn attention to the fact that, in 2020, the most common diagnosis was depression. According to the Swiss psychiatrist Jung, mental states in adults such as restlessness, meaninglessness and emptiness may be the beginning of a deeper process of personal development – *the process of individuation*. According to Vedfelt's cybernetic psychology, these mental conditions can be viewed as the beginning of the phase of life he refers to as the *professional master crisis*. The chapter explains the internal processes and external circumstances that are typical of the development. The chapter shows that it is possible to achieve greater complexity, spaciousness and inclusiveness in the personality, and thereby greater meaning in life. Bearing in mind the worldwide prevalence of depressive tendencies, Vedfelt's life phase, the *professional master crisis*, is explored and considered in relation to Jung's *process of individuation*.

Crises, Life Transitions and Potential Personal Development

According to the analytical psychology of the Swiss psychiatrist Carl Gustav Jung (1875–1961), restlessness, meaninglessness and emptiness, which are conditions increasingly experienced in the population, may just be the beginning of what he refers to as the *process of individuation*. According to Jung, when these states of suffering are experienced, most people are unaware of where they originated, and what possibilities lie ahead, and therefore suppress them. The mental states are then explained away, often with rationalisation about how the external circumstances in life are the cause of the crisis. Jung, however, perceives it differently, viewing the mental conditions as calls from *the self*, referring to the centre and whole of the psyche, and he encourages looking inward and listening to the unconscious (Jung, 1991, p. 166).

According to the Danish psychotherapist and author Ole Vedfelt, all new stages of personal development in life begin with the introduction of new, incomplete forms or schemas, from a new and higher level, exerting pressure from the *unconscious intelligence*. Vedfelt describes the unconscious intelligence as a superior

DOI: 10.4324/9781003360247-13

intelligence in us all, forming our lives in so many ways. The development itself consists of having one's view of the world nuanced and differentiated to fit the external reality, while at the same time integrating new creative potentials (Vedfelt, 2002, p. 342). He describes the phases of life that occur most frequently in adulthood. He refers to them as *"from apprentice to journeyman"*, *"parenthood"*, *"the professional master crisis"* and *"midway turn"*. The *professional master crisis* phase, which according to Vedfelt often begins with feelings of emptiness and meaninglessness, reflects growing tendencies in society. According to cybernetic psychology, crises are an inevitable part of life. In theory, life transitions therefore always contain the possibility of developing a more spacious, empathetic and, in a positive sense, complex personality and a chance of getting closer to one's inner core (Vedfelt, 2002, p. 345).

Carl Gustav Jung

The originator of analytical psychology was the Swiss psychiatrist Carl Gustav Jung. He worked with both the conscious and the unconscious aspects of the psyche. He perceived the psyche as layered, where consciousness 'lies at the top', followed by the personal unconscious and the *collective unconscious*.

Jung worked rigorously with the unconscious, both theoretically and in practice, putting intense focus on dream analysis and symbols. He saw dreams as a form of creative power that holds ancient wisdom. He concentrated particular attention on opportunities of personal development in the future. In the bigger picture, the task of dreams was to make the personality more whole. Jung described how all people have a potential personal plan of development that strives to make the personality unique and whole. He examined and studied personal development in the adult stage of life and called the whole personality development, or the realisation of the personal development plan, the *process of individuation* (Jung, 1991, p. 160).

Jung also contributed several therapeutic theories and methods that are still in use today: Typology, for example, where he divides people into the functions of feeling, thinking, intuition and sense, and their orientation of introvert or extrovert. He also worked with alchemical symbolism, especially from dreams, as well as the phenomenon of *synchronicity*, which, according to the theory, is experienced more frequently when working with individuation. He described synchronicity as causal events that are independent of each other and yet experienced as meaningful coincidences (Vedfelt, 2002, p. 355).

Jung's Personality Model

Jung's personality model describes an *ego*, which represents both consciousness and the unconscious mind. The ego is the part of the personality that thinks, feels and remembers. Attached to the ego is the *persona*, the Latin word for mask, which points to the face shown to the outside world and the image intended. In contrast, the *shadow*, the other side of the ego, is known to be undeveloped or repressed.

According to Jung, the shadow refers to the unconscious aspects of the personality that, for one reason or another, have not yet been integrated. The name *shadow* is said to have been chosen because, in dreams, it often appears in a personified form (Franz, 1991, pp. 168–169).

The model also includes Jung's highly significant notion that every human being has innate qualities of the opposite gender, which are referred to as *anima*, the feminine qualities in the man, and *animus*, the masculine qualities in the woman.

The self is perceived as the whole of the psyche and the centre of inner guidance during the process of individuation (Jung, 1991, p. 162).

The unconscious part of the personality contains, in theory, both a personal and a collective element. Jung perceived the *collective unconscious* as a giant ocean of universal symbols representing different universal experiences, behaviours, roles, common human life situations and personality development. He regarded it as the common psychic heritage of humankind and the eternal symbols or *archetypes* (Jung, 1991, p. 107).

Jung described the archetypes as inherited imaginative possibilities, as empty or blank forms. Their purpose is to bring the individual into contact with life tasks. For example, an archetype can be a universal symbol of motherhood, paternity or of the transition from child to adult. Sexuality can, archetypically speaking, symbolise the union of male and female characteristics, integration and the opportunity to develop creatively and spiritually (Vedfelt, 2007, pp. 65–66).

Ole Vedfelt

The psychotherapist and author Ole Vedfelt developed the theory of cybernetic psychology. He is head of the Vedfelt Institute for Cybernetic Psychology and Integrated Psychotherapy, together with his wife Lene Vedfelt, and has well over 40 years of experience with therapy and working with dreams.

Cybernetic psychology is the doctrine of how complex information is regulated and processed in the human psyche. The theory integrates elements from various psychological schools, including Freud's psychoanalysis, analytical Jungian psychology, body therapy, gestalt, Imago and cognitive therapies. The theories form an integrated framework, an overall and new theory. According to Vedfelt, the main thesis in cybernetic psychology is that the more complex systems can potentially regulate the less complex systems. Since the unconscious has a far greater capacity for information and complexity than our everyday consciousness, extensive regulation of the personality can only take place in cooperation with the *unconscious intelligence* (Vedfelt, 2002, p. 35). The theory can be described as progressive, as it focuses more on resources and personal development opportunities than on postulated inner errors (Vedfelt, 2001, p. 304).

Vedfelt's Personality Model

In cybernetic psychology, Vedfelt explains that there is an *unconscious intelligence* within the personality which allows us to use our resources optimally and get in balance with ourselves. The unconscious intelligence is an intelligence in the unconscious that is superior to our everyday consciousness. It shapes our actions, our interactions with other people and our basic experience of reality. According to Vedfelt, the unconscious intelligence is thus the driving force in life, constantly present in all of us, and orchestrates the various transitions and phases we go through (Vedfelt, 2002, p. 17). The unconscious intelligence enables self-organisation and self-regulation, as well as guiding the personality through several predetermined developmental stages, including the professional master crisis, and thereby helps with the self-formation of the personality (Vedfelt, 2003, pp. 31–33).

According to Vedfelt, the *cybernetic self* refers to the overall system, the personality in total, which coordinates the overall governing processes in the personality. The cybernetic self thus encompasses the whole personality, in contrast to the subjectively experienced self or self-perception, which denotes personified self-experience (Vedfelt, 2002, p. 264). In cybernetic psychology, the personality is regarded as a multilayered self-regulating cybernetic system in which the more complex levels have a greater capacity for information and can regulate the less complex levels. Less complex levels may support or interfere with the higher levels but not regulate them. The unconscious intelligence has greater complexity and capacity than the everyday consciousness and can regulate more complex structures. The overall psychic control systems are protected against the everyday consciousness but can be influenced and supported – for example, in a therapeutic process and with training in altered states of consciousness such as in meditation and visualisation (Vedfelt, 2002, pp. 192–194).

According to the cybernetic personality model, the psyche organises itself in natural subsystems, which often manifest themselves in subpersonalities. Together, they form a distributed intelligence that can store and handle large, holistic amounts of information, simultaneously and on many levels (Vedfelt, 2002, pp. 252, 264–265). Vedfelt describes how the individual's innate ability to enter a relationship with the primary caregiver, most often the mother, forms the basis of the formation of a mother network, which collects and structures information about maternal qualities. The information sinks in as tacit knowledge and unfolds as a subpersonality (Vedfelt, 2000, pp. 545–548). The development of subpersonalities will, in most cases, start with the mother and expand concurrently with the development of the personality, continuing with the father network, siblings and so on. The subjectively experienced self can also be perceived as a personified system, a subpersonality. According to cybernetic psychology, the various functions within personality are viewed as a system of subsystems or subpersonalities that carry out various tasks in our lives: A distributed intelligence (Vedfelt, 2003, pp. 26–29).

Vedfelt perceives the human being as an open network that thrives on incomplete information and always seeks the input that best matches the inner conditions. The human reality is therefore viewed as an interpreted reality (Vedfelt, 2002, p. 312). Upon cross-border psychological stress, such as traumatic events or excessive adaptation to the environment, the possibilities of self-regulation are limited in terms of complexity and spaciousness, and personality development is complicated in critical phases. This may result in a more excessive personality, which results in more rigid patterns (Vedfelt, 2002, pp. 312–313).

The Development of the Personality and the Purpose

The Jungian Approach

From a Jungian perspective, one central concept is the process of individuation, which depicts natural, universally grounded personality development. This starts around midlife and is a matter of developing into one's own indivisible self by directing one's attention towards an awareness of the relationship with the self. Over a long period, Jung examined approximately 80,000 dreams, collected from many different people. He found that all the dreams followed a recognisable form and structure, a pattern of psychic growth. In the dreams, Jung identified a kind of hidden underlying process that was occupied with creating a slow, almost invisible psychic growth towards the wholeness and unity of the personality. According to Jung, this process, the process of individuation, involved a gradual emergence of a more nuanced and mature personality, based on the formation of a bridge within the psyche between the conscious and the unconscious (Franz, 1991, pp. 160–162).

Seen from a Jungian approach, the very purpose of the process of individuation or self-realisation is to find one's own inner personality core through which to develop one's highest potential. Achieving contact with the self has the potential to lead to fulfilling one's purpose in life (Skogemann, 2013). According to Jung, the self is the inner guiding, spiritual centre of the individual. It is the sum of the psyche and the whole, as opposed to the ego, which is only a small portion of the sum. Among other things, the self organises the development that Jung refers to as the process of individuation. For Jung, the process is best supported through work with one's dreams (Jung, 1991, p. 162).

The actual confrontation with the unconscious is described as a harsh and difficult process. During the process of individuation, control of the personality gradually moves from the persona and the outer world to the self and the inner world. During this process, a person progresses from being guided from the outside to personal guidance from the inside. Over time, the individual becomes less dependent on the feedback and reflections of the outer world. Thus, a feeling of resting within oneself emerges (Franz, 1991, pp. 160–162).

Jung describes the necessity of being consciously and actively involved in the individuation process. The ego must be trained in listening attentively to the unconscious in order to hear what the guiding impulse in the process of individuation, the self, wants to happen next (Jung, 1991, p. 38).

The Vedfelt Approach

As stated by Vedfelt's cybernetic psychology, during the course of a human life there is constant pressure from within towards integration, differentiation and development of the personality. This pressure can evolve creatively in all phases of life, both in practical action and as inner processes. The conductor of this development is, according to Vedfelt, the unconscious intelligence (Vedfelt, 2002, p. 329). Natural transitions and new phases in life are often linked to a specific age, to social tasks of importance for human development and to the *ecological niche*, understood as institutions, customs and personalities in the life of the individual (Vedfelt, 2002, p. 337).

Vedfelt's cybernetic psychology states that development of the personality always occurs from a lower to a higher complexity. Since the unconscious has far greater information complexity and capacity than the normal consciousness, extensive regulations of the personality can only take place in cooperation with the unconscious intelligence. At new stages of life, higher and more complex control systems are activated. Potentially, they have a greater degree of freedom and more choice than the lower levels and are therefore capable of including the whole personality.

The systems that are to control the new phase of life are forms yet without content, empty. In order to be usable, they must receive input from the ecological niche and from life experience itself. The unconscious intelligence has already collected material for the conversion by, for example, experiencing other people in this phase of life, which makes it possible to take such a large, extensive leap without everything ending in chaos (Vedfelt, 2002, p. 327).

For the sake of understanding, the actual 'filling in' of the forms, with input from our ecological niche, can be compared to the passage of the year with the regular cultural events and holidays that are common to Danes: for example, birthdays, Midsummer's Eve, Easter, Christmas and New Year. We all know the empty form prior to a birthday celebration. There should be guests, gifts, flags, cake and a song. We have to fill in the blanks ourselves: The guest list, which songs to sing, what gifts to give – from content to wrapping and when to open them – what kind of cake to serve with regard to taste, colour and size, and whether the cake should be homemade or store-bought.

In the same way, humankind has inherited forms, yet without content, for becoming an adult, becoming a parent and finding an exclusive professional indicator. Those forms must also be filled in, with experience from life. In this way, according to Vedfelt, all people have both their individuality and many of the same empty forms, which must be filled in individually and developed throughout a lifetime (Vedfelt, 2002, p. 327).

Vedfelt describes how transitions to new phases of life are, in most cases, difficult and filled with conflict, and how it is often necessary to work with previous experiences in order to overcome the challenges (Vedfelt, 2002, p. 328). For example, if a man has been told throughout his upbringing that it is a sign of weakness to show any emotion, he will find it difficult suddenly to have to contain his own child's tears, which is, of course, necessary in the new phase of life as a parent.

According to Vedfelt, personal development continues from birth to death. It is initiated by a higher-level management system that prevails and starts a reformatting of the previous personality structure. The process is prepared in the unconscious and reflected in symbolic processes, which can be observed in dreams, as somatic manifestations and in visualisations during meditation (Vedfelt, 2002, p. 329). According to Vedfelt, the unconscious intelligence uses symbols as code for transformation. In dreams, for example, the snake, which sheds its skin, and the fire that transforms solid matter into gases may symbolise a form of transformation of the personality (Vedfelt, 2012, pp. 184–185).

Vedfelt points out that intense, information-dense states of consciousness often arise in the predictable transitional phases of life, such as puberty, parenthood, vocation, midlife crises and death. In Vedfelt's theory, the phenomena *states of consciousness* are regarded as states comprising psychic patterns of fluid tension within a defined area. The different states of consciousness are dynamic patterns of psychological systems and subsystems. According to the theory, states of consciousness must be actively maintained by certain processes in order not to switch to another state (Vedfelt, 2002, p. 98). Cybernetic psychology maintains that the intense, information-dense states can be experienced as preparatory waves sent towards the consciousness. They can be considered an inner process of creation that is visible in the unconscious – in dreams, for example – long before the transition itself takes place.

The high intensity often depicted in dreams before life transitions is viewed as an expression of the much greater capacity for information which, according to the theory, is essential for recoding overall control systems in the personality (Vedfelt, 2002, pp. 332–333). In cybernetic psychology, therefore, high-intensity, information-dense states of consciousness are perceived as both natural and necessary conditions for important life transitions (Vedfelt, 2002, p. 335). When these conditions occur, it is often in the context of an expected transition. Vedfelt therefore describes these intense states of consciousness as potential personality-changing processes that are produced by the predictable transitions in life rather than being the very cause of these transitions (Vedfelt, 2002, p. 332).

Vedfelt also explains that all transitions translate into observable signs. In the midlife years, for example, the transitions often appear as emotional crises, wild love affairs, openness to everything different and total conversions of views on life. When these impulses and experiences are not recognised, then, instead of leading to development, they can lead to a more rigid and fixed personality (Vedfelt, 2002, p. 335). In Vedfelt's theory, he describes how the development of the personality consists of being able to relate to increasingly complex experiences, both internally and externally (Vedfelt, 1996, p. 113).

In cybernetic psychology, development of the personality is considered a form of creative and fluid process, in which development can take place in several areas simultaneously. There is not necessarily a specific sequence of events that must be followed in order to develop the personality. The process follows a more dynamic trajectory and can take place on many levels and stages at the same time. A human being, viewed in cybernetic psychology as a living system, is generally flexible and can thus follow many paths to the same goal. Vedfelt refers to this concept as *equifinality* (Vedfelt, 2002, p. 314).

The Professional Master Crisis Viewed in the Light of the Individuation Process

Encounter with the Unconscious

According to Jung, the process of individuation itself usually begins with a crisis, often experienced as unbearable and challenging owing to overriding feelings such as emptiness and meaninglessness. He describes how most people have an experience of searching for something that is at first untraceable and cannot be identified. The self's purpose with this crisis is both unpredictable and hidden and only manifests itself via messages from the unconscious. Therefore, the aim of the crisis is to start a process in which our attention is turned inwards. This initiates the task of raising awareness and accepting and processing all harsh facts which a confrontation with the unconscious entails. The human conscious self-image is often experienced as being quite far from what the self wants to initiate, which further complicates the process (Franz, 1991, pp. 160–162). The only thing that works at this stage, according to Jung, is to look directly towards the advancing darkness, without prejudice, and completely and naively try to discover the nature of the secret goal and what the self wants from you (Franz, 1991, p. 167).

Life's Phases

In cybernetic psychology, Vedfelt describes a phase of life between the ages of 35 and 45. This period contains many of the same patterns as other phases but is also unique in terms of internal psychic and external social dynamics alike. The phase is about finding one's professional calling in life, and Vedfelt refers to it as the *professional master crisis* (Vedfelt, 2002, p. 345).

According to Vedfelt, in our mid-30s, we all enter a new phase of life which often builds up to a crisis around the age of 40. This crisis lasts for approximately 4–5 years, after which the transition itself is over, and the new role is implemented. During this phase, work commitment emerges in a new way and may manifest itself as a desire to develop a more independent attitude within an already established area or, more comprehensively, as a desire to switch to a completely different line of work (Vedfelt, 2002, p. 345).

In detail, the phase involves finding one's unique contribution to the community, career-wise, as well as finding oneself at ease with one's social contribution to life. In Vedfelt's experience, we all have an impulse to find our exclusive brand, where we can do things in our very own way and find our own professional personal style and uniqueness. The whole person must be developed and involved in the work as much as possible by balancing ambitions with real abilities, within the existing societal framework (Vedfelt 2002, pp. 345–346).

According to cybernetic psychology, parts of our natural progression, development, qualities and traits that did not fit into our world when we were growing up have sunk into the unconscious. Now the time has come to get in touch with some of these aspects, since the professional master crisis is about realising oneself and doing so by raising awareness of unconscious parts of the personality (Vedfelt, 2002, p. 346).

Jung and Vedfelt agree that development demands release of the current governing forces of the personality so that a new order can emerge. According to both, at the beginning of the process, this is often symbolised in dreams as a process of death – for example, dreams of cemeteries, funerals, collapsed buildings and experiences of drowning, or an encounter with black dogs, ravens or other harbingers of death. Symbolically speaking, this could be indicating that major personality changes are on the way. The intimidating nature of the symbols indicates that the dreamer is at a point in the process where fear is present and where it is very difficult to let go of the safe and familiar way of life (Vedfelt, 2012, pp. 184–185).

An Awareness of the Shadow

Jung describes how adults, owing to their ego development and socialisation, identify too much with their social role, the *persona*. Therefore, qualities that do not fit into this role – attractive as well as less attractive – have been displaced and hidden away. However, those qualities are still essential for the whole of the psyche and must therefore be rendered alert at this stage (Franz, 1991, pp. 168–169).

To become aware of the *shadow*, we must look at the unconscious sides of our personality through working with our dreams. In dreams, the shadow is usually of the same sex as the dreamer. Awareness often reveals that qualities in people looked down on or looked up to are a part of the dreamer's own personality. The shadow encompasses values that the personality needs in order to become whole, but these qualities exist in a form that proves challenging to integrate. These characteristics are often subconsciously projected on to people with whom we interact, as they are difficult to hold within ourselves. Integrating the parts, according to Jung, means that they must be recognised as a part of ourselves and thereby consciously drawn back to ourselves, so that the personality becomes more composed and complex. For example, if your parents have taught you that feeling angry is not okay, then you might find it difficult to be aware of and admit to yourself that you are angry. The anger will be repressed and projected outwards instead, so that anger in others may be viewed as wrong or inappropriate. Integration of anger means that we must acknowledge our own anger by learning to accept, feel, hold and express it. This element of the work with development of the personality is often a long and painful process leading to soul-searching and then to insight that calls for changes in one's life. Jung believes this to be the very reason many people choose to neglect the new knowledge and insight they have gained, as the work ahead can seem far too overwhelming (Franz, 1991, pp. 168–170).

According to Vedfelt, in order to work your way through the professional master crisis you must let go of everything you have learned from your earlier teachers: Their ideas, thoughts and patterns which have previously provided support while you perform various tasks. It is time to stand on your own two feet, otherwise it will be impossible to realise the individual, the unique and different and take charge in your personal domain, which is the purpose of the crisis. On these grounds, it is not possible to seek advice from outsiders in this phase, as the individual and original must come from within (Vedfelt, 2002, p. 346). Since you can only seek guidance in your inner world, the phase is often associated with a feeling of loneliness and isolation. In this part of the process, Vedfelt describes how you feel a need to be free to do as you wish, without being subject to control from above, but at the same time you are unable to identify your goal. On the one hand, you know more than your teachers do and, on the other hand, you need guidance.

The very insistent energy felt during this transition is described as being impossible to identify. The only option, according to Vedfelt, is to turn your attention inwards and towards the unconscious intelligence, which fortunately assists with the transition and development. Vedfelt points out how working with dreams can be helpful for the process, as the dreams can indicate direction, draw attention to unused resources and point to where support can be found (Vedfelt, 2002, pp. 346–347).

In dreams, according to both Jung and Vedfelt, the shadow is most often depicted as a person of the same gender as the dreamer. In men's dreams, the shadow might be experienced as, for example, a biker, a Don Juan, a vagabond, an artist, a gay man or a Native American man. In women's dreams, the shadow is known to be symbolised as, for example, a witch, a fury, a prostitute or a Madonna. The shadow constantly depicts the repressed side of the personality. In both approaches, in dreams, the shadow can prove to contain valuable qualities and characteristics, and in these cases it must be consciously integrated. In other cases, *the shadow* can represent forces that dominate the personality and cause the more nuanced and finer parts to be overlooked, and then *the shadow* must be challenged and reined in. Certain concessions made to our *shadow* will often render it more manageable (Franz, 1991, pp. 168–170; Vedfelt, 2012, pp. 254–256).

Integration of the Innate Qualities of the Opposite Sex: Anima and Animus

According to Jung's analytical psychology, the next step – although not necessarily followed in strict order – in the process of individuation is to integrate the inner, innate qualities of the opposite gender. Jung refers to the male qualities in the woman as animus, and the female qualities in the man as anima. The aspects of the opposite gender personify the opposite gender's tendencies in the psyche. For example, during this transition, the man has the potential to develop and refine his compassion, spaciousness and relational competence. The woman can develop her willpower, drive and decisiveness. In the personal form of expression, the woman's animus is often characterised by her father complex, and the man's anima by his mother complex (Franz, 1991, pp. 177–179).

In his theory, Jung describes how, in dreams, the feminine aspect can appear as symbols experienced as feminine – for example, as a sister, an old lady, a virgin, an angel, a cow, a ship or a witch. The masculine aspect in the woman can be experienced as male symbols – for example, a brother, a craftsman, a male helper, a lion, a tower. According to Jung, the integration of the inner qualities of the opposite gender requires that the person be made consciously aware. After the integration, it will be possible to add several new characteristics to the personality, which then becomes more spacious, nuanced, complex and whole (Franz, 1991, pp. 177–179).

In Vedfelt's theory, the development of men and women does not follow the same path. Since gender roles are not the same in culture or society or on a personal level, the unconscious material that must be integrated is therefore not the same either. Nevertheless, during the professional master crisis, both genders will have an opportunity to integrate the inner qualities of the opposite sex. When the man finds himself in transition to the professional master crisis, he usually experiences it as a midlife crisis. He seeks to open out professionally, to find a niche that is original and unique, on a more comprehensive basis. He frequently enters the process with masculine energy, which often takes an aggressive and competitive approach to established authorities and competing peers. The potential challenge here is that the search may result in projecting the resistance he encounters outwardly, and he then ends up seeing enemies everywhere. In dreams, too, this struggle can become visible, manifesting itself in the form of threatening male personalities or symbols, which points to the male aspects of the personality that are not yet integrated (Vedfelt, 2002, pp. 346–347). As the phase and integration consciously progress, the male symbols in the dreams will change character, becoming friendlier over time. Finally, if the development has proceeded as intended, the dreams will present symbols of wholeness and growth (Vedfelt, 2012, pp. 254–256).

According to Vedfelt, the woman encounters the professional master crisis in a somewhat different way. She must find her female individuality in her work and then transfer it to her female consciousness. This calls for her to engage in a process, as opposed to establishing a creative energy. Owing to the female role in our society, she may experience being divided between family and work to a much greater degree than the man may. She is able to spend a longer period stifling the inner calling that wants work-based self-realisation. On those grounds, this inner calling is seen to manifest itself abruptly, completely unexpectedly and with great force. The woman must acquire knowledge and expand her field of work if she is to fulfil the inner calling. Her dreams now include female figures, which are manifestations of the opportunities for growth that this phase entails. When the integration has fully transpired, symbols of wholeness will appear (Vedfelt, 2002, pp. 347–348).

Contact with the Self

When the process of individuation has reached a point at which awareness and integration of all the unconscious aspects of our personality have occurred, a feeling of spiritual reorientation may set in, infusing the psyche with energy, life and adventure (Franz, 1991, p. 196). The self is now activated, and from here on the job is to be aware and listen to its messages, which deal with the direction of our flow of life and can be expressed in dreams and external events alike. The hazard of the contact with the self now established is that it may result in madness and grandiosity if contact with reality, humour and the ability to reflect and enjoy human interaction are lost (Franz, 1991, p. 216).

Jung depicted symbols of the self that now begin to appear in dreams as the circle in many different forms – for example, the mandala or the four points of the compass – and in personified form as the wise old man, the sorcerer, the sorceress, the guru, the master and the goddess (Franz, 1991, p. 213).

According to Vedfelt, adaptation to the new phase of life will inevitably raise emotional and personal memory material, enabling the personality to restructure old patterns. The nature of the outcome of the professional master crisis is largely based on how the inner subpersonalities relate to one another, as well as the very structure of the inner psychic network and, obviously, our ability to listen to the unconscious intelligence (Vedfelt, 2002, pp. 346–348).

Vedfelt reports how the literature describes ingenious inventions and artistic breakthroughs that have arisen from a sudden revelation in this phase. In these special cases, where it is a matter of scientific innovation or artistic genius, it is often a so-called conscious high-intensity and information-dense state of consciousness that prevails. Vedfelt describes how the mental state during the breakthrough is totally clear, as well as how the singular scheme itself crystallises in a single flash and with complete conviction. This type of revelation is associated with a reorganisation of material, where the result is greater than the combined parts. In cybernetic psychology, the process is referred to as *emergence* and it affects the whole personality (Vedfelt, 2002, p. 346). In theory, when this type of experience occurs, enough capacity of information is released to activate a new comprehensive, overall organisational level and control system, which give the personality greater spaciousness, complexity and inclusiveness (Vedfelt, 1996, p. 116).

Both theoreticians believe that the contact with our inner self, established by listening inwardly, provides the opportunity to be guided by something far greater and more intelligent than the everyday consciousness. This 'something' is described as the unconscious intelligence by Vedfelt and as the self by Jung. They agree on the result of the process: The development of a more whole, spacious, empathetic and, in a positive sense, complex personality so that it becomes possible to fulfil one's purpose in life.

Hannah's Psychotherapeutic Course

The Encounter with the Unconscious

When Hannah, at the age of 38, began her therapeutic course, she found life meaningless, difficult and lonely. It was impossible for her to define what she wanted in life. At the beginning of the therapy, she was having dreams in which she was given a life-threatening diagnosis, was chased by black dogs, ancient gates had to be opened, and buildings were undergoing extensive renovation.

In relation to the theories of personality development, her dreams can be viewed as reflections of the beginning of the therapeutic process. In particular, the life-threatening diagnosis and the black dogs testified to the great horror Hannah associated with encountering the unconscious and the need to let go of familiar patterns for the benefit of the unknown, exactly as described by both Jung and Vedfelt.

An Awareness of the Shadow

After a while in treatment, with an intense focus on dreams, Hannah began to sense a growing creativity within. Now, she felt she was able to get in touch with her creativity, which had been absent since childhood. She had reconnected, and creative ideas emerged. In fact, she questioned whether to stay in her current profession with the fire department or to follow new paths of creativity. After one session, Hannah dreamed about a golden-coloured snake sticking out its tongue. In the dream, she was not afraid.

As Vedfelt's description of the professional master crisis shows, our profession will manifest itself in a new and more individualised way and, in rarer cases, as a desire to change the field of work completely. Hannah's experience indicates that repressed creative aspects of her personality, which had been shut down for one reason or another in childhood, had now surfaced and appeared in the process of being integrated. Owing to the integration of the creativity, Hannah's personality had developed towards wholeness, which is precisely the intention of the individuation process itself.

The dream about the snake, which often symbolises transformation (Vedfelt, 2012, p. 185), could suggest that the client was no longer as afraid of developing her personality in treatment as was the case earlier. The dream might symbolise that Hannah had a greater openness towards working consciously with the process.

Integration of the Innate Qualities of the Opposite Sex: Anima and Animus

After a few years in treatment, Hannah dreamed the following dream: She was renovating her apartment, and her father had already done a great job with the basics. In the waking world, Hannah had started producing the shoes that she had designed. She had launched her creative project, hoping to make a living from it in the future and eventually be able to quit her job at the fire department. The whole project was a source of great joy and energy. The dream highlighted positive male qualities in Hannah, which might have been the reason she was able to move forwards and thus accomplish her 'shoe project'. The integrated male qualities could be courage, action, structure and creative boldness (Vedfelt, 2012, p. 234).

Later in the process, Hannah described being able to make decisions no longer based on the fear of being abandoned but instead based on what was best for her. This led to Hannah choosing to leave her boyfriend and to do so with firm conviction. From a cybernetic point of view, what Hannah experienced is equivalent to a client in the transition phase to the professional master crisis managing to restructure old patterns and schemes that are no longer appropriate from the perspective of the self, thereby creating a more spacious and whole personality.

Although Hannah continues to work simultaneously with all the phases of the individuation, and the process is far from complete, it becomes clear that listening to the unconscious intelligence through therapy and dreamwork assists the personality in becoming more whole and thus closer to its inner core.

Therapeutic Treatment

Dreams played a major role in Jung's therapeutic work, which often consisted of raising awareness and substantiating the process of individuation. When interpreting dreams, he applied his profound understanding of symbols derived from mythology, fairy tales, religion, the initiation rites of primitive peoples and alchemy. The process itself, which developed concurrently with the deep therapeutic work, was reflected in the dreams by means of symbols that could then be incorporated into the therapy (Franz, 1991, pp. 160–162). Jung regarded the analyst's own individuation and personal development as a fundamental tool in connection with the client's resistances and transferences and in the very act of being a Jungian analyst, which he described as a calling in life and a lifelong process (Vedfelt, 2001, p. 289).

In cybernetic psychology, work is undertaken in several ways to support the constant pressure towards differentiation and making the personality more whole. This also applies in relation to the professional master crisis as well as other life transitions and phases. Dreams are a very important tool, as are visualisations, meditations, bodywork, drawing therapy and gestalt therapeutic and psychodynamic methods, all depending on what the therapist finds to be most useful and appropriate in the unique situation (Vedfelt, 2002, p. 299).

Both Jung and Vedfelt engage with symbols from dreams when working with the development of the personality. They agree that the symbols contain a transforming power when they are experienced rather than just being thought, and therefore the work in the therapy room places great emphasis on the actual experience of the symbols (Vedfelt, 2002, p. 329). In addition, they both find that the personality of the therapist is fundamental to the very quality of the therapy. Vedfelt emphasises – like Jung – that the therapist's development of his or her own personality and relational competence are the most important tools in therapy.

Summary

Throughout this chapter, a potential answer has crystallised as to how personality development in adulthood can be viewed. Both in cybernetic and analytical psychology, the development of personality in adulthood, including the professional master crisis and the process of individuation, can be viewed as part of the natural development process in every individual's path through life.

The very purpose of the professional master crisis is clear: To achieve a more whole, spacious and, in a positive sense, complex personality by integrating the unconscious parts of the personality. The directing parts thereby attain a higher level, which results in a shift taking place: We progress from being guided from the outside to being guided by ourselves from the inside, thus getting in touch with life's deeper meaning.

In light of Jung's and Vedfelt's theories and experiences of personality development in adulthood, a conscious listening to our inner wisdom and an immersion in personal development processes, supported by a therapeutic course, may be a potential response to the restlessness, meaninglessness and emptiness that pervade the people of the world. It is a necessity for all of us to look inwards when identifying the causes of our personal crisis.

References

Franz, M.-L. von, 1991. "Mennesket og dets symboler", in C.G. Jung (Ed.), *Individuationsprocessen*. Lindhardt & Ringhof, Copenhagen.

Jung, C.G. 1991. "Mødet med det ubevidste", in *Mennesket og dets symboler*. Lindhardt & Ringhof, Copenhagen.

Skogemann, Pia. 2013. "Individuation", in *Den Store Danske*, Gyldendal. Available at: http://denstoredanske.dk/index.php?sideId=97364 [accessed 2 February 2017].

Vedfelt, Ole. 1996. *Bevidsthed – Bevidsthedens niveauer*. Nordisk Forlag, Copenhagen.

Vedfelt, Ole. 2001. "Fra Jung til kybernetisk psykologi", in Pia Skogemann (Ed.), *Jungiansk teori og praksis i Denmark*. Lindhardt & Ringhof, Copenhagen.

Vedfelt, Ole. 2002. *Ubevidst intelligens. Du ved mere end du tror*. Nordisk Forlag, Copenhagen.

Vedfelt, Ole. 2003. *Manden og hans indre kvinder*. Nordisk Forlag, Copenhagen.

Vedfelt, Ole. 2007. *Drømmenes dimensioner*. Nordisk Forlag, Copenhagen.

Vedfelt, Ole. 2012. *Din guide til drømmenes verden*. Nordisk Forlag, Copenhagen.

Vedfelt, Ole. 2000. Delpersonligheder, objektrelationer og kybernetisk netværksteori. *Psyke og Logos*, 21(2), 542–563.

13

Shame

When Something Crucial Is at Stake

Lone Nissen

In this chapter, I put the focus on *shame* from a cybernetic psychological perspective, looking at the ways in which the therapist can work with shame in the therapeutic arena, and the ways in which feelings of shame occur in the client–therapist relationship. Explanations are given as to how and why, in a cybernetic psychological perspective, shame cannot, either theoretically or in practice, be considered a malfunction but can, on the contrary, be seen as signals from the unconscious, overarching, self-regulating and self-healing forces in the personality. Discussion will also address the ways in which, from a cybernetic psychological resource-oriented perspective, transference and countertransference are essential therapeutic tools in working with feelings of shame. This also applies to the therapist's personality, experience and capacity for listening to his or her own unconscious intelligence.

The Manifestations of Shame

Danish psychologist Lone Frølund describes shame as an ambiguous and complex phenomenon, given that a sense of shame often goes unacknowledged or unspoken, remaining unconscious. Being subject to shame triggers feelings of being ashamed, but the feeling of being ashamed is also triggered by witnessing someone else feeling ashamed. Frølund adds that it is difficult to identify shame, because shame ranges from milder forms, such as being shy, self-conscious, awkward, embarrassed, timid and modest, to more severe forms, such as being violated, humiliated, despised, degraded and in disgrace. For someone feeling ashamed, the shame is manifested in emotional confusion, which impedes rational thought and action. In addition, shame is manifested in physical reactions, such as blushing, pallor, increased perspiration and trembling.

The response to shame is to bow the head and lower the eyes, feeling exposed in an agonising and degrading manner that makes it necessary to hide. Attention turns inwards, as an agonising self-consciousness resulting from a sudden unexpected exposure of vulnerable sides of the self (Kaufmann, 1989). Personal experience, which is usually the background for a person's thoughts and actions,

DOI: 10.4324/9781003360247-14

suddenly assumes a profile, and the person feeling shame is aware of being seen both by eyes within and by the eyes of others (Lewis, 1987).

(Frølund, 1999, p. 137)

Frølund also describes the way in which psychoanalysis has developed towards a broad theory of personality evolution, and that it has contributed to 'shame' progressing from being an exclusively *intrapsychic* concept to also being an *interpersonal* concept. In this light, a differentiation can be made between two types of shame: The early, externalised type, which is linked to the mother–child relationship, and the mature internalised type, which is linked to incorporation of prevailing norms and rules.

[S]hame is both about the experience of flaws and shortcomings vis-à-vis personal goals and ideals and about experiences of failure in relation to others (Rizzuto, 1991). The experience of personal weakness and inferiority occurs in parallel with the experience of being the object of scorn, disdain and rejection. Along with the experience of self-doubt (Erikson, 1971) and social inadequacy, which results in the need to hide, shame gives rise to a longing for reunification with the person or persons who caused the shame, in the form of the need to feel accepted and as part of a community. Shame thus involves a contradiction: the ashamed person wishes to vanish while also longing for acceptance and acknowledgement.

(Frølund, 1999, p. 137)

Shame is also described as having a positive impact, since 'small doses' of shame would appear to have a regulating effect on the development of a stable self, whereas shame in 'large doses' disrupts the development of the self. Frølund also refers to two types of shame – *normal* and *pathological*. In cases of normal shame, an individual is capable of enduring the feeling, and the self remains intact, whereas pathological shame creates an ongoing heightened predisposition to experiencing shame, which becomes an all-embracing condition with a feeling that one's entire psychic existence is endangered (Frølund, 1999).

The essence of Frølund's description of shame is identical to that of psychologist Lars J. Sørensen's concept of the phenomenon, although Sørensen gives a more comprehensive account in his book *Skam medfødt og tillært* (Shame – Innate and Acquired). The main thread running through the book maintains that "shame relates to 'being', and there is a risk of shame emerging when experiences of being are disrupted". And he goes on: "Shame is an actuality when lack of harmony disrupts the possibility of intimacy, and far too often the result is a sense of being 'wrong', which is an intense outage of intimacy" (Sørensen, 2013, p. 63).

Shame can be inflicted on you by being made to feel 'wrong', but you can also be spontaneously, automatically and within yourself confronted with the feeling of wrongness when happiness becomes an impossibility. This is highly subtle and (again) a consequence of shame as both an innate feeling and an accommodated feeling; trimmed by surrounding preconceptions as to what is perceived as human and natural.

(Ibid., p. 119)

Clarification is provided as to how shame affects self-image, which is formed in the encounter/mirroring with the child's close caregivers and which thereby becomes an element of the child's perception-of-self-in-the-outside-world (Sørensen, 2013, p. 100). If a child's need for mirroring is not met, the child feels wrong and unacknowledged; the ashamed feeling of wrongness grows and affects the child as an individual. Being acknowledged and seen causes the child to grow, feel authentic and in harmony with his or her self-perception. The opposite, being overlooked, causes the child to lose inner balance and self-perception; the child feels lonely, not worthy of love, and ashamed. That is a painful and heavy weight, and shame becomes a covert feeling (ibid., p. 73), the shrouded impact of which is so disconcerting that it remains shrouded (ibid., p. 69). Shame thus also becomes an active factor of socialisation, for better or for worse (ibid., p. 21).

Sørensen describes how shame is transmissible, that there is a *relational* feeling, and, via a conscious/unconscious registration of the other's body language, this other's feelings are mirrored in our own body.

Consequently, we will feel this shame, or perhaps we will swing to the opposite of shame and be shameless by becoming cynical or denigrating (Sørensen, 2013, p. 57). Shame and intimacy do not exist simultaneously. Shame speaks of a person's desire for intimacy and authenticity, and, if that is not fulfilled, shame steps in. Sørensen explains how a harmonious interaction with someone else can cause shame to disappear, without shame having to be formulated at all (ibid., p. 140), and he elaborates:

When something becomes unbearable, a certain level of physical intimacy and cognisance evaporate. For the therapist, this means it is not possible to give help or undertake psychotherapy with someone 'who is not there'. The assignment is to follow the person without pursuing the person concerned.

(Sørensen, 2013, p. 152)

The symptoms and physical manifestations of shame are classified as an attempt at self-healing; the symptoms reveal an imbalance in the person requiring balanced and understanding attention. The feeling of shame is so delicate that 'pawing' – as Sørensen puts it – instantly reinforces the feeling of wrongness in the person. On the other hand, if the shame is handled with gentleness, and the symptoms are looked at overtly, they will show the route to health just as often as they will show something unhealthy.

Cybernetic Psychology and Psychotherapy

Cybernetic psychology is the theory of how complex information is regulated and processed in the human psyche (Vedfelt, 2007, p. 502). Cybernetic psychology has been developed by Ole Vedfelt, integrating theory from various main schools of psychological thought, including Freud's psychoanalysis, analytical Jungian psychology, body and gestalt therapy, Imago therapy and cognitive therapy. Within an integrated framework, cybernetic psychology forms a conceptually coherent theory.

Vedfelt describes the way in which, between them, consciousness and the unconscious form a multilayered, hyper-complex information system with many subsystems working in parallel and simultaneously, where their continuing collaboration and merging with one another are necessary for the personality's self-organisation, self-regulation and relationship to the outer world (Vedfelt, 2007, p. 502).

The central thesis of cybernetic psychology is that the more complex systems can potentially regulate the less complex systems. Since the unconscious, according to Vedfelt, has a far greater information capacity and complexity than the normal consciousness, then comprehensive regulating of the personality can only occur in collaboration with the *unconscious intelligence*.

The unconscious intelligence is an intelligence in the unconscious that is superior to consciousness. It has a self-regulating and self-organising function which contributes actively and constructively to personal development throughout life.

> A fundamental assumption of cybernetic psychology, as formulated by a pioneer cyberneticist, Ross Ashby, is the "law of requisite variety" (requisite complexity). This states that the regulating capacity of a system is potentially increased the larger its information capacity and complexity. [...] In terms of life philosophy, this corresponds to only being able to solve a problem if you can look at it from a higher level than the level upon which the conflict is being played out.
> (Vedfelt, 2002, p. 34)

Cybernetic psychology is also described as the theory of self-regulating and self-healing forces in the personality, and of the healing and development potential in relationships between individuals. The theory put into practice is termed cybernetic psychotherapy.

Cybernetic psychotherapy integrates, as described, methods from various therapeutic schools of thought, and the therapy is like a laboratory to which people who are experiencing inner problems and conflicts come when they cannot solve those problems on their own. From a cybernetic viewpoint, these problems and conflicts cause disturbance in the overall integrated psychological functions and hinder the self-regulating and self-healing forces from working under optimum conditions.

In a therapy situation, the therapist senses that something is at stake in the client. This will appear as something *other* seeking dialogue both with the client's self and with the therapist (Vedfelt, 1998, p. 112). This other is manifested via, for example, body language and dreams and in relation to the therapist. Vedfelt does not perceive this other as a malfunction; on the contrary, he sees it as a signal from the overall self-regulating levels in the client.

The signals can be seen as transient and variable and, in the therapeutic work, they might move, vanish or shift; with further work, they then emerge as unpredictable transference processes, jumps in a line of coherent associations or new corporeal reactions.

Any signals identified by the therapist as meaningful will be seen as leading to a higher and more essential level of organisation in the client's personality. Of the meaningfulness of the signals, Vedfelt explains that working with them can reveal:

> not merely a solution to the problem, but also a new way forwards; ultimately, therefore, it can seem that the symptom or the problem was produced in order to force the inflexible self to change direction and submit to a more comprehensive self-regulation than had been imagined possible.
>
> (Vedfelt, 2002, p. 69)

The therapist's relational skill plays a central role in cybernetic psychotherapy and is regarded as the principal instrument in the therapy situation. In a cybernetic sense, relational skill means the therapist's ability to be personified as a 'good person' or perhaps several 'good people' in the client's imagination. A 'good person' is a trained individual who offers the client acceptance and challenge, while being the role model that the client needs (ibid., p. 299). Relational skills are characterised by, for example, empathetic capacity, the capacity for insight and understanding of the client's body language and self-observation.

Vedfelt also describes how negative feelings in the therapist are a requisite element of the therapy, and that it is only through acceptance of these that the therapist can capture the intensity encapsulated in the feelings. This requires a two-way consciousness, which ought to be an element of therapy training and which, via introspection, allows the therapist an opportunity to detect personal blocks. The therapist is then able to listen to his or her own *unconscious intelligence* (ibid., p. 292).

Shame from the Perspective of Cybernetic Psychology

Frølund explains how the feeling of shame usually remains *unconscious*. Seen in the perspective of cybernetic psychology, the unconscious – in this case, shame – is understood as an unconscious intelligence that is superior to consciousness. Shame should therefore be seen as an attempt by the self-regulating and self-organising functions in the personality to be heard and contribute to an active and constructive development of the personality.

In the therapy situation, the therapist will discern an issue at stake, and it will appear, as described by Vedfelt, as something other. This other can appear as, for example, shame, which as we have seen can be manifested in blushing and an attempt to hide oneself by avoiding eye contact, and non-rational thought/action. In a cybernetic perspective, this other – here, shame – should not be seen as a malfunction but as signals from the overarching, self-regulating and self-healing forces in the client.

If the therapist understands the signals – shame – the result of the therapeutic relational situation will lead to a higher level of organisation in the client's personality. Elevation of this in a higher cybernetic perspective is due to comprehensive regulation of the personality only being possible in collaboration with the unconscious intelligence, which, according to Vedfelt, has far greater information complexity and capacity than the normal consciousness.

According to the cybernetic personality model, personality consists of "many systems and subsystems with differing yet overlapping memory systems, with varying degrees of function similar to consciousness or unconscious, and each with its set of options and limitations" (Vedfelt, 1998, p. 113). The systems are in constant development and communicate with one another in order to establish the balance that will ensure the continuance and function of the whole, the personality. Personality development occurs in stages from lower to higher levels; this development means that the control system of a higher level will emerge and be filled with energy previously invested at a lower level. In this way, the higher control system has the opportunity to integrate the lower level, facilitating development of the personality.

Vedfelt describes how consciousness is necessary to the processes of personal development: A consciousness that expresses itself via body language, dreams, verbal language and other therapeutic material (Vedfelt, 1998, p. 113). In this perspective, shame is seen as an expression of unconscious communication from a higher organisational level in the individual, appearing as an attempt to create balance in the personality.

In a development process – a therapeutic relationship, for example – imbalance in the client will be able to develop from this lower level to a higher control level. One example of this process is the integration of the client's shame by the higher control system, which in therapy comprises the two systems, of the client and the therapist, put together to create greater complexity and capacity of information than the two systems separately. This higher level activates the client's overarching control systems, leading to development of the personality.

Therapy thereby functions as a systemic relation, a cybernetic system of a second order, in which the client's shame unconsciously communicates by bypassing the client's conscious self, attempting to communicate independently with the therapist (Hass, 2015, pp. 92–93). This corresponds to the problem being resolved from a higher level than that at which the issue is playing out (Vedfelt, 2002, p. 34).

Shame in Cybernetic Psychotherapeutic Practice

In order to gather the threads between cybernetic theory and practice, I will give a short account of a case study from Vedfelt's own practice, showing how Vedfelt works with shame in a psychotherapeutic process (Vedfelt, 2002, pp. 243–244).

The case study is an example of cybernetic theory and personality model and the theory of transference and countertransference in practice.

The case concerns Randi, a 40-year-old woman; for some time, she has been lacking the desire for sexual intimacy with her husband. While Randi is relating a dream she has had, Vedfelt observes signals of embarrassment and shame behind her neutral body language. When she draws images of the dream, her body language becomes more distinct. Randi is encouraged to go over the emotions again, and she is suddenly struck by memories of her uncle's advances and fondling when she was a young girl. She now realises how bewildering these situations had been, and the sense of shame they had instilled. She says that she had acquiesced, and that it had been pleasurable; subsequently, Randi can feel herself becoming "a little angry". Vedfelt intervenes by giving the uncle, on the drawing, a slap and exclaiming: "Shame on you. Keep your hands off Randi". Randi reacts with intense rage and is supported in expressing her feelings. She smudges out the picture of her uncle, tears him from the drawing, rips him to pieces, joyfully stamps on him and breaks down, weeping intensely while being comforted and held. Afterwards, Randi is infused with a feeling of liberation and she subsequently reports that her desire for sexual intimacy has returned (Vedfelt, 2002).

Transference and Countertransference in a Cybernetic Perspective

In cybernetic psychology, *transference* is not regarded exclusively as an echo from traumatic experiences in the past. It must also be understood as an attempt by the self-regulating and self-healing forces in the personality to have a say in relation to the healing and development potential of the therapeutic relationship.

Vedfelt writes:

> Transference often takes the form of idealisation of the therapist. It mirrors a fixation to a requisite developmental phase in childhood, but it is also the projection of a process on a higher level, which cannot as yet fulfill itself as a stance in everyday life.

> (Vedfelt, 1998, p. 145)

He even concludes: "If transference does not work, nothing works" (ibid., p. 296).

A client's fantasies about his or her parents are transferred and relieved in relation to the therapist, and the therapist is thereby the object of the same emotions. When, in the therapeutic process, the client encounters a different understanding and empathy, the old fantasies about the parents are transformed, and the therapist becomes the new inner mother or father in the client. In this situation, the client transfers a higher level of processing to the therapist, and *that* is the healing and developmental aspect of *transference*, facilitating development in the client.

With reference to his own therapeutic practice, Vedfelt explains that it is important to process transference and countertransference, to be a step ahead in the therapy, to be able to see the resistances before the client plays them out and to bring the energy from the transference and countertransference into the therapy.

In his article "Den nødvendige kompleksitet" (The requisite complexity), psychotherapist Henrik Hass elaborates on the systemic relationship between client and therapist: Cybernetic psychotherapy looks upon the therapeutic situation as a system, a second-order cybernetic system, in which an imbalance in the client's system cannot be communicated through the client's conscious self and is therefore communicated via the overarching control system, bypassing the client's conscious self. He writes about how Vedfelt's *the other* attempts to communicate independently with the therapist in part of a communicative process accounted for as transference. Hass explains that the second-order cybernetic system is of greater complexity than the client's and the therapist's systems are individually, which causes the therapeutic relationship to activate the client's overarching control levels (Hass, 2015, pp. 92–93).

Psychotherapies of a more recent date make far more use of the therapist's emotions and experiences than was the case earlier; of countertransference, Vedfelt writes that transfer of the therapist's emotions to the client is inevitable (Vedfelt, 2007, p. 48). Countertransference is inevitable because the individual, while growing up, develops an intuitive expertise in reading other people's emotions and body language. Countertransference is regarded as a sensitivity and insight into the client, which the therapist must learn to use consciously rather than being swept along.

A differentiation is made between *syntonic* (harmonious) and *dystonic* (disruptive) countertransference. In syntonic countertransference, the therapist feels something personally – shame or sadness, for example – that the client cannot contain and therefore transfers to the therapist. Via the transference, the therapist senses these feelings within his or her own person. It is then the therapist's job to bring this into the therapeutic process by, for example, asking what the client is feeling and sensing, or by asking directly if the client is feeling, for example, sad. If the feeling finds resonance in the client, then it is a case of syntonic countertransference.

Dystonic (disruptive) countertransference is the opposite process. If sadness is a prominent character trait in the therapist, or if something has occurred in the therapist's private life to cause the therapist sadness, the feeling of sadness will not be recognised or find resonance in the client, and therefore the feeling relates to the therapist.

The therapist, it is emphasised, does not have to interpret transference reactions for the client. On the other hand, the therapist can activate the underlying feelings by using drawing, bodily experiences or psychodrama, moving the energy from the therapist and over to the inner processes in the client, as we saw in the case study with Randi. Following this procedure, the client will have far greater facility in differentiating between personal material and transferences to the therapist. A transference interpretation by the therapist, on the other hand, can perhaps be understood intellectually but not acknowledged in the same way as when the material has been worked on therapeutically.

The therapeutic work activates the higher progressive level of processing, and the conflict is thus lifted above the plane on which it was created (Vedfelt, 2007, pp. 296–297). Vedfelt points out that this requires the building-up of positive transference, and that the client needs to have confidence in the personal inner resources before being ready to acquire new methods of experience.

Sara and Shame

Sara, who is 49 years old, contacts me for a consultation because her inner and outer life lack coherence. She expresses a wish to find out *what is wrong with her*, so that she can have a good relationship with herself and with her family.

Sara grew up in a typical nuclear family. Her mother was frail, her father was irascible and violent, and her older sister did all the 'right' things. The family members were always needling Sara. She felt 'wrong' and lonely; as a child and now as an adult, she was and is in doubt about everything. The family endured many conflicts, and Sara was thrown out of the home when she was 16 years old; she has had to fend for herself ever since. Fierce conflicts still rage between Sara on the one side and her parents and sister on the other side.

In therapy, the family dynamics and Sara's relationship with her mother are mentioned frequently. Sara then reddens across her chest, throat and face and looks away. She typically avoids contact by changing the direction of the conversation and she makes many and long associative detours.

In one session, Sara talks about her feeling of 'wrongness' and her relationship with her mother, who has never been satisfied with her. I see an emerging insecurity and discomfort in Sara. She blushes and breaks eye contact with me, while her narrative about the relationship with her mother slowly grinds to a halt. She gazes out at the balcony railing and 'escapes' across the balcony, down to the street and the birds beyond. She stops in her tracks, for a second insecure and irresolute, whereupon she exclaims: "Oh, the birds are such fun!" She becomes absorbed in a lengthy association about birds, smiling and chuckling. She spends time 'out there' and only comes 'back' to the therapy room once she has, as I see it, regained control of the situation. She then continues unnoticed along her association route.

Seeing Sara exposed in her insecurity and bodily reaction causes me immediately to break eye contact, pause the situation and 'escape' with her out on to the street. I am affected and ashamed by witnessing Sara's reaction. I recognise the reaction, the feeling and discomfort, in myself and, when Sara comes 'back' to the therapy room, I go along with her on the associative detours.

Shame in the Therapeutic Relationship

In order to be able to identify the way in which shame emerges and the feeling of shame is manifested in the therapeutic relationship, it makes sense to start by considering whether or not Sara (and I) can be thought to suffer shame at all.

Sara has the feeling of being 'wrong'; she constantly wonders if she is doing the right thing and what is wrong with her. If she fails to live up to her parents' expectations, she is excluded, as when she was thrown out of the family home. Despite this exclusion, Sara wants to be reunited with her family, but the feeling of wrongness and of being left out stays with her when she is together with her family. Her self-doubt is thereby increased, and, as she expresses it, her inner and outer do not add up. She wants to find out what is 'wrong with her', so that she can have a good relationship with her family; this highlights her longing for acceptance and acknowledgement and her desire to be 'one of the family'.

I see the family dynamics as a contributory factor in Sara's issue with shame, here with reference to Frølund's description of shame as involving the experience of faults and shortcomings vis-à-vis personal ideals and of failure in comparison with others – for Sara, in relation to family. Frølund also describes how the experience of weakness and inferiority occurs parallel to the experience of being the object of scorn, disdain and rejection, here seen in connection with Sara and the family dynamics.

I imagine that Sara's exclusion triggers feelings of shame and loneliness and, at the same time, according to Frølund and Sørensen, a longing for reunification with the person who, or the circumstances that, caused the shame, in the form of the need to feel accepted and as part of a community. Shame thus involves a contradiction: The ashamed person wishes to vanish while also longing to be seen.

Sørensen describes how, via conscious/unconscious registration of the other's body language, this other's feelings are mirrored in the subject's own body, and shame is thereby induced by witnessing the shame of others. I experience feelings of wrongness and a feeling of not being able to stay in the contact. The situation becomes uncomfortable; I 'escape' with Sara and stay 'out there' until Sara again involves me. In the light of this, I assess that we are both experiencing shame.

Sara reacts physically, with reddening across her chest, throat and face and evasive eye contact manifested in turning her gaze and head to look out over the balcony railing. This response in Sara resonates with Frølund's description of the bodily manifestation of shame, with blushing, pallor, perspiration and trembling, lowering the head and gaze, hiding from the eyes of the world.

Sara's split second of uncertainty and doubt can be understood as making contact with a painful self-consciousness that exposes her vulnerable sides. The reaction could be about her feeling of wrongness in relation to her mother. This feeling of wrongness is a central and hypersensitive theme for Sara, stretching back to a childhood during which she never received her mother's recognition. A more explicit reading could point to Sara being concerned about how she and I perceive her (am I good enough?), an issue perhaps unexpectedly exposed in the therapy session, causing her to be overcome by the feeling of wrongness. She spots the birds and 'goes off' with them. She continues the dialogue via an association route following the birds; from the perspective of cybernetic psychology, this can be seen as an attempt by the self-regulating and self-healing forces (the unconscious intelligence) to have a say. The presence of feelings of shame is thus manifested between us.

Transference and Countertransference in the Therapeutic Relationship

Sara has felt wrong and lonely and has often been kept out of the family during childhood. Despite this, she wants to find out what is 'wrong with her' so that she can be 'let inside' her family. During the session, Sara talks about her feeling of wrongness and her problematic relationship with her mother. At this point, Sara is affected by shame.

Vedfelt describes how the client's fantasies and feelings about parents are transferred and relieved in relation to the therapist, and that this is called transference.

In this perspective, Sara's feeling of shame is seen as transference. When Sara talks about her mother, we can imagine that she is suddenly subjected to feelings she experienced in her childhood relationship with her mother, and that these feelings are transferred to me. The shame can therefore be a matter of feeling 'wrong' and can be a signal that the unconscious intelligence wants to have a say.

The issue is vitalised and animated in the transference to me. I take on the role of the mother and, in so doing, gain awareness that something important is in action. The transference thereby becomes therapeutic material and a valuable therapeutic tool.

Vedfelt also writes about the other – in this instance, shame – that attempts, in an unconscious and independent manner, to communicate with the therapist and is explained as transference. According to Vedfelt, the transference can mirror a fixation to a developmental phase in childhood (Vedfelt, 1998, p. 145).

The fixation asserts itself in connection to Sara's problematic childhood relationship with her mother/family, but also as a current issue. The fixation tells me about Sara's relationships and indicates that Sara's problems relate to her process coming to a standstill at precisely this level in her childhood. This can be the explanatory model for why Sara reacts with shame. The shame thereby mirrors an inner conflict between equally strong and contradictory forces. The conflict is located at a point where changes and solutions cannot occur and thus has to be resolved at a superior level – that is, in a therapeutic relationship.

Sara's feelings and reaction could be shielding the exposure of her vulnerability, for which reason she becomes concerned about her own experience of inadequacy. It is too painful for her, and she more or less consciously attempts to protect herself. She breaks eye contact and 'escapes' out to the birds, where she remains until she has reached a safe place within herself. From this spot, she can again face and involve me, without the painful inner state taking over.

When encountering different understanding and insight from an empathetic therapist, a client will, according to Vedfelt, transform old fantasies and feelings. The therapist will thereby be a new inner mother in the client, which is the healing and developmental element of transference (Vedfelt, 2002, p. 299).

When Sara blushes, avoids eye contact and 'goes' down to the street, I feel 'wrong' and ashamed and flee the situation. I experience difficulty maintaining the contact and immediately choose, with no internal debate – unconsciously – to 'hide' myself.

Of *countertransference*, Vedfelt writes that transfer of the therapist's emotions to the client is inevitable (Vedfelt, 2007, p. 48). My feelings of wrongness and shame can therefore be said to be my countertransference in reaction to Sara's transference to me.

I intuitively recognise her body language and feelings and I let Sara have her time 'out there'. I am thereby unconsciously avoiding confrontation with my own feelings of shame – be they involving a personal theme or professionalism – and giving us time out. This exhibits an intuitive sensitivity on my part which does not intimidate Sara or contribute to intensifying her feeling of wrongness and shame.

In a subsequent supervision session, the importance of 'going' with the client so that the client does not feel 'wrong' was made explicit. Feeling wrong is a central theme for Sara. Activation of the wrongness feeling, with resulting shame, is therefore not expedient in a therapy setting. In Sara's context, 'going' with the client means 'going' on to the street and looking at the birds in order to remain in supportive contact with her – to stay in the shift of level and in the attempt by Sara's unconscious intelligence to have a say.

In the session with Randi, when she talks about the dream, Vedfelt sees her affected by embarrassment and shame. She is encouraged to go over the emotions again; when she does this, she suddenly makes contact with just how much shame had been associated with these situations. Vedfelt felt the other in himself, this being the feelings that Randi cannot herself contain and therefore transferred. This other proved to match the feelings Randi experienced in herself. In this situation, Vedfelt was able to examine what he describes as a syntonic countertransference.

I did not question Sara about her emotions, what she was feeling, and did not bring it into the therapeutic process. On the other hand, I took gentle care of Sara and went along on her escape detour without putting her in the wrong. In relation to Sara, my attention was not focused on whether my countertransference was syntonic or dystonic, but I felt and recognised the shame in myself!

Shame as Unconscious Intelligence

Shame is often not acknowledged or verbalised, and so shame remains unconscious. Shame can be manifested via many physical reactions, such as blushing, pallor, increased perspiration and trembling, but can be extremely difficult to identify given that it assumes many forms and degrees. Therefore, shame does not necessarily appear in full view, but is perhaps more visible in the client's body language and in evasive behaviour. Feelings, too, are manifested in a reaction to shame; in the therapeutic relationship, these will become apparent as feelings of wrongness, self-doubt, emotional confusion and emotional flooding, experience of faults and shortcomings, inferiority, social inadequacy and loss of intimacy, which result in the need to flee and hide.

If this explanatory model of shame is put in a cybernetic perspective, which takes a fundamental resource-oriented view, shame can be understood as an unconscious intelligence which shows the way to a possibility of personal development and which has a self-regulating and self-organising function that opens up for the self-healing forces in the personality.

Cybernetically, the appearance of shame and the presence of the emotions (the client's unconscious intelligence) show the therapist a resourceful route to understanding that something important is at stake. Shame thereby becomes important therapeutic material and an important therapeutic tool. In the same way, the personal feeling of shame gives the therapist the possibility, via self-observation, reflection and supervision, to gain insight into, and understanding of, the client's and the therapist's reactions and feelings.

The Therapist's Focus on Transference and Countertransference

Shame is a relational feeling that is transmissible. Shame is thereby also about the therapeutic relationship, about transference and countertransference, and about how the therapist can work with shame. The case study involving Randi shows an example of the way in which cybernetic psychology approaches shame via transference/countertransference. We have looked at two examples of work in practice. In the first, the therapist (Vedfelt) checks up on his countertransference and uses it as a therapeutic tool by activating the underlying emotions in the client. In the second example, I am advised in supervision to 'go' with the client when she 'escapes' down on to the street and thereby – via this sensitivity – not render the client more 'wrong'. From a cybernetic perspective, the 'escape' – here, shame – is seen as a meaningful route leading to potential development. From the vantage point of cybernetic psychology, the client's reactions to shame will not – theoretically or in practice – be considered a malfunction but as signals from the overarching layer in the personality, thereby showing the resource-oriented approach taken by cybernetics.

Sørensen describes how a candid view of the symptoms and harmonious contact can make shame vanish, whereas 'pawing', as he calls it, reinforces the feeling of wrongness. Feelings of shame are thereby significant indicators pointing up what is essentially important for the person and can thus be crucial to healing. Sørensen also describes shame as an attempt at self-healing of imbalance in the individual, and that it is the therapist's job to take a sensitive approach when accompanying and helping the client make sense of the reaction/shame.

Conclusion

We have seen how shame emerges in therapeutic work, and that, in the perspective of cybernetic psychology, shame should be viewed as an instruction to the therapist that something important is at stake in the client. Shame requires gentle therapeutic handling, given that it is an exposed and overwhelming feeling.

We have also seen that transference and countertransference are valuable thera-peutic tools, and that it is important to be aware of this in order to be a step ahead, so that the energy of countertransference and transference alike are brought into the therapy.

The therapist's personality, experience and ability to create safety and trust in the relationship make for valuable tools, and it is equally important that the thera-pist, via self-observation and reflection, can listen to his or her own unconscious intelligence.

References

Erikson, E.H. (1971) *Identitet. Ungdom og kriser*. Hans Reitzels Forlag, Copenhagen.

Frølund, L. (1999) The Psychoanalytic Shame Concept. *Nordisk Psykologi*, 51:2, 135–150. DOI:10.1080/00291463.1999.11863944

Hass, H. (2015) Den nødvendige kompleksitet, in T. Hansen (Ed.), *Det ubevidstes poten-tiale*. Frydenlund, Copenhagen.

Kaufman, G. (1989) *The Psychology of Shame*. Springer, New York.

Lewis, H.B. (1987) Introduction: Shame—the "Sleeper" in Psychopathology, in H.B. Lewis (Ed.), *The Role of Shame in Symptom Formation* (pp. 1–28). Lawrence Erlbaum, New Jersey.

Rizzuto, A.-M. (1991) Shame in Psychoanalysis: The function of unconscious fantasies. *International Journal of Psychoanalysis*, 72, 297–312.

Sørensen, L.J. (2013) *Skam medfødt og tillært*. Hans Reitzels Forlag, Copenhagen.

Vedfelt, O. (1998) *Bevidsthed*. Nordisk Forlag, Copenhagen.

Vedfelt, O. (2002) *Ubevidst intelligens*. Nordisk Forlag, Copenhagen.

Vedfelt, O. (2007) *Drømmenes dimensioner*. Nordisk Forlag, Copenhagen.

14

Complexity, Learning and Music Therapy

Cybernetic Psychology as a Tool for Understanding the Therapist Student's Learning Processes

Charlotte Lindvang

As a future therapist, it is of vital importance to achieve therapeutic competencies so as to be able to help future clients in the best way possible. This not only involves acquiring knowledge and understanding theory, it also involves developing the ability to reflect as well as acquiring knowledge of practice and method through self-experience. This chapter focuses on the experiences of music therapy students regarding their learning through training therapy as an integrated part of education and training. The chapter gives the therapy students a voice through a series of quotations from interviews, where the students describe their learning processes. This illustrates how the students can expand and practise awareness and increase their knowledge of themselves and their own relational patterns. The cybernetic approach offers a way to understand more deeply the layers of complexity in therapeutic learning processes.

Complex Learning Processes

Research shows that training therapy is important for therapists' personal as well as professional development. A common argument for this, agreed upon by many therapists with different theoretical orientations, is that the therapist, by taking the role as client, improves the ability to be empathic with the clients. The therapist also practises and trains sensitivity to dynamics and nuances in the therapeutic process. This can be a guide in the role of therapist, as the student will have experienced first hand, as a client, the tools and effects of therapy (Bike, Norcross & Schatz 2009; Grimmer & Tribe 2001; Hougaard 2019).

Most psychotherapy training programmes have training therapy as an important, integrated part of training. In the five-year music therapy programme at Aalborg University, Denmark, experiential training processes are integrated into the programme as a track running parallel to musical and academic training. Training therapy is a special learning environment where the student, during his/her training, has the role of client, individually as well as in groups. At a later time in the programme, the student experiences having the role of therapist under supervision. This part of the music therapy training programme is called training therapy, because it is a mandatory part of training and thus is different from therapy chosen by the student as a private individual. In self-experiential training, the aim is for

DOI: 10.4324/9781003360247-15

the student to develop professional competence as a therapist through personal development. In other words, the focus of this work is preparation for a future professional *integrated and experienced identity* as a music therapist (Lindvang 2013, 2015; Pedersen 2002; Murphy 2007; Pedersen, Lindvang & Beck 2022).

It is difficult to investigate the training and education of therapists empirically, and studying the learning achieved through training therapy may be particularly difficult, which can be owing to the fact that experiences cannot always be verbalised completely, as part of the therapeutic process is stored as tacit knowledge. My PhD thesis "A Field of Resonant Learning" (Lindvang 2010) focuses on the relationship between learning and therapy and is based on a qualitative study of how music therapy students at Aalborg University experience and describe learning processes generated by situations in which the student takes the role of client.[1] Part of the study involved understanding the common characteristics found in the group of students, and the results from this part of the analysis, from which I have taken quotations, form the basis of this chapter. In working with the analysis, there was a need for a theoretical frame of reference that was broad enough to include the many dimensions and themes that were illuminated and the *intersection* between learning process and therapy that was represented in the study. The theory of cybernetic psychology and consciousness was suitable to meet this need (Vedfelt 2000, 2002).

The cybernetic analysis of the interview study showed that, in learning processes as clients in therapy, the students build competence in *containing and acting* in relation to the complexity of a therapeutic process. The analysis revealed the complexity of the learning processes in the following areas:

- *The interactive levels of consciousness*: Some of the learning is below the threshold of consciousness and is stored as tacit knowledge. At the same time, the abilities to reflect, create cohesive meaning and understand and communicate one's own experiences are all in focus. It is the interrelationship between the forms of consciousness that is central to the learning process.
- *The multimodality of perception*: The student develops receptiveness, ability to contain and flexibility of perception, which correspond to using different sources of information and modalities in the field of contact. These are, for example, inner images, bodily sensations and the timbre of the voice, corresponding to develop*ment of "the supramodal space" in cybernetic terminology.*
- *The necessity and diversity of relationships*: Learning takes place in a relational field, as the student enters into relationship with the training therapist as well as fellow students, while at the same time working through patterns from other important relationships, both current and past.

Cybernetics and Complexity

Cybernetics is a transdisciplinary approach that explores regulation and control of complex systems – it could be a machine or it could be the human nervous system. The word *cybernetics* comes from the Ancient Greek *kybernetikos* ('good at steering'), referring to the art of the helmsman. If we look more closely at the word 'steer', we find that it has to do with movement; to steer means to make something move in a particular direction or to direct efforts in the right direction. When human beings fail to steer, we are thrown into turbulence or confusion – we get 'disturbed' (*Webster's New Universal Dictionary of the English Language*, 1976). Similarly, the Danish word *forstyrret* (to be disturbed) means being physically or psychologically off balance owing to failing physical or psychological function. In other words, the individual is, to a certain degree, 'pushed' out of a natural ability to 'steer' and self-regulate. A music therapy student describes her learning process as a *movement*, where she lifts herself to a new level of clarity and direction (steering):

> This kind of consciousness and this process of becoming aware has made me able to see through, to see through the fog – kind of like seeing myself clearly, and, with that as a starting point, being able to take control of and steer in my own life.

Complexity is a central concept in cybernetics: When a system is developing, it is characterised by moving towards a higher degree of complexity, where increasingly more components are contained and come into play. According to the *Oxford Advanced Learner's Dictionary* (2005), 'complexity' is defined as a state of being formed by many parts – possibly opposing – or as a state of being difficult to understand. It is interesting that, historically, the word 'complex' comes from the Latin word *complexus/complecti*, which means to 'encircle' or to 'embrace'. *Com* means with, and *plectere* means to weave or braid. In a psychological context, a complex means having a specific system of more or less conscious emotional thoughts or perceptions – for example, an exaggerated dislike or fear, an obsession (*Webster's New Universal Dictionary of the English Language*, 1976). A complex can also refer specifically to a feeling of inferiority and shame. Complexes are complicated, and a great deal of responsiveness, enquiry, empathy and support is required to dissolve a complex. When the future therapist develops complexity through self-experience, it can be described as a process that weaves together many parts and helps the person to embrace more of the self and more of the other person in any encounter, even when it is complicated. In the following quotation, a music therapy student describes how, during the course of her therapy, she gradually overcame a psychological complex and embraced inner conflicting elements:

> There is being small, but also being big and ugly. But it was like none of it was accepted, in me, I mean. Because I wasn't allowed to be small and weak, and I wasn't allowed to take up too much space or make too much noise, either. But you really are both of those as a human being. And now I have gradually understood that, and integrated it.

The more complexity a person can contain, the greater the ability to manage disturbances – and the more it takes to cause confusion and imbalance. A system/ person who is knowledgeable, experienced, has awareness of his/her own body and sensuousness and is able to reflect is better at maintaining closeness, can discriminate and choose and thus act and navigate in the complexity of being a human being relating to other people. The future therapist's training therapy creates the setting and possibility for growth in many areas, including the emotions. When the student succeeds in reducing inner disturbances, his/her freedom of movement is optimised, as is, thus, the ability to navigate and meet future clients 'where they are'. According to the Danish theologian and philosopher Søren Kierkegaard, this is an ethical act and the secret to the entire art of helping. Kierkegaard stated, "If one is to truly succeed in leading a person to a particular place, one must first and foremost take care to find him where he is and begin there" (Kierkegaard 1859, p. 96).

Learning and the Interactive Levels of Consciousness

Using cybernetic theory makes sense in the context of learning theory. In Vedfelt's book *Unconscious Intelligence* (2000), the author moves in the direction of learning theory, integrating concepts such as 'practice learning', 'tacit knowledge', 'intuitive expertise' and a clear reference to theory about apprenticeship. The close connection between consciousness theory and learning theory is emphasised by the Danish professor of learning Knud Illeris, as he acknowledges that it is possible to learn without being conscious of it in a way that can be expressed in everyday language. Illeris quotes Vedfelt:

> Unconsciously we are able to store both cognitive and emotional experiences in our memory for a long period of time, and the unconscious receives information much quicker and much more comprehensively than the normal state of consciousness [...] At first this is shocking to common sense because it indicates that the self (and the normal state of consciousness) is like a small boat on a huge ocean of unconscious information.
> (Vedfelt 2000, p. 28, author's translation, quoted in Illeris 2006, p. 31)

Much of the knowledge that we use in therapy as well as in our daily lives is tacit knowledge. We can recognise a face among thousands of other faces or a voice in a multitude of other voices without being able to say exactly what makes this possible. "We know more than we can tell", as philosopher Michael Polanyi stated in 1966 as the first person to conceptualise the tacit dimensions of learning and science (Polanyi 1966). Polanyi describes tacit knowledge as a fundamental kind of knowledge that is the basis for all other knowledge. With Polanyi's work, the unconscious element in learning has been included in discussions regarding theory of learning, and, in line with a number of scholars of learning theory, Vedfelt is interested in how information and learning are acquired tacitly through practice and rooted in bodily experiences. Through the body and through experience in practice-oriented learning arenas, the learner develops an 'action-borne knowledge', which is also known as the principle of 'learning by doing' formulated by the American philosopher and educational reformer John Dewey in the 1930s (Wackerhausen 2008). This phenomenon was apparent in the therapy students' descriptions of how they experienced acquiring therapeutic knowledge and competence through bodily therapeutic processes:

> it is a very strange thing, finding out how music therapy works. And you have to experience it, I think, you have to experience for yourself these processes in your body along with the music, before you completely understand it.
>
> (Student)

Action-borne knowledge is associated with the cybernetic concept of 'unconscious intelligence'. Unconscious processes are extensive, and they play a vital role in the human psyche, where there is intense unconscious activity parallel to everyday consciousness. It is important for the student to develop the ability to let go and surrender him/herself to the therapy process, where being present physically and emotionally opens access to the unconscious intelligence. A student describes how she gradually developed trust in the process and in the knowledge of what felt right and wrong, without necessarily being able to verbalise it:

> So what I learned was – that, in time, what I feel in the moment turns out to be right. Maybe I can't see in that moment why I should do it. ... And it is this feeling of peace – by doing what I feel I need to do – that I've clearly gotten from training therapy.

Several therapy students describe how they experienced personal change primarily through the music and body – that is, the nonverbal processes in training therapy. At the same time, one of them emphasises how important it was for their learning to reflect on their own process, at home, when listening to the recorded sessions from individual therapy:

> It was really good to be able to listen to the sessions afterwards. So there was actually a three part process for every session. Because the music often was a way to process the verbal content, and so I listened to the whole session again when I got home. So there was one more process, where I looked back at and learned from what had happened.

Another student expresses something similar: "For me it was important to reflect on what happened – the transformation wasn't only in the music, it was really important to have the reflective process too".

An unreflective practitioner who does not give careful consideration during and about the specific meeting with a given client risks 'being on autopilot' – meaning driven by habit and, in the worst case, losing full empathic resonance with the client. The unreflective practitioner may avoid dialogue with colleagues and miss the opportunity for the right professional feedback that can open new ways of understanding. When the practitioner 'is left to his/her own devices', there may be, instead of tacit knowledge and action-borne knowledge, a practice characterised by 'tacit unknowledge' and 'action-borne unknowledge' (Wackerhausen 2008).

The professional therapist, then, needs to be able to navigate through a process that is at times chaotic and still achieve clarity (Fog 1995). There is a reciprocal interaction between the competence to surrender to the processes of unconscious intelligence, including the varied and unpredictable emotional landscape, *and* the competence to pause, reflect on and verbalise the processes. This reciprocal interaction, then, contributes to the dynamic that creates a high degree of complexity in the learning of the future therapist. In the role of student-client, this dynamic between sensing something and realising something can be trained from the start. A music therapy student expresses her experiences with steps in her process of achieving understanding and insight in the following way:

> I can sense a new part of myself, or I can sense myself more clearly, or have this 'aha' experience: Ah, that's the way it is, or: This is how it also can be, and all in all I'm more aware and in tune with myself after an improvisation fades out and I've allowed myself to sense it.

According to cybernetic theory, the human feedback system is a second-order system, which means that we are able to meta-communicate – we can reflect on ourselves and the communication we are engaged in, and this is precisely what is used in training therapy, where students learn to reflect on their own systems with their components and relational patterns.

Now and then, a student can find that full understanding of his/her emotions and the therapy process emerges quite a bit after the moment when the experience is unfolding, which can be frustrating. Developing complex therapeutic insight and competence requires both courage and patience, as many experiences are pieced together over a period of time, and much of the learning remains tacit knowledge. This can be described metaphorically as seeds that are sown to sprout later and become healthy plants that can give nourishment to the therapist, or building blocks that will gradually be joined into a form that, with time, will support the therapist's professional identity.

The Multimodality of Learning and Perception

In cybernetic psychology's view on therapy, there is a greater probability that clients will feel understood and benefit from therapy if more elements are contained and brought into play in their therapeutic process; these can be emotions, inner imagery, memories, sensations or parts of the personality. This section focuses on how development and refinement of cross-modal sensory perception increase the future therapist's ability to bring many components into play in the therapeutic process, which corresponds to being consciously aware on several levels simultaneously.

Empirical infant research shows that the ability to transfer information across sensory modalities is innate (Meltzoff & Moore 1999; Stern 2000, 2010; Malloch & Trevarthen 2009). Sensory modalities are, for example, the visual, auditory and tactile senses. This phenomenon is called cross-modal perception, intersensory coordination, cross-modality or multimodality. In the analysis of interviews with therapy students, it was found that this innate ability is further developed in the learning process of therapeutic training. One student describes this in the following:

> I had gotten to where I had a deep sense of myself when I was present in the music – I felt this very much in my body, felt it and was very close to myself – in my backbone – and I have been able to remember these feelings again through the sensitivity I experienced in the music and at the same time in my body.

When the music therapist is in the role of client and experiences how therapy works, it seems that the student trains cross-modal perception and processes. There is a continuous and flowing awareness of sensing the body, touching instruments and listening to the music and the sound of the therapist's and one's own voice; the student has inner imagery and access to emotions and memories. The therapy student expands, so to speak, his/her experience so that he/she is present on several levels at the same time and receives a richness of information:

> Yes, it is simply an image of a kind of movement I feel inside of me while I'm singing, and it becomes a visualisation of what is happening to me [...] I have an inner image of a fairy sprinkling dust in my heart. And I can relate to it much better when there is imagery.

As mentioned earlier and exemplified in the selected quotations, the body has great significance for understanding and achieving competence, and experience shows that we remember better when the body is involved. The body provides a kind of resonance for learning and growth, which the student can experience tangibly, for example in vocal improvisation in training therapy:

> This is how it moves together: The movement of the voice out through the mouth, out through the body, out through the mouth, while at the same time sensing the feeling moving downwards, that is moving down and really feeling the feeling (...) – and then I am there, back in the living room, where I'm standing silently and looking at my mother, who is just lying on the sofa.

Here, a student expresses how she experienced a flowing connection between her vocal expression and bodily sensations. She exemplifies how self-awareness is deeply rooted in the body. Simultaneously, she becomes aware of and expresses her emotions, experiences bodily sensations and resonates with painful memories from her childhood. The result, in other words, is that the student learns to contain the complexity of the verbal and nonverbal communication that is expressed simultaneously. The capacity for empathy or empathic resonance is developed here, as training opens awareness of her own and others' diversity and richness and the many different ways of communicating information and expressing oneself. In this way, it is an advantage for future clients that the therapist, through the experiential part of her training, has acquired a well-developed sense of cross-modality in interaction, which in a cybernetic psychological sense means moving in the supramodal space. This is a multidimensional psychic space from which there is access to several types of experiences, and, at the same time, a great deal of information can be processed at a fast speed.

In the professional therapeutic relationship, this means that the therapist seeks to obtain a picture of the specific client and his/her process that is as complete as possible. This corresponds to developing a kind of synaesthetic sense that is experiencing sensory input in several modalities at the same time. In her/his interaction with the client, the therapist transforms the many nuances in the client's expressive communication into other modalities. In this way, the client can experience being seen, heard and responded to without the therapist mechanically repeating or imitating the client. This kind of creativity forms the basis of affective attunement, where the therapist and client share inner emotional movements through very fine nuances and changing rhythms. In affective attunement, the partners seek to reflect each other's emotional dynamics cross-modally (Lindvang & Bonde 2012; Trevarthen & Malloch 2000; Trondalen & Skårderud 2007).

As seen in the selected interview quotations, the experiencing of self through the music opens the student to experiencing multimodality, as the music is made up of sound waves that can be felt in the body and, often very quickly, give rise to inner imagery and inner movements in the form of access to emotions, memories and so on.

Learning and the Necessity and Diversity of Relationships

The capacity for cross-modal perception and communication is an innate human capability that is further developed through relationships. As mentioned, this is already seen in the interaction between parents and the newborn child. In the therapeutic process, much information will be shared nonverbally, and many experiences may never be verbalised. A student expresses in the following how complex learning is in each particular group session, where there is an extensive network of relationships:

> In group therapy – I definitely learn a lot through experiencing my own reactions to the rest of the group members, and through my reaction to how the therapist tackles what I bring up, and what the others bring up, and also by seeing the others' reactions to each other.

A recurring element in the interviews with music therapy students was that they had experienced the necessity for the therapist's presence, and several of them expressed a feeling that the therapist's mirroring and feedback were essential for their growth and development, which is described by a student in the following:

> You really can't do it alone, you can't [...] it's important that there is an experienced therapist beside you. That made it safe for me.

In the interviews, several students described how they had experienced first hand how important for the process it is to have faith in the therapeutic relationship, and how vulnerable it can make them feel to work with this theme. In early childhood, the most basic relational competencies are developed through nonverbal communication with the closest caregivers, and this relationship is "the first human apprenticeship" (Vedfelt 2000, p. 70). Based on these close relationship experiences, an inner 'network' of working models ('patterns' or 'schemes') is created regarding how one communicates with and relates to different situations. In training therapy, elements from the early human apprenticeship are integrated; the student adds new, fundamental experiences in relationships to those experiences that are already there.

A student describes the feeling of the importance of the therapist's presence as someone who supports without 'taking over':

> I'm playing me, that is, what is going on inside of me, and there is someone who supports me in that, I think it's exciting to experience first hand what it leads to, and the fact that the therapist is there for me in the music, while I'm actually the one in control.

The connection between self-development and relationships is an important dynamic factor. The students got to know themselves better and, *at the same time*, developed a sense of the meaning, dynamics and healing potential of relationships. A music therapy student tells of her experienced understanding of the connection between her relationship to herself and her relationship to others:

> I have realised that if I can do this – be 'on my side' – then I can do a lot more [...] I've started looking after my own interests and needs also, instead of just other people's. And I can see that this is the only way I can be a therapist, I have to nourish myself, I have to give myself something, something I can live on, on many levels, before I can help others.

The student expresses here her recognition of the fact that her own self-development and ability to care for herself will be significant in future therapeutic relationships.

A professional therapist who is not able to, or does not have the personal resources to, open up and be resonant in relation to his/her client and the complex landscape the person contains risks creating distance from the client, and the client may miss the opportunity to be met. A therapy student described this as follows:

> If we didn't have the therapeutic track in the programme, and had only read about therapy, it would all have been fragmented inside me. I wouldn't have resonated emotionally […] It would have been more separated, I think – maybe more 'them and us' – that some are clients and some are therapists.

It is not possible to reduce therapy to be only about the client. The therapist is part of the complex relational system – there is an 'I' and a 'thou' (Buber 1997). Therapeutic competence, then, is about having the courage to immerse oneself in the giant ocean of information, response and responsibility that flows between the partners. In cybernetic theory, learning means optimising a system as a result of the feedback the system has received from the outside. The human system/individual creates him/herself and self-regulates – not independently and isolated from the world, but rather deeply connected to and dependent on influences and contributions from the outside world. A student describes the dynamics with the therapist in this way:

> The therapist does something to the improvisation by being so stable, with one single note, that is, she brings me down to something calmer. What I can remember, the memories that are still with me from the improvisation, is this part where we – where one note is very dominating. So this is what made an impression on me […] I think she was very brave.

We are *not* self-sufficient, but we do have the potential to guide and regulate our interaction with our surroundings. In other words, individuals are, at the same time, self-sustainable and dependent on being part of a community. In Niklas Luhmann's theory, we find an understanding of the individual as alternating between being receptive to information from the outside world and withdrawing to a state where external impulses are temporarily muted in order to be able to evaluate, organise and integrate information (Luhmann 1998). For the future therapist, it is important that self-regulating dynamics work – that is, to balance between openness and limitations (Vedfelt 2000).

Knowledge and Experience – between Past, Present and Future

In conclusion, I will mention yet another dynamic that adds to the understanding of the relational dimension of learning processes and contributes to complexity in learning processes. This is the relationship between what happens in the present moment, when students and training therapist interact, and the patterns embedded in the student (as well as the therapist) owing to the history that the person brings with him/her. These patterns influence the present, and the present influences the patterns. In other words, the learning process is a meeting place for the past, present and future, as a student expresses:

> Some of the things I brought up in therapy from my past, from my childhood, were painful, and it was hard, but it wasn't hard in a bad way – it was hard in a good way, I'd say – that points forward.

And the world is constantly changing, which means that the past, present and future are also constantly changing. We are not, in every way, the same people we were. As humans, we are influenced by each other, by our environment, and – at times almost imperceptibly – we change. Therefore, receptiveness and flexibility are an important part of therapeutic competence. The professional therapist must meet a complex reality from an awareness of the fact that, regardless of the level of theoretical understanding, one cannot, in advance, know with certainty what is needed in a particular therapy session. This is a kind of 'qualified ignorance', which is quite different from the 'unknowledge' identified earlier in this chapter as risk, when the therapist is on autopilot and has not yet developed sufficient reflective skills. In qualified ignorance, the therapist has direct access to his/her complex ground of experience and theoretical preparedness and he/she maintains an openness to the possibility of learning something new (Willert 2007). This attitude requires curiosity but also courage – the courage to learn to express dilemmas and uncertainty in a way that, for example, can help the therapist to act sensitively and relevantly in a given therapeutic situation.

The theoretical analysis in the interview study that I included in this chapter showed that the student, through therapeutic processes, builds trust in the present moment and trust in his/her own readiness to act. Development of the ability to be self-aware and grounded in oneself can bring certainty and readiness with regard to being receptive and flexible in relation to the client (Lindvang 2013; Pedersen et al., 2022). The complexity also lies in the fact of changeability – that we cannot and should not prevent movement in the client, our common environment or ourselves. The therapist must learn to follow, trusting the process, without losing his/her balance on the way.

Closing Remarks

In all learning processes, a dynamic between something old and something new emerges, something that is *given* and something that is *possible*. Therapy training is about building and attaining competence in perceiving the given conditions and possibilities regarding the specific client, situation and relationship, while still keeping in view one's own position and possibilities as a therapist (Fog & Hem 2009). In other words, a practical wisdom evolves – a capacity to be engaged in the special, the specific, and to assess relevantly in a given situation whether actions are needed and, if so, which ones. The real world is full of unpredictable situations where the most relevant and ethical behaviour and actions cannot always be figured out in advance (Brinkmann 2007).

In three areas, this chapter describes how the future therapist gradually goes through a growth process that is complex – where therapy and learning come together as a whole. The first area, about learning and the interactive levels of consciousness, described how, through training therapy, the student can develop flexibility of consciousness and integration between 'mind and body', so that the intellect and bodily awareness come together. The next area of learning was about the multimodality of perception: Development of the ability to communicate supramodally means that many types of information can be perceived simultaneously, information can be transferred between different sensory modalities, and a broad variety of rapidly collaborating orientation channels are developed. The third area shed light on the fact that learning takes place in relationships and over time. When the future therapist is engaged in, develops through, and gradually integrates these three dimensions, the person is well on the way to crystallising a complex and unique therapeutic competence.

The crystal symbolises the diverse and complex in balance. Through the crystal, the clear light of consciousness can refract and shine in all directions. Although learning and building therapeutic competence do not have a final goal but can continue throughout life, I will conclude with a quotation from a student who describes how she, through a training therapy process, reached renewed and balanced clarity:

> I had a sense of some crystals [...] rock crystals, transparent beautiful ones. I had the sense that the crystals that were facing the wrong way, now were facing the right way. It was like the crystals fell into place.

Note

1 Nine music therapy students in their final year of studies volunteered as contributors to my interview study. The thesis is in English and can be downloaded at: www.mt-phd.aau.dk/digitalAssets/6/6465_dissertation_c_lindvang.pdf. Readers interested in qualitative methods should see Chapter 4. Cybernetic analysis is described in Chapter 6.

References

Bike, D.H., Norcross, J.C. & Schatz, D.M. (2009). Processes and outcomes of psychotherapists' personal therapy: Replication and extension 20 years later. *Psychotherapy: Theory, Research, Practice, Training, 46*, 19–31.

Brinkmann, S. (2007). The good qualitative researcher. *Qualitative Research in Psychology, 4*(1–2), 127–144.

Buber, M. (1997). *Jeg og du*. Hans Reitzels Forlag.

Fog, J. (1995). At komme til klarhed. Om bevidst-blivelsesprocessen hos terapeuten. *Psyke & Logos, 16*(2), 374–409.

Fog, J. & Hem, L. (2009). *Psykoterapi og erkendelse. Personligt anliggende og professionel virksomhed*. Akademisk Forlag.

Grimmer, A. & Tribe, R. (2001). Counselling psychologists' perceptions of the impact of mandatory personal therapy on professional development – an exploratory study. *Counselling Psychology Quarterly, 14*(4), 287–301.

Hougaard, E. (2019). *Psykoterapi. Teori og forskning* (3rd ed.). Dansk Psykologisk Forlag.

Illeris, K. (2006). *Læring*. Roskilde Universitetsforlag.

Kierkegaard, S. (1859). *Synspunktet for min Forfatter-Virksomhed. En ligefrem Meddelelse, Rapport til Historien*, vol. 18. C.A. Reitzels Forlag.

Lindvang, C. (2010). A field of resonant learning. Self-experiential training and the development of music therapeutic competencies. PhD thesis, Aalborg Universitet, Institut for Kommunikation. www.mt-phd.aau.dk/digitalAssets/6/6465_dissertation_c_lindvang.pdf

Lindvang, C. (2013). Resonant learning: A qualitative inquiry into music therapy students' self-experiential learning processes. *Qualitative Inquiries in Music Therapy, 8*, 1–30.

Lindvang, C. (2015). Group music therapy – a part of music therapy students' training at Aalborg University. *Group Analysis, 48*, 36–41.

Lindvang, C. & Bonde, L.O. (2012). Følelser i bevægelse. Om læreprocesser i musikterapeutens uddannelse. *Psyke og Logos, 33*(1), 87–116.

Luhmann, N. (1998). Erkendelse som konstruktion, in M. Hermansen (Ed.), *Fra læringens horisont – en antologi*, pp. 163–182. Klim.

Malloch, S. & Trevarthen, C. (Eds.) (2009). *Communicative Musicality: Exploring the Basis of Human Companionship*. Oxford University Press.

Meltzoff, A.N. & Moore, M.K. (1999). Persons and representations: Why infant imitation is important for theories of human development, in J. Nadel & G. Butterworth (Eds.), *Imitation in Infancy*, pp. 9–35. Cambridge University Press.

Murphy, K. (2007). Experiential learning in music therapy: Faculty and student perspectives. *Qualitative Inquiries in Music Therapy, 3*, 31–57.

Pedersen, I.N. (2002). Self-experience for music therapy students – experiential training music therapy as methodology – A mandatory part of the music therapy programme at Aalborg University, in J.T. Eschen (Ed.), *Analytical Music Therapy*, pp. 168–189. Jessica Kingsley.

Pedersen, I.N., Lindvang, C. & Beck, B.D. (Eds.). (2022). *Resonant Learning in Music Therapy: A Training Model to Tune the Therapist*. Jessica Kingsley.

Polanyi, M. (1966). *The tacit dimension*. University of Chicago Press.

Trevarthen, C. & Malloch, S. (2000). The dance of wellbeing: Defining the musical therapeutic effect. *Nordic Journal of Music Therapy, 9*(2), 3–17.

Trondalen, G. & Skårderud, F. (2007). Playing with affects – and the importance of affect attunement. *Nordic Journal of Music Therapy, 16*(2), 100–111.

Stern, D.N. (2000). *The interpersonal world of the infant. A view from psychoanalysis & developmental psychology*. Basic Books.

Stern, D.N. (2010). *Forms of vitality: Exploring dynamic experience in psychology, the arts, psychotherapy, and development*. Oxford University Press.

Vedfelt, O. (2000). *Ubevidst intelligens. Du ved mere end du tror*. Gyldendal.

Vedfelt, Ole. (2002). *The dimensions of dreams. The nature, function, and interpretation of dreams*. Jessica Kingsley.

Wackerhausen, S. (2008). Erfaringsrum, handlingsbåren kundskab og refleksion. *Refleksion i Praksis, Skriftserie*, no. 1/2008. RUML Institut for Filosofi og Idéhistorie, Aarhus University.

Willert, S. (2007). Psykologi som håndværk – psykologistudiet som håndværkeruddannelse? tre utopier og en brugervejledning, in S. Brinkmann & L. Tanggaard (Eds.), *Psykologi: Forskning og profession*, pp. 249–278. Hans Reitzels Forlag.

15

The Ecological Niche in Cybernetic Psychology and Therapy

Christian Uhrskov

When I commenced my acquaintance with cybernetic psychology 20 years ago, the significance of the creative element only gradually became clear, and not only in relation to psychotherapy work in general: Systems theory, on which it is based, uses concepts such as 'emergence', 'self-regulation' and 'self-organisation'. These are concepts that point to the inherent, creative properties of life itself and to development that takes place in living organisms.

Although we are individuals and experience ourselves as separate entities, we are always part of larger entities. Those closest to us – family, our circle of friends, the work environment, society, culture – all together are in turn woven into the biosphere. The 'ecological niche' is an expression of this and denotes our living conditions and surroundings. The concept has – like systems theory itself – roots in biology and originally describes not something that is environmentally friendly but rather the interplay, interaction, relationship and dependency between living organisms.

Organisms of different complexity interact with each other and are, according to systems theory and cybernetic psychology, perceived as self-regulating and self-organising, which gives us a new definition of the concept of human development in psychotherapy. The question, therefore, is how we as psychotherapists best stimulate and support these creative qualities. Cybernetic psychology emphasises collaboration with unconscious intelligence, primarily owing to the fact that it has access to far greater information and complexity than our waking everyday consciousness. The superior intelligence of the unconscious is not a new insight, but, with cybernetic personality theory, it proves itself to be a substantial discovery enriching psychotherapeutic practice.

Introduction

Most illnesses heal themselves, an old saying goes. Without our awareness, our body takes care of an extremely complex regulation of life functions and physiology. The wound heals itself, the sore throat goes away, and the body can even, up to a certain point, overcome serious injuries and diseases. Our psyche, too, is self-regulating. As we are complex beings, we switch, in just over a day, between many different – more or less extroverted – states of consciousness with varying

DOI: 10.4324/9781003360247-16

intensities, as well as the completely introverted ones, such as sleep and dreams. All of them are essential to our health. The different states of consciousness regulate our personality and are important for the natural self-regulation of our organism as a whole (Vedfelt 2003, p. 97).

Every living organism is connected to its surroundings and the environment that conditions its existence. The ecological niche is of as great importance to the human organism as upbringing is to psychic regulation and early development. Everything from the atom to the universe is seen as a system, or an organised whole, from a systems theory point of view (Ølgaard 2004, p. 30). When applied to human beings, a more holistic view may be achieved with the eradication of a distinction between body and psyche. One can imagine

> The psyche and the body as complementary expressions of the same phenomenon, just like wave and particle within quantum physics.
>
> (Vedfelt 1996, p. 226)

The living organism is not seen in isolation, but as part of other systems – there is interaction/communication between a systemic unit and the environment which influences and conditions its existence.

Our connectedness and connection to the surrounding world are crucial in all respects. Especially in the earliest stages of life, when we are particularly vulnerable, patterns are engraved that shape us so deeply that psychotherapy may become necessary later in life. Whether it is a child's neurobiological development, general ability for contact or traumatic imprints, *attachment* is singled out as a crucial factor for psychic well-being.

Attachment disorders are cured through "re-parenting" or re-attachment (Sørensen 2005, pp. 35, 210). Psychodynamic-oriented therapy refers to a "corrective emotional experience" as the central corrective element.

> Ultimately, it is this personal attachment to the therapist that is the prerequisite for the corrective emotional experiences.
>
> (Fog & Hem 2009, p. 270)

The therapist must dare be the attachment figure the client's parents, for various reasons, could not or did not dare be (ibid.).

Vedfelt describes how the therapist can step into the role of "the adult who was not there" by actively providing the input that was missing and

> the therapist, as systemic partner for inner self-regulatory forces, effects an overarching interpretation framework which is missing […] The therapist forms an integrative background and a self-regulating ecological niche.
>
> (Vedfelt 2003, pp. 243–246)

An overall goal for a psychotherapist, therefore, must be to provide a new and better functioning integrative ecological niche – a situation where focus is on inner processes – learning, creative and healing processes – in the service of the self-regulating and self-organising properties.

The Client at the Centre

Instinctive long-term planning/programming results in us having to go through certain developmental phases, and the *unconscious intelligence* checks to see if we are up to date with our development potentials. Dreams, for example, can contain important information about past conditions in life, the current life phase as well as future prospects (Vedfelt 2017, p. 105). Changing conditions in life or landmark life transitions indicate that, throughout life, we must both redefine and reorient ourselves. Different parts of our system must become parts of new connections, and self-organisation signifies the creation of new complex structures of greater cohesion and capacity.

In the early stages of childhood, the response from the environment (the ecological niche) is particularly decisive for whether, later, more complex levels of development can fully be realised. If the ecological niche does not provide the necessary response, the unconscious intelligence will signal that there is conflict. When the child cries, for example, the adult may or may not be responsive to the signals.

At times, the child needs a certain type of contact, and the self-organising tendency will, throughout life, try to re-establish a relationship that can compensate for the lack of this contact.

While *self-organising* refers to inherent *epigenetic potentials* throughout life, understood as the psyche's ability to meet the challenges of the various phases of life, *self-regulating* refers, in particular, to the constant, often unconscious, adapting to – and balancing of – inner needs in relationships to the pressures and developmental opportunities of the ecological niche.

Contemporary humanistic psychology speaks of *the need for self-realisation* and a *self-actualisation tendency*. The concept of 'self-actualisation' has philosophical roots dating back to Aristotle but was introduced in modern times by the American psychologists Abraham Maslow and Carl Rogers.

With his development model, Maslow pointed at the need for self-actualisation as the top of a hierarchy of needs. At the top level, one has the strength to meet the needs to realise one's goals, to realise innate or later acquired abilities. This is in accordance with an 'inner core' or 'the inner self' and thus the possibility of reaching human and personal essence (Maslow 1968, p. 213).

With Rogers, a *self-actualising tendency*, understood as an internally observed directional force, is asserted in all organic life. It is seen as the first, basic effort/need to which all other psychological, as well as organic, needs are subordinate and it thus includes Maslow's hierarchy of needs (Rogers 1951, p. 488).

In Roger's personality theory, it is described as a

> basic tendency and striving – to actualise, maintain, and enhance the experiencing organism.

> (Rogers 1951, p. 487)

Ten years later he writes:

> The mainspring of creativity appears to be the same tendency which we discover so deeply as the curative force in psychotherapy – man's tendency to actualise himself, to become his potentials.
>
> (Rogers 1961, p. 350)

The hypothesis of the self-actualising tendency – that the client has the answers and an implicit knowledge of what is most important – forms, in Rogers, the starting point for a non-controlling, client-centred form of therapy. The therapist does not try to change the client or manipulate the process by persuasion, advice, comfort or solutions to the client's problems, but is basically neutral. 'Holding back' in favour of the client and what the client brings out is also entirely in the spirit of the cybernetic method.

This emphasises how important both the client's and the therapist's commitment is to a successful course of therapy.

From Biology and Technology to Cybernetics

Ludwig von Bertalanffy, a biologist (1901–1972), first presented systems theory[1] in 1937. With his description of "the new philosophy of nature", the living organism was now considered an *organised whole* (Hammond 2010, p. 105). Contrary to fundamental mechanistic thinking, which claims that we understand an entity when we understand the mechanics of each individual part, general systems theory (GST; hereafter, just systems theory) is seen as a paradigm shift.

The paradigm considers the complex system *in itself*, as the scientific subject area and the new way of thinking enable a new understanding of laws in hyper-complex systems. *Complexity* is singled out as an essential property that cannot be reduced without affecting the whole (Ølgaard 2004, p. 52). The parts of the system and their interaction with each other are just as important as the elements themselves. The fact that the system may have properties that do not exist in the individual parts – for example, life or consciousness – means that one can claim that "the whole is much greater than the sum of its parts" (Hammond 2010, p. 134).

One of von Bertalanffy's most important contributions is the understanding of organisms – living systems (as opposed to machines) – as *open* systems capable of "Maintaining a state of equilibrium by constantly interacting with [their] environment" (Hammond 2010, p. 105).

The term 'homeostasis' refers to a system's ability to regulate itself in the pursuit of optimal inner balance and in relation to the environment that forms the conditions for the organism's survival.

The success of systems theory is largely due to a change in science's approach to, and strategy for, entities that are "complex organised".

The changing aspects, such as regulation and direction (directedness), are also referred to as "teleological behavior, i.e. appropriate or purposeful behavior"

(Ølgaard 2004, p, 52). The uniqueness of all living matter, with its striving and choosing, means that biology can never be reduced to physics.

Norbert Wiener, a mathematician (1894–1964) and Bertalanffy's contemporary, studied a more mechanistic side – that is, electrical circuits and control systems in weapons. The underlying principle related to the regulation and control of information in complex communication systems was named *cybernetics* by Wiener in 1948. *Cybernetes* is the Greek word for helmsman.

A thermostat can regulate temperature and turn heating on when it gets too cold or turn it off when a certain temperature is reached – an example of first-order cybernetics. The system corrects itself, based on the feedback from the environment. Concepts such as 'self-reference' and 'feedback' in mechanical systems, were, with the new technology, seen as analogous to similar phenomena in living systems – here called *second-order cybernetics*. Second-order cybernetics, where the observer influences the observed, has many implications in the cybernetic method. The systemic unity makes it imperative to focus on the cognising subject's states and levels of consciousness. When training the therapeutic skills, deeper motivations, prejudices or blockages are sought to be uncovered so that the client may be observed without prejudice (Vedfelt 1996, p. 110).

A third pioneer in the cybernetic field, and an important one in this context, was the psychiatrist William Ross Ashby (1903–1972). With the *law of requisite variety*, Ashby showed that, in a game between two systems, the system with the greatest variation possibilities will easily beat the one with fewer. By analogy, deleting the overall operating system of a computer will have far greater consequences than deleting a smaller program with more limited features. This means that systems with higher complexity can regulate or control a less complex subsystem, provided the possibilities are exploited.

According to cybernetic personality theory, personality is understood as a layered, hyper-complex information network. The psyche consists of many different systems with varying degrees of complexity. They are simultaneously active, and some have greater control than others.

> In a normal state of consciousness, the ego does not possess the complexity and capacity needed to regulate the complete psycho physical system.
>
> (Vedfelt 1996, p. 114)

It follows that activation of higher control systems with a greater degree of complexity can affect and regulate larger psychic areas, including the rational self. Being able to see more perspectives, understand with greater nuance or be more inclusive towards a problem expands or 'moves' the consciousness to another, higher level of complexity. This implies greater freedom of choice and greater flexibility.

The English anthropologist Gregory Bateson (1904–1980), like Vedfelt, used systems theory and cybernetics as principles to develop his theories and concepts. Communication and an interest in how all living matter experiences knowing formed Bateson's great interest and overall project in everything he worked on. With the help of systemic thinking, he wanted to create a new meta-science about the "mental" and its "pattern" – "A science of mind and order" (Ølgaard 2004, p. 21).

Contrary to positivist science, which believes it can describe phenomena objectively, Bateson believed that all knowledge only represents ideas of reality or, popularly expressed: "The map is not the terrain", and "we do not experience the world as it is, we experience a model of the world".

The inner maps are our subjective experience of what the world is like. Epistemology is the science and process of knowledge that examines the subject, but, with Bateson, there is an expanded understanding of the subject. Not only the human but all living matter – animals, animal communities, ecosystems, organisations and so on – is self-referential and an expression of "mind processes". The "self" is therefore not something one has but a "system of thought", a "process" the boundaries of which do not coincide with the body or consciousness but are understood just as much "in the network of causal paths along which transformed differences are led" (Ølgaard 2004 p. 242).

We constantly send and receive messages and signals to and from the outside world. All we do (and do not do) is communication, which is why communication is understood as much more than our spoken language. In the company of others, all our behaviour can be perceived as communication; we cannot 'not-communicate'. The most significant ways we do this are by reading body language, facial expressions and the tone of voice.[2] All our attitudes, such as reluctance, dominance or interest, are expressed through our body language, and we read all this partly unconsciously. Body language in itself can act as a kind of end result and give clues to different emotions or memory experiences which can be explored (carefully) in dreamwork and dialogue with the client.

By the term the *cybernetic self* we understand the complete or total personality system that coordinates the higher, self-organising, governing processes in the personality (Vedfelt 2003, p. 264).

> The personal self comes into being by the cybernetic self personifying a segment of the psyche in a special way.
>
> (Vedfelt 2003, p. 315)

The cybernetic self is the whole of consciousness and unconsciousness and therefore holds far greater capacity for information than our personal self. The self is a much smaller part of the whole and is perceived as a personified system, a subpersonality.

> The personal self, or ego, manifests itself at a stage in development as the experience of a certain identity, a fixed memory structure, with a special life story and a constant feeling of being the same.
>
> (Vedfelt 2000 p. 287)

According to Vedfelt, the psyche can be understood as a many-layered, decisive, self-optimising, hyper-complex information system that organises itself spontaneously in a network of various subsystems, each of which appears more or less clear to consciousness. The subsystems make up different memories. Many of the units are active simultaneously and overlap or operate on parallel lines. Subpersonalities and object relations can be described as manifestations of the activity of the subsystems (Vedfelt 2000 p. 549). They have varying degrees of consciousness-like or unconscious functions, each with their own set of choices or limitations (Vedfelt 1996, p. 113). Like all cybernetic systems, they are self-correcting and self-regulating.

Unconscious Intelligence

Whereas the unconscious, in Freudian psychoanalysis, was primarily perceived as a more or less chaotic domain of repressed and infantile impulses, C.G. Jung viewed the unconscious as "a great guide, friend and adviser of the of the conscious" (Jung 1964/1991, p. 12).

Cybernetic psychology is inspired by the Jungian way of thinking, and work with dreams – which, according to Vedfelt, constitutes a kind of "X-ray image" of the inner world – is an integral part of the cybernetic method. Nocturnal dreams are full of symbolism and deal with what is important to us in life (Vedfelt 2017, p. 45). In waking life, unconscious intelligence is also expressed through intuitive skills and creative work. Vedfelt explains how unconscious intelligence, as an inner creative force, presses forth from within, "so we may use our resources to their fullest and be in balance with our surroundings" (Vedfelt 2003, p. 31).

The one-to-one therapeutic relationship involves interaction between the two systems on many levels. The increased complexity of a second-order system means that consciousness bandwidth is increased compared with the relationship's higher control system – the unconscious intelligence.

Relating to the unconscious means, among other things, an understanding – and recognition – of the fact that emotions, inner fantasies, body sensations or body language contain as much information as rational consciousness. In psychotherapeutic work, it occurs through awareness of being able to be in conscious dialogue with bodily, sensory and the more irrational aspects of the personality. These can be clues and meaningful expressions of higher integrating levels of the unconscious and they thus become expressions of the natural self-regulation of the personality.

The unconscious, by virtue of its much higher complexity and capacity for information, can regulate our rational consciousness (Vedfelt 2003 p. 33). Collaboration with unconscious intelligence is therefore a key element in working with cybernetic psychotherapy methodology.

Recent research shows that the unconscious is both practice- and intelligence-focused (Vedfelt 2003, p. 34). The practical refers, among other things, to everyday skills and more or less automated practices that have sunk into the unconscious and thus relieve the awake consciousness, which can focus on more important things. For example, it is difficult to cycle until it is 'learned by heart', so to speak. The competence becomes 'automated' and is seen as an expression of a tacit knowledge – a skill and intelligence rooted in the body. The awake consciousness has only a certain 'bandwidth', which is why a large part of the enormous amount of information we receive from the outside world is sensed, stored and processed below the threshold of consciousness. This is called subliminal perception, and extensive research in the field confirms that we both navigate and make a wide range of decisions in our lives based on unconscious perception. The overwhelmingly large unconscious domain, as well as its impact on our lives, speaks its own clear language of how deeply connected we are to the environment – our ecological niche.

Resistance and Self-regulation

Sigmund Freud defined the central challenges in therapeutic practice with the concepts of *defence mechanisms* and *resistance*, which refer to a form of refusal of a deeper self-exploration. The resistance, according to Freud, is expressed through a wide range of defined defence mechanisms, and, in psychoanalytic therapy, these are important diagnostic and therapeutic aids. Linguistically, the concepts of 'defence' and 'resistance' have a tinge of battle, and several psychotherapeutic schools of thought have, since Freud, used methods that are very controlling in relation to wanting to 'confront' the unconscious. Freud saw defence mechanisms as crucial obstacles to achieving the aim of psychoanalytic therapy, defined as "an increased self-understanding and increased ability for independent conscious action" (Mousten 1980, p. 181) and where old repressions and unconscious mechanisms are exposed, remembered and integrated.

According to Vedfelt, defence mechanisms and the understanding of resistance may be reformulated in cybernetic understanding or even rejected altogether as an explanatory model (Vedfelt 1996, p. 119). Resistance and defence are, first and foremost, described through a somewhat broader concept of *constraints* – which here are translated into the necessary framework of the psyche. Instead of seeing resistance only as stubbornness towards change or healing, constraints point to a self-sustaining function – a condition and property of any system that ensures it does not collapse or disintegrate. A system does not know what to do if it does not have sufficient constraints. This is seen, for example, in learning processes, where limitations play a crucial role.[3]

The fewer restrictions a system has, the greater its freedom of choice, also called *contingency* (Vedfelt 2003, pp. 203–204). Too many choices, however, can lead to paralysis or the opposite happening: The personality stiffens in previously learned constraints.[4]

As an illustration, one could think of the (main) character Mads Skjern from a classic Danish TV series. Despite the desire to do away with his missionary background, he fails to do so. When his wife leaves him because of his stiffness, he has a sort of breakdown and is paralysed. When his wife returns, after all, his only wish is for everything to be as it was (the Swedish playwright Ingmar Bergman used the term "When the mask burns into the face").[5]

From a systems theory point of view, it must first be stated that, when the outside world is more complex than the individual organism, the possibilities for influencing it are limited (cf. Ashby). If the organism is disturbed or feels threatened, it reduces its surroundings and the affected potentials in itself. Since it is a matter of survival, the organism restricts itself to the part of the ecological niche that it needs for its self-regulation.

Viewed in the perspective of human personality system, this is understood as problem-solving behaviour. The neurosis or personality disorder is therefore seen as an expression of necessary, creative survival strategies that were once best.[6] Vedfelt describes how aspects of ourselves that we have difficulty recognising can regain their dignity:

> it makes it easier for us to give them acceptance that is the condition for coaxing them out of hiding and cooperating with them.
>
> (Vedfelt 1996, p. 115)

Central aspects of us, which for various reasons have been detached or have had to go into hibernation, can again be brought to life and integrated by being met, seen, understood and accommodated in a neutral appreciative field/relationship via a new, more optimal ecological niche.

According to cybernetic psychology, serious psychic disorders, such as trauma, will always affect control systems at a high level. The resistance experienced in the unveiling of previously unresolved conflicts or traumatic experiences is therefore seen as the self, in the normal state of consciousness, not having the complexity and capacity needed to regulate the total psychophysical system (Vedfelt 1996, p. 114). Resistance and defence now arise when we encounter a situation where we must integrate information from a higher system/level than what we, with our normal consciousness, recognise ourselves in – or understand ourselves as. The constraints of normal consciousness make sure to slow down the self-regulating processes with experiences of, for example, anxiety, pain and discomfort in the face of what apparently threatens the survival of the personality.

Hypothetically, Mads Skjern might be able to access a new emotional register, with all that entails, through a longer psychotherapy programme. In the initial phases, a cautious reference to careful, inconspicuous body signals could gradually lead to inclusion of larger entities and parts of the consciousness content and, in time – perhaps – the beginning of a new relationship with his son Daniel, whom he threw out because of his homosexuality. Later, greater contingency can be achieved, greater freedom of choice and flexibility when we manage to allow the more complex system to take control: Mads again includes his beloved son in the family. A self-organising at a higher level of complexity takes place.

Vedfelt explains how the combination of various methods – for example, body therapy and drawing therapy – makes it possible to get behind the resistance and activate higher-level systems. However, in other cases, it may be appropriate to strengthen the ego (Vedfelt 1996, p. 118).

In work with negative experiences or traumatic events, trust must be established that the internal resources can bear, which is why the focus is on building these resources. The work with positive or negative transference on the therapist can also, over time, develop the consciousness in the direction of increased contingency, but requires therapeutic ingenuity and understanding of the nature of interaction.

Defining the client as having resistance may be convenient, but the therapist's co-responsibility for the breach of contract should be always considered. Vedfelt mentions that resistance is like a coin with two sides and is not just stubbornness in the face of change but an area that contains intensity and possibilities for transformation, both for the client and the therapist (Vedfelt 2003, p. 292).

In connection with dreamwork, it is emphasised that this creative process may be slowed down by premature 'wise' interpretations with which the client may disagree.

> I understand it as a breach in the relationship between myself and my client, and between waking consciousness and self-organising variables hidden behind the dream.
>
> (Vedfelt 2017, p. 49)

In the situation, it is important to be alert and approach the theme on a different level. Maybe the therapist is too busy, has a far too ambitious approach or even blockages and blind spots. The therapist's own inner work – or self-examination – contains a constant confrontation with sore points and continual assessment, along with an analysis of the therapy process through supervision.

The Inner Maps

In our upbringing, "we are apprentices as human beings" and we practise through time shared with our closest caregivers (Vedfelt 2003, p. 78). The first basic relational skills and patterns of interaction are especially formed between mother and child. Everything we go through, experience, register and sense, consciously as well as unconsciously, is stored in our psychophysical system.

Based on these events and experiences, a large number of internal networks develop – also called *neural networks*. The neural networks form working models (patterns or schemas) for how to relate to and communicate with the surrounding world (Vedfelt 2003, p. 343). Norms, behaviour and patterns of experience make us tend to choose environments that suit our expectations. When they do not live up to our expectations, we often experience them as if they do, thanks to transference mechanisms. Freud called this the "compulsion of repetition".

These experiences and impressions function as our theories about the world and are sorts of unconscious pre-understanding or schemas. The schemas can be seen as the very "building blocks of cognition" and understood as a knowledge structure that organises and interprets the sensory data we receive (Vedfelt 2003, p. 196). In other words, the pattern constitutes a *perception* – an *interpretation* – that gives an idea of how 'something' in a particular context is likely to behave. The patterns often last fairly unchanged, right into adulthood, and can, depending on their flexibility, have negative consequences for our perception of ourselves and our relationships with our surroundings, here and now.

Our ways of reacting when meeting other people, therefore, happen through what is called holistic pattern recognition. It is the preconceived approximate image or notion of a situation or relationship that governs our perception until the opposite is proven (Vedfelt 2003, p. 196) The patterns largely operate unconsciously in our lives but can be made conscious.

If, when meeting a random woman, there is any resemblance to the client's mother schema, it may activate key aspects of the early pattern of 'mother' – the mother network.

A pattern is activated, perhaps via transference (or projection) on to one's female therapist but can also be detected via recalling forgotten memories. An optimal relationship will now provide an opportunity to nuance impressions and gain new experiences.

> In therapy, a new memory matrix is formed, which supports the development of an altered personality structure.
>
> (Vedfelt 2003, p. 246)

New experiences, or new memory structures, allow the self-regulating properties to form new, more general schemas. The more flexible, or more stable patterns

> provide space for the integration of old memories into newly created more comprehensive wholes.
>
> (Vedfelt 2003, p. 246)

The absorbed schemas, also called working models, can, as we have seen, have far-reaching consequences for our understanding of ourselves and the world around us. The same goes for our interpretation and understanding of inner emotions set in motion in the encounter with a client.

Modalities and the Supramodal Space

Jung wrote the following on meeting a patient:

> Through this presentation, his system is set in relation to mine, thereby triggering an effect in my own system [...] This effect is the only thing that I, both as an individual and legitimately, can offer my patient.
>
> (Jung 1993, p. 191)

The quote from Jung could be interpreted in the sense that "an effect that is triggered in my own system" means there is *something that manifests itself* in the interconnection. *Something* of significant importance, at the same time as this effect, becomes a guiding or supporting element in the exchange with the patient.

This could allude to transference mechanisms, where the client attributes characteristics to the therapist that stem from the previously mentioned schemas, built up early in life. The phenomenon is an expression of communication, but from a higher operating system, beyond the client's conscious self.

We inevitably become emotionally affected owing to subliminal perception, our unconscious understanding of body language and, in general, of the other person's presence (Vedfelt 2003, p. 39). This circumstance is present in all close contact between people, and the inner emotions that are set in motion are important markers of what is happening in the relationship.

For the therapist, it is *counter*transference that constitutes the therapist's own prejudices and assumptions about the client. Projection (or transference) of unconscious religious beliefs and transpersonal experiences are also believed to resonate in the therapist's system (Vedfelt 2007, p. 696).

In other words, we constantly transmit our states of consciousness, which are perceived beyond language.

> We can perceive the imperceptible and involve it in the process of cognition.
>
> (Vedfelt 2003, p. 73)

In our normal, rational, everyday consciousness, we may have most confidence in verbal thought processes, but non-intellectual understanding, which is our non-verbal 'sense' of contact, is based on a wealth of inner *modalities* that manifest themselves and communicate in the field of consciousness – compare Bateson: We cannot non-communicate. Inner modalities in the form of emotions, thoughts, imagination, body sensations and so on come into play, and the modalities are encoded as entities, as different aspects of any given experience.[7] Dreams are also encoded in entities, where body sensations and body language, for example, can be approaches and promote resourceful states and new insights (Vedfelt 2017, pp. 137–141). The various modalities also act as clues to memory. Being open to inner images that may manifest themselves or other notions, such as associations, can drive the process forward.

Normal consciousness, as a rule, is aware of only one sensory modality (or one channel) at a time. We either think or feel or see images or feel body sensations. This condition is intended to maintain adequate constraint and control over our state of consciousness (Vedfelt 1996, p. 130). This may be necessary, for example, when we are driving a car.

By drawing the client's attention to other process channels in therapy, in connection with a current theme, the field of communication, and thus the bandwidth of consciousness, is expanded. It may seem a form of interruption – for example, being asked how a belief or other verbal expression is sensed in the body – but, during this break, while sensing, consciousness spreads to other parts of the human personality system.

The switch between different process channels expands the bandwidth, thereby weakening the system's constraints. This can activate a higher level of consciousness or states of greater information density, which enables the self-regulating processes from higher levels to regulate and integrate the personality. When communication includes several process channels simultaneously, several associative networks can be activated. Perhaps unpleasant or traumatic memories press forward, which can be seen as a sign of a self-regulatory tendency (Vedfelt 2003, p. 73). This can create increased reflexivity, deeper introspection and, eventually, greater clarification.

Supramodal Sensing

Vedfelt calls the psychic space or 'place' where multidimensional experiences occur the *supramodal space* (2003, p. 68).

Being aware of present communication on several channels at the same time – and being able to consider, for example, body sensations, emotions or inner images that may arise simultaneously with reflections in a conversation – is called supramodal sensing (Vedfelt 2003, p. 73). The point is to be able to relate to the various modalities with a neutral observing attitude, in the same way as in mindfulness meditation practice, where consciousness content is witnessed and recorded. An increased awareness of what may arise from one's client or from oneself could be countertransference – for example, excessive sympathy or the opposite. Neutral observation of the various modalities, forming large entities of the information field and arising in the supramodal space, is considered a core competence in therapy.

Vedfelt mentions the obligation to work with self-examination so that one may consider one's clients as open-mindedly as possible and emphasises the importance of meditative practice.

Case

Peter became more and more aware of how difficult it was for him to feel, notice and stand by his own feelings and needs. Being aware that his own feelings had value proved to be important to him in terms of being able to give his surroundings a more optimal response. He had a very developed "radar function", to use his own expression, which enabled him to read others, and Peter outwardly appeared to be a very polite, sociable and sympathetic person.

As a survival strategy and necessary adjustment behaviour in his childhood, with a chronically ill mother, this pattern had major consequences in relation to his family, his changing jobs and, on the whole, for his self-esteem. Through psychotherapy, which created the opportunity to rediscover the forgotten complex of emotions from his upbringing, contact with his own needs became simpler, yet, from being 'alter-centric' – primarily focused on others – Peter now became more and more egocentric, among other things, in his relationship to his family. This could seem to be a setback, as it presented a wide range of new problems, but, overall, it could also be seen as a natural reaction to a life lived with a primary focus on the needs and premises of *others*.

In time, during the process, it also became a challenge for Peter to work with his needs management while constantly being aware of accommodating himself, managing himself and being able to manage himself in a constructive way within social relations.

In Peter's case, it was of major consequence that his mother almost never had the energy to take an interest in or engage with him. As a child, it was almost impossible, for obvious reasons, to communicate his sense of deprivation to his mother. Peter's pronounced focus on caring for her and her depressive state (and early death), therefore, gave him problems as an adult. The early adapting could be seen as a necessary reduction in flexibility and freedom of choice. The outcome was a one-sided image of women – a rigid mother network.

The self-regulatory properties were present both in Peter's problem-solving behaviour as a child and in his journey through therapy, from over-adapted to maladapted. Today, he appears far more nuanced and emotionally balanced. Peter's *working models* for the female were mostly inflexible, and, on the whole, he was insecure in his relationships with women. His incentive to start in therapy had also been relationship problems.

Relationship Skills

The therapist's personality and ability to become emotionally involved in the client are considered the most important of the various factors acting in common in psychotherapy (Vedfelt 2003, p. 299). Vedfelt emphasises the therapist's relational skills and ability to be personified as a "good person" or even several "good persons". He/she is not a nice, idealising, caring person, but a trained person with professional qualifications that distinguish the therapist from ordinary friendly and understanding people; a person who spars with the client on many levels (Vedfelt 2003, p. 299). According to Vedfelt, the development of relational skills best takes place through apprenticeship and self-therapy.

The expansion of attention to what is going on in the other has to do with the development of one's own 'empathy muscle'. The better we are aware of our own blockages and life themes, the better we are able to understand what is being expressed and thus respond constructively.

Summary

As we have seen, the self-regulating and self-organising properties of the human organism are central to mental balance and potential development opportunities. The human system's integral characteristics and strategies for survival and development call for an ecological niche that responds with the right care and empathy. Understanding the human psyche as a self-regulating, self-organising system is important on many levels. Not only can we trust that our inner self is always seeking to balance our psyche, something nocturnal dreams also express, but our system even encourages and pushes us further towards the necessary development that our changing lives and new phases of life inevitably offer us.

Taken together, the two concepts could be an expression of what is called the *evolutionary impulse*. In Greek mythology, it is the god Eros who symbolises man's pursuit of perfection – of the good, the true and the beautiful. In contemporary speech, Eros denotes the evolutionary impulse and a drive towards higher degrees of complexity, diversity and consciousness (Wilber 2017, p. 133).

In the imagined example, with the character from the Danish programme, the development is characterised by an ever-increasing capacity for compassion and love. Peter's therapy and development show, among other things, that there may be bumps on the road ahead when self-regulating and self-organising forces become active. Evolution is beautiful but not always pretty, Wilber might comment.

Cybernetic psychology and its methods, with extensive understanding of both systems theory and depth psychology, can inspire psychotherapists to develop even better conditions for therapeutic practice and, in addition, help us all to be able to offer a more optimal ecological niche. This applies both to our work life and our private life, so that we strengthen the necessary developmental opportunities in our fellow human beings.

Notes

1 He did this at a seminar in Chicago; however, the ideas were not well received. The lecture was put aside until after World War II.
2 Experiments have documented that the significance of what is said has least importance. What matters most is the voice and facial expression. Mimicry, according to most attempts, signifies as much as 58%, the tone of voice 35% and the verbal meaning only 7% (Vedfelt 2003, p. 37).
3 It can be confusing, for example, to have too many musical notes to choose from when taking the first steps in improvisation. Built-in limitations (dogmas) can often be inspiring frameworks for creative enterprise.
4 Or 'restrictions'.
5 From the movie *Fanny and Alexander*. In Jungian terminology, the "mask" is our persona – our outer face.
6 From this follows the "salutogenic" perspective, where the disorder is seen as motivated by problem-solving behaviour rather than as a pathological (sickness) phenomenon.
7 According to cybernetic theory and network models, every experience is encoded in many experience parameters, which is why they are information codes that contain far more information than linear, verbal consciousness (Vedfelt, 2000, p. 551).

References

Fog, Jette & Hem, Lars (2009) *Psykoterapi og erkendelse. Personligt anliggende og professionel virksomhed*. Akademisk Forlag, Copenhagen.

Hammond, Debora (2010) *The Science of Synthesis: Exploring the Social Implications of General Systems Theory*. University Press, Colorado.

Jung, Carl Gustav (1991) *Mennesket og dets symboler*. Lindhardt og Ringhof, Copenhagen. (J.G. Ferguson, 1964)

Jung, Carl Gustav (1993) *Den analytiske psykologis grundlag og praksis*. Walter-Verlag AG, Olten. (Danish ed., Gyldendalske boghandel, Copenhagen, 1993)

Maslow, Abraham H. (1968) *På vej mod en eksistenspsykologi*. Nyt nordisk forlag, Copenhagen. (Danish ed. 1970, Åge Haugland)

Mousten, Leif (1980) *Psykologi*. Leif Moustens Forlag, Copenhagen.

Rogers, Carl R. (1951) *Client-Centered Therapy*. Houghton Mifflin, Boston.

Rogers, Carl R. (1961) *On Becoming a Person. A Therapist's View of Psychotherapy*. Constable, London.

Sørensen, Lars J. (2005) *Smertegrænsen. Traumer, tilknytning og psykisk sygdom*. Psykologisk Forlag, Copenhagen.

Vedfelt, Ole (1996) *Bevidsthed*. Gyldendal, Copenhagen.

Vedfelt, Ole (2000) Delpersonligheder, objektrelationer og kybernetisk netværksteori. *Psyke & Logos*, *21*, 542–563.

Vedfelt, Ole (2003) *Ubevidst intelligens – du ved mere end du tror*. Gyldendal, Copenhagen.

Vedfelt, Ole (2007) Religiøse højdepunktsoplevelser i Transpersonligt, psykodynamisk og kybernetisk perspektiv. *Psyke og Logos*, *28*, 675–705.

Vedfelt, Ole (2017) *A Guide to the World of Dreams*. Routledge, London.

Wilber, Ken (2017) *The Religion of Tomorrow. A Vision for the Future of the Great Traditions*. Shambala, Boulder, CO.

Ølgaard, Bent (2004) *Kommunikation og økomentale systemer. En introduktion til Gregory Batesons forfatterskab*. Akademisk Forlag, Copenhagen.

Index

Note: *Italic* page numbers refer to figures and page numbers followed by "n" denote endnotes.

For Product Safety Concerns and Information please contact our EU
representative GPSR@taylorandfrancis.com
Taylor & Francis Verlag GmbH, Kaufingerstraße 24, 80331 München, Germany